# Sense and Respond: Industrial Applications of Smart Sensors in Cyber-Physical Systems

# Sense and Respond: Industrial Applications of Smart Sensors in Cyber-Physical Systems

Editors

**Javier Villalba-Diez**
**Joaquin Ordieres Meré**

MDPI • Basel • Beijing • Wuhan • Barcelona • Belgrade • Manchester • Tokyo • Cluj • Tianjin

*Editors*

Javier Villalba-Diez
Management und Vertrieb
Hochschule Heilbronn
Schwäbisch Hall
Germany

Joaquin Ordieres Meré
Industrial Engineering School
Universidad Politécnica de Madrid
Madrid
Spain

*Editorial Office*
MDPI
St. Alban-Anlage 66
4052 Basel, Switzerland

This is a reprint of articles from the Special Issue published online in the open access journal *Sensors* (ISSN 1424-8220) (available at: www.mdpi.com/journal/sensors/special_issues/industrial_applications_smart_sensors).

For citation purposes, cite each article independently as indicated on the article page online and as indicated below:

LastName, A.A.; LastName, B.B.; LastName, C.C. Article Title. *Journal Name* **Year**, *Volume Number*, Page Range.

**ISBN 978-3-0365-3814-3 (Hbk)**
**ISBN 978-3-0365-3813-6 (PDF)**

# Contents

# About the Editors

**Javier Villalba-Diez**

Javier Villalba-Diez, PhD., aims to empower individuals and organizations to achieve their strategic goals while increasing trust.

Dr. Villalba-Diez is a Mechanical Engineer with Technische Universita t Mu nchen, Germany and Industrial Engineer with Technical University Madrid, Spain (2003). He received his PhD in Engineering, Economics and Organizational Innovation with a focus on Strategic Organizational Design from the Universidad Polite cnica de Madrid in 2016. His PhD was awarded with the prize for the best doctoral thesis. In March 2022, he received a second PhD in Engineering from the Universidad Polite cnica de Madrid and Applied Physics with a focus on industrial applications of Quantum Computation.

His current research interests include Quantum Computing, Deep Learning, Hoshin Kanri, Strategic Organizational Design, Business and Artificial Intelligence. He has 15 years'worth of experience as a lean consultant and production manager in a number of positions related to manufacturing operations in German, American and Japanese manufacturing facilities.

His research and work, currently performed at Hochschule Heilbronn in Germany, has brought him to numerous companies and hundreds of factories, where he collaborates with people to test ideas and share lessons learned.

He splits his time between Germany, USA, Japan, and Spain.

**Joaquin Ordieres Meré**

Prof Ordieres-Meré is a full professor at the Industrial Engineering School of the Universidad Politécnica de Madrid, Spain, and his research aims are to increase the understanding of Integrated Manufacturing processes and their identification and optimization with the help of Business Analytic tools, including artificial intelligence and quantum computing.

In particular, complex processes involving human and technological devices as well as complex socio-technical systems are targeted. The aim is to be able to translate the gained knowledge into advanced tools helping decision-making processes that managers need to carry out, by providing them with either support or guidance.

Different type of processes and industries have been explored, such as building physics, steel-making, and rubber industries. In addition, some interest was also paid to more scientific fields, such as pollution prediction or digital astrophysics, where similar tools helped to bring additional value and knowledge.

His research has been cited more than 8000 times, and he has published more than one hundred and fifty journal papers and a similar number of conference papers as well as fifteen patent applications.

# Preface to "Sense and Respond: Industrial Applications of Smart Sensors in Cyber-Physical Systems"

Over the past century, the manufacturing industry has undergone a number of paradigm shifts: from the Ford assembly line (1900s) and its focus on efficiency to the Toyota production system (1960s) and its focus on effectiveness and JIDOKA; from flexible manufacturing (1980s) to reconfigurable manufacturing (1990s) (both following the trend of mass customization); and from agent-based manufacturing (2000s) to cloud manufacturing (2010s) (both deploying the value stream complexity into the material and information flow, respectively).

The next natural evolutionary step is to provide value by creating industrial cyber-physical assets with human-like intelligence. This will only be possible by further integrating strategic smart sensor technology into the manufacturing cyber-physical value creating processes in which industrial equipment is monitored and controlled for analyzing compression, temperature, moisture, vibrations, and performance. For instance, in the new wave of the 'Industrial Internet of Things'(IIoT), smart sensors will enable the development of new applications by interconnecting software, machines, and humans throughout the manufacturing process, thus enabling suppliers and manufacturers to rapidly respond to changing standards. This reprint of "Sense and Respond"aims to cover recent developments in the field of industrial applications, especially smart sensor technologies that increase the productivity, quality, reliability, and safety of industrial cyber-physical value-creating processes.

This reprint is dedicated to Moritz Seydler, a boy with great talents. Remember that discipline is the root of all good qualities.

**Javier Villalba-Diez and Joaquin Ordieres Meré**
*Editors*

sensors

MDPI

Article

# Geometric Deep Lean Learning: Deep Learning in Industry 4.0 Cyber–Physical Complex Networks

**Javier Villalba-Díez [1,2,3,*], Martin Molina [2], Joaquín Ordieres-Meré [3], Shengjing Sun [3,4], Daniel Schmidt [3,5] and Wanja Wellbrock [1]**

1 Fakultaet fuer Management und Vertrieb, Campus Schwäbisch-Hall, Hochschule Heilbronn, 74523 Schwäbisch-Hall, Germany; wanja.wellbrock@hs-heilbronn.de

2 Department of Artificial Intelligence, Universidad Politécnica de Madrid, Campus de Montegancedo, 28660 Boadilla del Monte, Madrid, Spain; martin.molina@upm.es

3 Escuela Técnica Superior de Ingenieros Industriales, Universidad Politécnica de Madrid, José Gutiérrez Abascal 2, 28006 Madrid, Spain; j.ordieres@upm.es (J.O.-M.); shengjing.sun@alumnos.upm.es (S.S.); daniel.schmidt@saueressig.de (D.S.)

4 Exposure, Epidemiology, and Risk Program, Department of Environmental Health, Harvard T.H. Chan School of Public Health, Boston, MA 02115, USA

5 Lead Developer Quality Inspection, Matthews International GmbH, Gutenbergstraße 1-3, 48691 Vreden, Germany

* Correspondence: javier.villalba.diez@hs-heilbronn.de

Received: 31 December 2019; Accepted: 29 January 2020; Published: 30 January 2020

**Abstract:** In the near future, value streams associated with Industry 4.0 will be formed by interconnected cyber–physical elements forming complex networks that generate huge amounts of data in real time. The success or failure of industry leaders interested in the continuous improvement of lean management systems in this context is determined by their ability to recognize behavioral patterns in these big data structured within non-Euclidean domains, such as these dynamic sociotechnical complex networks. We assume that artificial intelligence in general and deep learning in particular may be able to help find useful patterns of behavior in 4.0 industrial environments in the lean management of cyber–physical systems. However, although these technologies have meant a paradigm shift in the resolution of complex problems in the past, the traditional methods of deep learning, focused on image or video analysis, both with regular structures, are not able to help in this specific field. This is why this work focuses on proposing geometric deep lean learning, a mathematical methodology that describes deep-lean-learning operations such as convolution and pooling on cyber–physical Industry 4.0 graphs. Geometric deep lean learning is expected to positively support sustainable organizational growth because customers and suppliers ought to be able to reach new levels of transparency and traceability on the quality and efficiency of processes that generate new business for both, hence generating new products, services, and cooperation opportunities in a cyber–physical environment.

**Keywords:** Industry 4.0; IIoT; geometric deep learning; lean management

## 1. Introduction

Today it seems almost a truism to talk about the fact that data surround us. According to recent studies, by 2025 humanity will have created about 163 zettabytes of information [1]. However, the alarming thing is not that we are going to be flooded with data, but that these data will be very different from the data with which we are used to dealing in classical disciplines such as signal or image processing, statistics, or machine learning. Beyond this, the data we will face are data that will emerge from the trillions of objects connected to the Internet of Things (IoT). In many cases, including the industrial IoT (IIoT), these data are produced by distributed sources, such as thousands of sensors in factories, i.e., data are distributed over networks. Managing large amounts of data in these ever-expanding networks raises nontrivial concerns about the efficiency of data collection, processing, analysis, and security [2,3]. Currently, data from processes and systems are collected and stored without a clear strategy, and this can be a barrier to implementing paradigms such as "social manufacturing" [4]. In addition to being distributed, these data may be unstructured, and therefore cannot generally be encapsulated in one table. A defined strategy is therefore needed on what kind of data to collect at the technical and the organizational level. Finally, in addition to numerical, data can be ordinal, categorical, or other. The aim of this work is to introduce the reader to a series of concepts that pave the way for processing these data by means of adapted deep-learning techniques [5].

The purpose of this work is to study the possibility of providing Industry 4.0 leaders with a theoretical model that allows for the extraction of relevant patterns embedded within their organizations by means of artificial intelligence. Specifically, the goal of this work is to provide the reader with mathematical models that adapt convolutional and pooling deep-learning operations, hence describing the possible use of geometric deep-learning architectures on non-Euclidean Industry 4.0 complex cyber–physical networks. The structure of this work is as follows: First, Section 2 provides relevant background information, clarification, and definitions. Second, Section 3 provides a framework of previous relevant concepts regarding deep learning, specifically geometric deep learning. Third, Section 4 provides mathematical models to compute geometric-deep-learning algorithms over Industry 4.0 lean-management complex-networked cyber–physical systems. Finally, Section 5 outlines the conclusions and managerial implications of this model, and its applications in the field.

## 2. Background

This brief section presents and defines fundamental preliminary concepts to the comprehensive understanding of the presented content in the following sections of this work:

- Industry 4.0. The term Industry 4.0 has gained large traction since it was first publicized [6], stating the need for a paradigm shift towards a less centrally controlled manufacturing structure. It is seen as the Fourth Industrial Revolution, with the first three being mechanization through steam power, mass production through electrically operated engineering, and the digital revolution through the integration of electronics and IT. Industry 4.0 enables more production autonomy as technology becomes more interconnected, and machines are able to influence each other by creating a cyber–physical system.
- Cyber–Physical Systems. The term "cyber–physical system" in the context of Industry 4.0 refers to the tight conjoining of and co-ordination between computational and physical resources. The impact on the development of such systems is a new paradigm of technical systems based on collaborative embedded software systems [7].
- Lean Management. Lean-management systems in an Industry 4.0 cyber–physical context have been described as sociotechnical entities that aim to systematically reduce the variability of value-creation processes [8–13]. These two fundamental dimensions, the social and the technical, are subsequently meant to symbiotically support each other to maximize value creation through the systematic elimination of activities that do not add value for the client. A series of models were presented by scholars that allow the analysis and quantification of these systems as complex networks [14,15].
- Complex-Networked Organizational Design. Under the organizational-network paradigm, modern Industry 4.0 cyber–physical lean-management-oriented organizations can be understood as a symbiotic sociotechnical ecosystem of social networks [16] that interacts with increasingly complex-networked physically distributed interconnected sensors [17], whose readings are modeled as time-dependent signals on the vertices, human or cyber–physical, respectively. This means that, on the nodes of the network, attributes can be found that describe them as having the form of a given time series.

Within this framework, a complex network is defined as a graph with nontrivial topological features that do not occur in simple graphs such as lattices and random networks [18]. For any given time $t$, lean complex cyber–physical networks can be formally described by time-dependent graphs $\Omega(t) = [N(t); E(t)]$ that can be understood as lists of $N(t)$ nodes and $E(t) \subset (N(t)xN(t))$ edges that represent its human and cyber–physical nodes, and its standard communication edges [19]. Given the static graph in $t$, $\Omega(t)$, each node and edge can be characterized by a series of typically two-dimensional signals $x = [x_1, \ldots, x_n] \in (\mathbb{R}^n x \mathbb{R}^m)$, where $n$ relevant parameters of the node or axis are described as the time series of $m$ elements. In the case of nodes, signals typically represent demographic, sociological, or competence information. In case that the nodes are human, and in the case of a cyber–physical node, relevant information on the state of the cyber–physical node expressed in time series of several key performance indicators. In the case of edges, signals typically represent information referring to the quality of measurable relationships of the individual with other stakeholders of the organization; in the case of human–human or cyber–physical-to-human edges, of the time series associated with relevant key performance indicators being reported to other stakeholders. Specifically, snapshots for the time-dependent graph can be built, that is, the time-dependent graph is considered as an ordered pair of potentially different sets. A time-dependent graph considered as a sequence of static graphs is given by Expression 1.

$$\Omega = [\Omega(t_1), \Omega(t_2), \ldots, \Omega(t_k)] \quad (1)$$

This method is most commonly used for modeling discrete time-dependent graphs, and is suitable for the time-dependent graph with a specific time structure, especially in real-time networks such as complex-networked cyber–physical systems [20]. This modelling method is assumed here, and the time sequence of static graphs is not explicitly mentioned when referring to time-dependent graphs.

As a consequence of these references, it can be stated that cyber–physical complex-networked lean-management systems in an Industry 4.0 context can be understood as management systems that systematically try to reduce the intrinsic variability of industrial value-creation processes by understanding them as complex networks of computational and physical elements.

## 3. Related Work

Within this framework, the work approaches the interpretation of strategic information contained in Industry 4.0 cyber–physical complex-networked lean-management systems from two main vectors: social and technical strategic organizational design complexity. As shown in the research overview in Table 1, these two research directions have been intensively examined at three (micro-, meso-, and macroscopic) levels of complexity. A better visualization of these organizational levels is in the graphical abstract of Figure 1 for clarity purposes, but it should be noted that this classification is purely synthetic; in reality, cyber–physical systems in an Industry 4.0 context present the continuous complexification of networks arranged in nested hierarchies. This by no means suggests that one level of aggregated complexity is more difficult to deal with than a less aggregated one. In fact, the opposite is often true. For example, in the study of value-creating cyber–physical systems, the study of shop-floor management has been done for decades with almost solely qualitative methods and common sense [21–23]. Deep learning has been recently used to extract statistical patterns from cyber–physical systems at certain microscopic local levels [24,25]; however, there is an urgent need for algorithms to be developed that ensure a holistic understanding of cyber–physical systems at the meso- and macroscopic level of complex-networked aggregation.

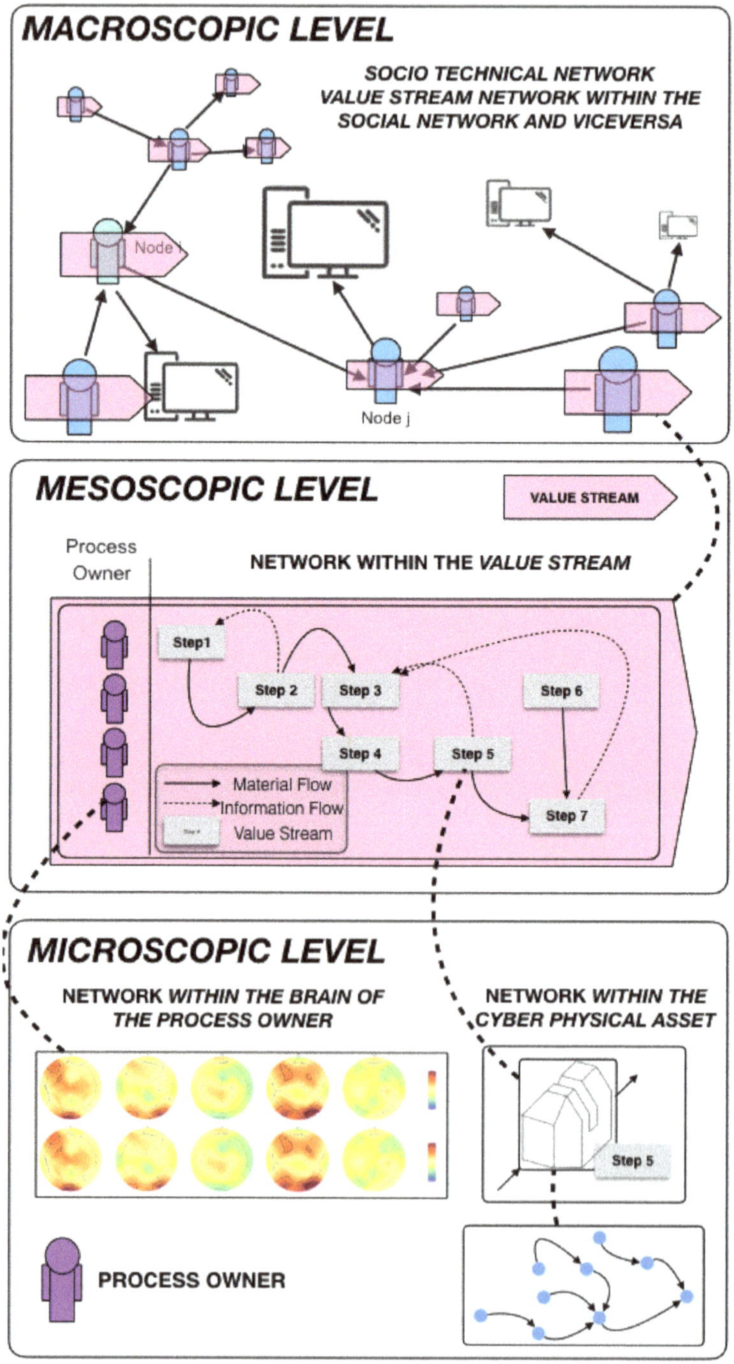


**Figure 1.** Macroscopic, mesoscopic, and microscopic levels of organizational sociotechnical complexity.

**Table 1.** Research overview.

| | Social | Technical | Socio Technical |
|---|---|---|---|
| Micro | Imai, 2012 [26];<br>Stock and Seliger, 2016 [27] | Takeda, 2009 [28];<br>Francis and Bian, 2019 [29];<br>Jabeur et al., 2015 [17];<br>Li et al., 2017 [30];<br>Aazam et al., 2018 [31];<br>Tao et al., 2018 [32];<br>Mushtaq and Haq, 2019 [33];<br>Shevchik et al., 2019 [34];<br>Al-Jaroodi and Mohamed, 2019 [35];<br>Sun et al., 2019 [36] | Villalba-Diez et al., 2015 [23];<br>Villalba-Diez et al., 2019 [24]. |
| Meso | Rother, 2010 [37];<br>Villalba et al., 2018 [13];<br>Birkel et al., 2019 [38] | Takeda, 2011 [39];<br>Davis et al., 2012 [40];<br>Gomez et al., 2015 [41];<br>Culot, 2019 [42];<br>Jimenez et al., 2016 [43];<br>Wang et al., 2018 [44];<br>Villalba-Diez et al., 2019 [25];<br>Jang et al., 2019 [45];<br>Ordieres-Mere et al., 2019 [46] | Villalba-Diez and Ordieres-Mere, 2015 [10];<br>Villalba-Diez et al., 2015 [9];<br>Villalba-Diez and Ordieres-Mere, 2016 [11];<br>Villalba-Diez et al., 2017 [47];<br>Davies et al., 2017 [48];<br>Kumar et al., 2019 [49]. |
| Macro | Womack and Jones, 2003 [50];<br>Toyota, 2014 [51];<br>Burton et al., 2015 [52];<br>Covey, 2004 [53];<br>Rabelo et al., 2019 [54];<br>Romero et al., 2017 [55];<br>Wang et al., 2019 [56];<br>Guo and Jyang, 2019 [57] | Lee et al., 2015 [58];<br>Wang et al., 2015 [59];<br>Goodfellow et al., 2016 [5];<br>Sisini et al., 2018 [60];<br>Zheng et al., 2018a [61];<br>Lu and Xu, 2019 [62] | Stock and Seliger, 2016 [27];<br>Villalba-Diez, 2017 [15];<br>Villalba-Diez, 2017 [14];<br>Kiel et al., 2017 [63];<br>Stock et al., 2016 [64];<br>Shang et al., 2019 [65]. |

Subsequently, a research hypothesis can be formulated. Due to the high potential shown by deep learning in a wide range of applications, we could hypothesise that deep learning can be used to find patterns within Industry 4.0 lean-management complex-networked cyber–physical systems, which takes us to the concept of geometric deep lean learning. The analogy of networks proposed in this work, as well as the global analysis of the evolving networks and, through the geometric deep lean learning of the local relations between agents, provide an adequate context to establish which data to collect, and how to structure their analysis in a general and systematic way.

Within this context, there are two main resource-organizing classes for integrating deep learning in Industry 4.0 cyber–physical contexts with regard to different assumptions on data acquisition:

- Offline training, and decision-support learning and predicting from a global and integrated way, for example, by extracting relevant information from an organization by means of deep-learning algorithms that analyze previously labeled text in organizational categories [66]. Alternatively, by combining deep learning with other computing methods that allow for more balanced datasets and, hence, better deep-learning performance [67].
- Digital twin and augmented reality. Creating virtual environments that, by recording, visualization, and interaction with cyber–physical assets, are capable of generating necessary tagged information in real time that is fed to deep-learning algorithms [68]. The creation of digital twins in combination with deep-learning algorithms was also proposed to enable the parallel control of cyber–physical value-creating processes [69].

Deep-learning algorithms are built by stacking data-processing filters—layers—in deep architectures [5]. These layers extract increasingly accurate representations of the data fed into them through a series of algebraic operations, such as convolution (learning local patterns of feature maps) and pooling (downsampling of feature maps). A key reason for the success of these classical deep-learning applications on time-series, images, or video processing, is on its underlying Euclidean or gridlike data-structure space. The ability to leverage statistical properties of such data through local statistics is possible because of the shift invariance, local connectivity and the multi-resolution of the dataset. For instance, in a color image, pixels are placed together (shift invariance), present local properties (local connectivity), and present a red–green–blue-layered color structure (multiresolution). The use of convolution and pooling imposes conditions on the dataset while extracting local features shared throughout images that make it suitable for the problem without sacrificing the expressive capacity of the network. In fact, the graph's Laplacian $\mathcal{L} = D - A$ that supports the information contained in the images is constant [70], where $D$ and $A$ represent the degree and adjacency matrix of the graph, respectively [19]. This allows a series of mass algebraic operations that make the magic of deep learning possible. However, at an organizational level, networks associated with Industry 4.0 lean-management cyber–physical systems are, by definition, dynamic and do not present these characteristics.

The fundamental idea of deep learning is that it is assumed that data to be studied came from the combination of different attributes at multiple hierarchical levels. An important underlining concept in this context is that of the manifold. A manifold can be intuitively understood as locally Euclidean space. Earth, for example, can be understood as a gigantic ellipsoid, but to a human at a point on its surface, it appears to be a plane. In other words, the manifold is an interconnected region: a series of points associated with its surrounding environment. From any of these points, the manifold appears to be locally Euclidean. Formally speaking, differentiable $X$ manifold of dimension $d$ is a topological space in which each point $x$ has an environment that is homeomorphic to a Euclidean space of dimension $d$ called tangent space $T_xX$ [71]. If the manifold is equipped with a Riemannian metric, such as an inner product $\langle \cdot, \cdot \rangle_{T_xX} : (T_xX)x(T_xX) \rightarrow \mathbb{R}$, then the manifold is called a Riemannian manifold. The set of tangent spaces at all points is known as tangent bundle $TX$ and is assumed to be smoothly dependent on the $x$ position. It is precisely this feature that is exploited by machine-learning algorithms. The condition for this is the implicit assumption that interesting points occur only in a collection of manifolds in directions tangent to the $TX$ planes, and with statistically interesting variations happening only when switching manifolds.

In other words, manifolds are topological spaces locally homeomorphic to Euclidean spaces. Complex networks, the object of this study, can be described by complexes of nodes and edges (i.e., triangles) that can be treated as discrete types of manifolds [72]. As has been described before [73–75], these can be understood as manifolds in order to explain the problems related to evolutionary manifolds using the theory of complex evolutionary networks. Specifically, deep learning applied to graphs usually considers these as manifolds; for this reason, we can consider deep lean learning as a manifold learning challenge. In the following sections, the consideration of graphs as manifolds is not geometrically rigorous, and might not be as smooth as previously defined. Classical applications of deep learning to graphs [76] focuses on static networks, but cyber–physical systems represented by complex networks are dynamic in nature, as nodes (both human and cyber–physical) and sociotechnical relations between them are constantly evolving.

For this reason, in order to discover statistical patterns within lean-management cyber–physical systems by means of deep learning, it is necessary to either transform existing data into figures that can be interpreted by classical approaches, or to generalize the concept of deep learning to dynamic networks. The first strategy was successfully implemented by one of the authors [13]. The second strategy follows in the footsteps of geometric deep learning.

Geometric deep learning is an emerging technique to generalize deep-learning models to non-Euclidean domains, such as certain graphs and manifolds [70]. The wide variety of domains in which geometric deep learning has so far been useful can be summarized in four categories:

- Graphwise classification. For instance, in the classification of molecules [77]. In this model, atoms represent the nodes, and chemical bonds are the edges of a graph. Research aims to extract certain features that predict certain properties of the molecule. This is relevant, for instance, to the pharmaceutical companies that are in the business of drug design. Some of these properties are toxicity and water solubility. Given a graph, researchers aim to classify a molecule graph. This is analogous to classical deep-learning-based visual image classification [78].

- Vertexwise classification. For example, in a social-network domain in which nodes are people of which we have certain demographic information, a researcher aims to predict how these people will vote in the next election. The analogy in computer vision is semantic image segmentation [79] in which the pixels of an image are labeled as belonging to a certain category.
- Graph dynamics. There are also domains that are described by fixed graphs, and others in which the graph changes with time [70]. Complex-networked cyber–physical systems belong to the second class.
- Known vs. unknown domain. In some cases, the graph can be known; in others, it is only partially known, *noisy*, or not known at all and needs to be learned. In these cases, the researcher aims to not only learn the graph features, but also the graph itself [80].

Existing approaches to implement geometric deep learning can be classified into two broad categories: spectral and local filtering methods.

- Spectral filtering methods.

  Spectral filtering methods make use of the spectral eigendecomposition of the Laplacian graph to elegantly mathematically define convolution-like operators. The fundamental limitation of the spectral construction is that it can only be used to single and static domains. This is because filter coefficients are dependent on the eigenvector- and eigenvalue-decomposition basis of the Laplacian graph, which is highly dependent on network architecture [70]. This approach is not suitable for our needs because of the dynamic characteristics of Industry 4.0 lean-management cyber–physical complex systems and their associated complex networks.
- Local filtering methods.

  Local filtering methods, on the other hand, are not topology-dependent, fall within the frame of signalling processing on graphs [81], and are more suitable in this setting, in particular, in order to define an operation similar to convolution in this domain [82].

## 4. Geometric Deep Lean Learning Over Industry 4.0 Lean-Management Complex-Networked Cyber–Physical Systems

According to Immanuel Kant, a science is not a science until there is a relation to mathematics. Although this characterization is provocative, and few would discuss such absolute numbers today, the implicit main question remains valid: can we find mathematical expressions that explain, process, and learn from network data, especially from complex-networked cyber–physical systems? This question is the motivator of this work, both for its practical and theoretical interest. On the one hand, empirically speaking, the processing of signals on graphs from complex cyber–physical networks has exponential importance due to the unstoppable emergence of technologies such as the IIoT and blockchain. On the other hand, the theoretical field of artificial intelligence constantly needs to develop new algorithms and computational architectures to later allow its practical application.

Applied to the analysis of complex-networked cyber–physical systems in the context of Industry 4.0, this leads to two classes of problem formulations that geometric deep lean learning theoretically solves:

- Strategic organizational design. Performing classical inference problems [76].

  Recently, it has been shown that this classification can be considerably improved by using information about the proximity environment [83,84]. Analyzing signals on graph vertices and edges could potentially help to learn inherent structures of the graphs, such as organizational clusters, with better accuracy than that provided by topological information alone—this is a strategic challenge to which organizational design tries to respond.

- Trust and power structures. Learning hidden organizational properties.

  Although deep learning has been employed in a wide variety of fields of knowledge, such as modeling social influence [85] and computer vision [86–88], it is important to incorporate knowledge about the domain to be treated in the model. For example, in order to build a deep-learning model for the study of a network of sensors in a cyber–physical system of industry 4.0, it might be useful, in a first approximation, to choose the edge weights of the graph as a decreasing function of the distance between nodes, as this would lead to a smooth graph signal model [89]; however, this would not be suitable for a lean structural network, because adjacency does not necessarily mean similarity [14]. For this reason, the model of the graph to be used can be superimposed on other structures, instead of being a pure unconnected abstraction. In other words, the graph that represents the complex-networked cyber–physical system in an Industry 4.0 context, can be studied from different perspectives, superimposing it to a specific sociotechnical environment that helps to better understand the statistical information that it contains. As a consequence, the integration of these priors is a fundamental challenge for the success of geometric deep lean learning. Some examples are the structures of power or trust between the different actors of an organization that are fundamental variables that influence the success of an organization, but remain elusive, since they often cannot be directly measured. Geometric deep lean learning could be applied to learn these parameters as weights between the nodes of the complex organizational network.

These problems reduce to fitting a time-dependent tensor $A(t)$, so that $\Omega(t+1) \approx A(t) \cdot \Omega(t)$ [90]. The hypothesis underlying this objective is that $x(t+1) \approx A(t) \cdot x(t)$ where $A(t)$ is constant in a window of time. The reason why we can take this assumption as true is that complex networks associated with cyber–physical systems in Industry 4.0 environments do not have very high variability [14]. As a result, a sufficiently small time window can always be found in which the hypothesis is sufficiently true.

Generalizing deep-lean-learning models to dynamic structured data in complex graphs requires a detailed description of the non-Euclidean equivalents to the basic elements of deep learning (convolutional layers and downsampling "pooling"), locally applied to each of the graph elements [70]:

- Convolution on non-Euclidean complex-networked cyber–physical graph time-dependent signals.

  As expressed in Expression 1, for weighted time-dependent directed graph $\Omega(t)$, a series of signals $x = [x(1), \ldots, x(n)] \in (\mathbb{R}^n x \mathbb{R}^m)$ expressed on its human and cyber–physical nodes, and on its standard communication edges, are considered, in which components of $x_a$ reside in or are protruding from node $a$.

  For each node, we define a proximity environment given by group $N_a = \{b : (b,a) \subset E\}$ that represents set of nodes $b$ connected with $a$. This $N_a$ set is characterized by an $\mathbb{R}^{NxN}$ matrix $S$ called the network-translation matrix operator that defines the manifold metric. We defined $S$ as the graph adjacency matrix, the Laplacian of the graph, or any other normalization of it, as a linear transformation to encode the structure of a graph. Without loss of generality, the singularity problem of the adjacency matrix, which is nontrivial, was not considered in this work [91]. As shown in Figure 2, group $N_a$ represents the manifold upon which the convolution acts.

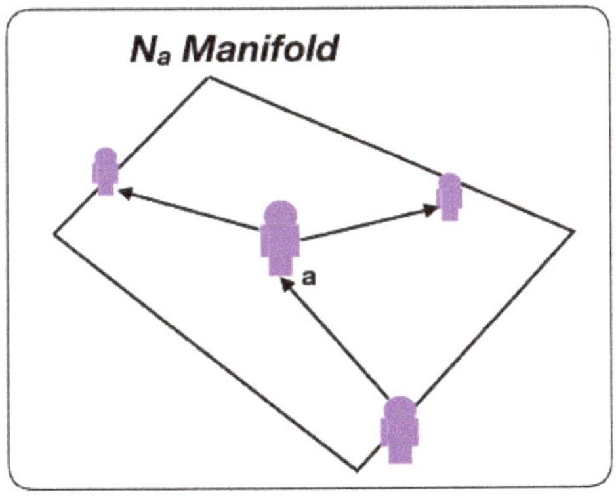


**Figure 2.** Local manifold upon which graph convolution acts.

The Fourier decomposition of graph $\Omega(t)$ is expressed by $\hat{x} = U^{-1} \cdot x$, where $S = \mathcal{U} \cdot \Lambda \cdot \mathcal{U}^{-1}$ and autovalues $\Lambda$ describe the frequencies of the graph [92]. Now, we can directly filter $x$ from the spectral domain by means of function $f : \mathbb{C} \rightarrow \mathbb{R}$ that allows to compute convolution $\hat{z} = f(\Lambda) \cdot \hat{x}$ by means of point-by-point multiplication in the spectral domain between filter $f(\Lambda)$ and the Fourier transform of the graph in $x$. Therefore, by inverting the Fourier transform of the graph, we obtain the extension of the convolutional operation to the non-Euclidean time-dependent graph in Equation (2).

$$z = \mathcal{P}(S)x \text{ and } \mathcal{P}(S) = \mathcal{U}f(\Lambda)\mathcal{U}^{-1} \tag{2}$$

The filter operation can be directly described on the node, resulting in an alternative formulation given by Equation (3), where scalar parameter $\phi_{a,b}$ is a representation of the information weights coming from neighbour node $b$ into or from node $a$.

$$z_a = \sum_{b \in N_a \cup a} \phi_{a,b} \cdot x_b \tag{3}$$

Due to the local properties of $S$, $z_a$ can be obtained in the domain of the node through local-information exchange. This means that the initial signal on the node is recursively transformed by $S$ a $K$ number of times until decomposition is obtained that determines $z_a$ as the convolution between the network filter with a polynomial transfer function and $x_b$.

By means of the Fourier transform of the network, the screening operation of Equation (3) has the transfer function given by Equation (4):

$$h(\Lambda) = \sum_{k=0}^{K} \phi_k \cdot \Lambda^k \tag{4}$$

This filter, based on local-information exchanges, captures information in K-radius proximity from the node representing the depth of the geometric-deep-lean-learning algorithm.

Taking into account this convolutional operation given by Equation (3), we are able to compute the $f$th level feature produced as output of the $l$th layer:

$$y_f^l = \sigma^l \cdot \left( \sum_{g=1}^{l-1} \mathcal{P}_{f,g}^l \cdot y_g^{l-1} \right) \tag{5}$$

where:

- $\sigma^l$ represents the nonlinear activation function (i.e., ReLU); and
- $\mathcal{P}^l_{f,g} \cdot y_g^{l-1}$ indicates the graph structure relating the $g$th input $y_g^{l-1}$ to the $f$th output $y^l_f$.

Now, we simply combine two cases to model the mechanism of a convolutional network applied to a non-Euclidean graph in each time slot: the case in which edges vary, and that in which nodes vary. This can be combined into a single expression to describe $\mathcal{P}^l_{f,g}$ given by Equation (6):

$$\mathcal{P}^l_{f,g}(S) = \sum_{k=1}^{K} Y^{l,(k:1)}_{f,g} + \sum_{k=0}^{K}\left(\prod_{m=0}^{k} Y_d^{(m)} + \phi_k \cdot \tau^k\right) \tag{6}$$

where:

- $\sum_{k=1}^{K} Y^{l,(k:1)}_{f,g}$ represents the edge-varying case, in which
    * $Y^{l,(k:1)}_{f,g}$ acts as a shift operator, and therefore represents a learning paradigm for data embedded within complex graphs, whose weights are known to some degree of ambiguity, are only partially known, or are unknown.
- $\sum_{k=0}^{K}\left(\prod_{m=0}^{k} Y_d^{(m)} + \phi_k \cdot \tau^k\right)$ represents the node-varying case, in which
    * $d \subset E$ is a special set of nodes (i.e., nodes with a degree above a certain threshold, nodes with a certain level of hierarchy in the organization, or any other relevant feature),
    * $\phi_k \in [0,1]^{Nxd}$ is a binary matrix, and
    * $\tau^k$ is a vector describing the node parameters in $d$.

- Pooling in non-Euclidean complex-networked cyber–physical graph time-dependent signals.

  As introduced earlier, downsampling pooling layers in classical deep-learning architectures that extract information from Euclidean domains such as speech, images, or videos typically report the maximal output within rectangular proximity [93]. In this way, it is possible to extract local characteristics that are shared by other areas of the images, thus considerably reducing the number of parameters that the deep network has to learn without sacrificing its learning capacity. Pooling can be described as a progressive coarsening of the graph. A simple way to do this is to collapse edges and reduce the size of the graph through a standard max-pooling operation on the nodes by just taking the maximum of each one of the feature tensors on each of the nodes being coarsened. This can be represented as a binary-tree structure of node indices. These pooling modules on graphs can be inserted between the convolutional modules in order to extract high-level graph representations, and thus be able to perform effective graph classification.

  Some alternatives in this field have not been to try to pool the whole network, but different hierarchies of the complex network in order to be able to learn which node groups have similar characteristics [94]. Once these groups are learned, clusters are made, and network pooling is carried out as described above or with an alternative method. This process is repeated for each of the network layers; thus, its classification is obtained. This presupposes, however, prior knowledge of the network structure.

  The extraction of shared local characteristics is not possible through this method in time-varying non-Euclidean domains, i.e., complex-networked cyber–physical graphs, because no stationarity or shift invariance can be found within these domains. Wu et al. [95], and Lee et al. [96] provided state-of-the-art surveying overview of this interesting open research question.

## 5. Conclusions and Management Implications

Geometric deep lean learning at a strategic level is expected to ensure sustainable organizational growth because customers and suppliers are able to reach new levels of transparency and traceability on the quality and efficiency of the processes, which generates new business opportunities for both, and new products, services, and co-operation opportunities in a cyber–physical environment. In a world of limited resources, increasing business volume can only be achieved by increasing the depth of integrated intelligence capable of successfully handling the emerging complexity in value streams. The future implications of geometric deep lean learning at an organizational level are yet to be fully deployed, but it is expected that the field of analysis of complex-networked cyber–physical systems in Industry 4.0 environments will attract intense attention from both industry and scholars who could develop tools to interpret, classify, and better understand the behavioral patterns of such networks through the application of this very exciting field of artificial intelligence.

Managerial implications of geometric deep lean learning on a mesoscopic level should try to integrate geometric deep lean learning in whole-value-stream processes to substantially improve resource optimization. Geometric deep lean learning at a value-stream level is expected to impact lead time and on-time delivery. At a mesoscopic level, producing only what the customer needs, when they needs it, in the required quality, the integration of deep-learning technologies is expected to not only allow the systematic improvement of complex value chains, but also the better use and exploitation of resources, thus reducing the environmental impact of Industry 4.0 processes. This technology could also be implemented at the customer side to increase defect-detection accuracy on products themselves. Such analyses provide sensitivity about operations and operational conditions, which also impacts value-stream-related efficiency and effectiveness.

The theoretical implications of the application of these geometric-deep-lean-learning models to data embedded within complex-networked datasets support researchers in departing from "crafted" features in modeling machine-learning models when dealing with geometric data. In the context of Industry 4.0 cyber–physical systems, these could be drone-positioning and decision-making algorithms, and the proper interpretation of wearable devices (i.e., physical sensors) on human or cybernetic process owners. Until now, models dealing with such problems required a certain amount of prior knowledge (e.g., the isometric-shape-deformation model), and often did not capture the full complexity and wealth of data. Geometric-deep-lean-learning methodologies could bring a breakthrough to the field and be the first indications of a coming paradigm shift by, for instance, expanding existing social-manufacturing knowledge into unknown territory through the contextual self-organizing of mass-individualization processes under a social-manufacturing paradigm through a cyber–physical–social system approach.

Some of the main potential applications can be clustered four categories:

- Graphwise classification. The classification of complex cyber–physical graphs by deep lean learning, thus creating product families and allowing automated decision making in real time in which products are developed, produced, and channeled to the final customer.
- Vertexwise classification. The classification of certain crucial nodes in the value-creation process by means of deep-lean-learning models that allows an improvement of organizational design to assure an increase of overall process performance.
- Graph dynamics. Learning complex-networked cyber–physical graph dynamics is of great interest when dealing with change management within non-Euclidean sociotechnical systems.
- Known vs. unknown domains. The learning, generation, and semisupervised design of value streams by learning the most suitable complex cyber–physical graphs for certain types of products, thus potentially generating high customization with high efficiency and effectiveness in resource use.

The data needed to implement these mathematical concepts are enormous and fall within the field of big data. The acquisition of data associated with the cyber–physical systems of Industry 4.0 is costly and of great strategic value to the involved organizations, which is why systems that increase the confidence of the involved actors and guarantee the security of these IIoT data, as the distributed ledger technology, are essential for the practical application of the exposed concepts. The quality of the obtained data essentially depends on the trust that the various value-creating actors have in each other. Achieving the necessary high degrees of confidence and successfully managing these parameters in an environment of interdependent supplier and customer networks is one of the challenges in the immediate future, and ought to be met by several blockchain and distributed ledger protocols. The Constrained Application Protocol is excellent for use with limited devices and low-power networks, such as those preferred in IIoT. To ensure greater security, applications known by the more important User Datagram Protocol, such as Voice over IP/Session Initiation Protocol, Datagram Transport Layer Security, can be run on User Datagram Protocol instead of Transmission Control Protocol. The Rivest–Shamir–Adleman hybrid algorithm can also be good, with high efficiency, better security and privacy protection, and is suitable for the end-to-end encryption requirements of the future IIoT. Future IIoT research within an Industry 4.0 complex-networked cyber–physical context should focus on, among others, the following characteristics: the open security system, the way in which individual privacy is protected, terminal-security function, and laws related to IIoT security. It is undeniable that IIoT security requires a set of policies, laws, and regulations, and a perfect security-management system for mutual collocation to ensure the success of this exciting and fruitful research endeavor.

**Author Contributions:** For research articles with several authors, a short paragraph specifying their individual contributions must be provided. The following statements should be used conceptualization, J.V.-D., M.M. and J.O.-M.; methodology, J.V.-D.; formal analysis, J.V.-D.; investigation, J.V.-D.; resources, S.S. and D.S.; writing—original draft preparation, J.V.-D.; writing—review and editing, J.V.-D., M.M. and J.O.-M.; visualization, J.V.-D.; supervision, J.V.-D.; project administration, J.V.-D.; funding acquisition, J.V.-D. and W.W. All authors have read and agreed to the published version of the manuscript.

**Funding:** This research was partially funded by the European Commission through the RFCS program, grant number ID 793505. This research was partially funded by the Ministerium für Wissenschaft, Forschung, und Kunst Baden-Württemberg (MWK), Germany, as part of idea competition "Mobility concepts for the emission-free campus 'NaMoCa'." The authors thank the China Scholarship Council (CSC) (no. 201206730038) for the support they provided for this work. The authors would also like to acknowledge the Spanish Agencia Estatal de Investigacion, through research project code RTI2018-094614-B-I00 into the "Programa Estatal de I+D+i Orientada a los Retos de la Sociedad".

**Acknowledgments:** J.V.D. would like to thank Paloma García-Lázaro (RIP), María Jesús Sánchez-Naranjo, and Eva Sánchez-Mañes for their magnificent job as professors of mathematics at the Escuela Técnica Superior de Ingenieros Industriales of the Universidad Politécnica de Madrid, for their inspiration, vitality, and energy in transmitting knowledge. All thanks to you, for teaching me these things that have greatly influenced my life and my work.

**Conflicts of Interest:** The authors declare no conflict of interest.

## Abbreviations

The following abbreviations are used in this manuscript:

| | |
|---|---|
| IIoT | Industrial Internet of Things |

## References

1. Reinsel, D.; Gantz, J.; Rydning, J. The Digitization of the World. From Edge to Core. 2018. Available online: https://www.seagate.com/files/www-content/our-story/trends/files/idc-seagate-dataage-whitepaper.pdf (accessed on 30 January 2020).
2. Ahmed, E.; Yaqoob, I.; Hashem, I.A.T.; Khan, I.; Ahmed, A.I.A.; Imran, M.; Vasilakos, A.V. The role of big data analytics in Internet of Things. *Comput. Netw.* **2017**, *129*, 459–471. [CrossRef]
3. Bhattacharjya, A.; Zhong, X.; Wang, J.; Li, X. Security Challenges and Concerns of Internet of Things (IoT). In *Cyber-Physical Systems: Architecture, Security and Application*; Guo, S., Zeng, D., Eds.; Springer International Publishing: Cham, Switzerland, 2019; pp. 153–185. [CrossRef]
4. Jiang, P.; Leng, J.; Ding, K.; Gu, P.; Koren, Y. Social manufacturing as a sustainable paradigm for mass individualization. *Proc. Inst. Mech. Eng. Part B J. Eng. Manuf.* **2016**, *230*, 1961–1968. [CrossRef]

5. Goodfellow, I.; Bengio, Y.; Courville, A. *Deep Learning*, 1st ed.; Adaptive Computation and Machine Learning Series; The MIT Press: Cambridge, MA, USA, 2016.
6. Hermann, M.; Pentek, T.; Otto, B. Design Principles for Industrie 4.0 Scenarios. In Proceedings of the 2016 49th Hawaii International Conference on System Sciences (HICSS), Koloa, HI, USA, 5–8 January 2016; pp. 3928–3937. [CrossRef]
7. Mosterman, P.J.; Zander, J. Industry 4.0 as a Cyber-Physical System study. *Softw. Syst. Model.* **2016**, *15*, 17–29. [CrossRef]
8. Shah, R.; Ward, P.T. Lean manufacturing: Context, practice bundles, and performance. *J. Oper. Manag.* **2003**, *21*, 129–149. [CrossRef]
9. Villalba-Diez, J.; Ordieres-Mere, J.; Chudzick, H.; Lopez-Rojo, P. NEMAWASHI: Attaining Value Stream alignment within Complex Organizational Networks. *Procedia CIRP* **2015**, *37*, 134–139. [CrossRef]
10. Villalba-Diez, J.; Ordieres-Mere, J. Improving manufacturing operational performance by standardizing process management. *Trans. Eng. Manag.* **2015**, *62*, 351–360. [CrossRef]
11. Villalba-Diez, J.; Ordieres-Meré, J. Strategic Lean Organizational Design: Towards Lean World-Small World Configurations through Discrete Dynamic Organizational Motifs. *Math. Probl. Eng.* **2016**, *2016*, 1–10. [CrossRef]
12. Villalba-Diez, J.; Ordieres-Mere, J.; Rubio-Valdehita, S. Lean Learning Patterns. (CPD)nA vs. KATA. *Procedia CIRP* **2016**, *54*, 147–151. [CrossRef]
13. Villalba-Diez, J.; Ordieres-Meré, J.; Molina, M.; Rossner, M.; Lay, M. Lean Dendrochronology: Complexity Reduction by Representation of KPI Dynamics Looking at Strategic Organizational Design. *Manag. Prod. Eng. Rev.* **2018**, *9*, 3–9. [CrossRef]
14. Villalba-Diez, J. *The Lean Brain Theory. Complex Networked Lean Strategic Organizational Design*; CRC Press: Boca Raton, FL, USA, 2017.
15. Villalba-Diez, J. *The HOSHIN KANRI FOREST. Lean Strategic Organizational Design*, 1st ed.; CRC Press: Boca Raton, FL, USA, 2017.
16. Cross, R.L.; Singer, J.; Colella, S.; Thomas, R.J.; Silverstone, Y. (Eds.) *The Organizational Network Fieldbook: Best Practices, Techniques and Exercises to Drive Organizational Innovation and Performance*, 1st ed.; Jossey-Bass: San Francisco, CA, USA, 2010.
17. Jabeur, N.; Sahli, N.; Zeadally, S. Enabling Cyber Physical Systems with Wireless Sensor Networking Technologies, Multiagent System Paradigm, and Natural Ecosystems. *Mob. Inf. Syst.* **2015**, *2015*, 15. [CrossRef]
18. Saleh, M.; Esa, Y.; Mohamed, A. Applications of Complex Network Analysis in Electric Power Systems. *Energies* **2018**, *11*, 1381. [CrossRef]
19. Barabási, A.-L. *Network Science*; Cambridge University Press: Cambridge, UK, 2016.
20. Wang, Y.; Yuan, Y.; Ma, Y.; Wang, G. Time-Dependent Graphs: Definitions, Applications, and Algorithms. *Data Sci. Eng.* **2019**. [CrossRef]
21. Suzaki, K. *The New Shopfloor Management*; The Free Press: New York, NY, USA, 1993.
22. De Leeuw, S.; van der Berg, J.P. Improving operational performance by influencing shopfloor behavior via performance management practices. *J. Oper. Manag.* **2011**, *29*, 224–235. [CrossRef]
23. Villalba-Diez, J.; Ordieres-Meré, J.; Nuber, G. The HOSHIN KANRI TREE. Cross-Plant Lean Shopfloor Management. *Procedia CIRP* **2015**, *32*, 150–155. [CrossRef]
24. Villalba-Diez, J.; Zheng, X.; Schmidt, D.; Molina, M. Characterization of Industry 4.0 Lean Management Problem-Solving Behavioral Patterns Using EEG Sensors and Deep Learning. *Sensors* **2019**, *19*, 2841. [CrossRef]
25. Villalba-Diez, J.; Schmidt, D.; Gevers, R.; Ordieres-Meré, J.; Buchwitz, M.; Wellbrock, W. Deep Learning for Industrial Computer Vision Quality Control in the Printing Industry 4.0. *Sensors* **2019**, *19*, 3987. [CrossRef]
26. Imai, M. *Gemba Kaizen: A Commonsense Approach to a Continuous Improvement Strategy*, 2nd ed.; McGraw-Hill Professional: New York, NY, USA, 2012.
27. Stock, T.; Seliger, G. Opportunities of Sustainable Manufacturing in Industry 4.0. *Procedia CIRP* **2016**, *40*, 536–541. [CrossRef]
28. Takeda, H. *Intelligent Automation Textbook*; Nikkan Kogyo Shimbun: Tokyo, Japan, 2009.
29. Francis, J.; Bian, L. Deep Learning for Distortion Prediction in Laser-Based Additive Manufacturing using Big Data. *Manuf. Lett.* **2019**, *20*, 10–14. [CrossRef]

30. Li, B.H.; Hou, B.C.; Yu, W.T.; Lu, X.B.; Yang, C.W. Applications of artificial intelligence in intelligent manufacturing: A review. *Front. Inf. Technol. Electron. Eng.* **2017**, *18*, 86–96. [CrossRef]
31. Aazam, M.; Zeadally, S.; Harras, K.A. Deploying Fog Computing in Industrial Internet of Things and Industry 4.0. *IEEE Trans. Ind. Inform.* **2018**, *14*, 4674–4682. [CrossRef]
32. Tao, F.; Qi, Q.; Liu, A.; Kusiak, A. Data-driven smart manufacturing. *J. Manuf. Syst.* **2018**, *48*, 157–169. [CrossRef]
33. Mushtaq, A.; Haq, I.U. Implications of Blockchain in Industry 4.O. In Proceedings of the 2019 International Conference on Engineering and Emerging Technologies (ICEET), Lahore, Pakistan, 21–22 February 2019; pp. 1–5. [CrossRef]
34. Shevchik, S.A.; Masinelli, G.; Kenel, C.; Leinenbach, C.; Wasmer, K. Deep Learning for In Situ and Real-Time Quality Monitoring in Additive Manufacturing Using Acoustic Emission. *IEEE Trans. Ind. Inform.* **2019**, *15*, 5194–5203. [CrossRef]
35. Al-Jaroodi, J.; Mohamed, N. Blockchain in Industries: A Survey. *IEEE Access* **2019**, *7*, 36500–36515. [CrossRef]
36. Sun, S.; Zheng, X.; Villalba-Diez, J.; Ordieres-Meré, J. Indoor Air-Quality Data-Monitoring System: Long-Term Monitoring Benefits. *Sensors* **2019**, *19*, 4157. [CrossRef] [PubMed]
37. Rother, M. *Toyota Kata. Managing People for Improvement, Adaptiveness, and Superior Results*; McGraw-Hill: New York, NY, USA, 2010.
38. Birkel, S.H.; Veile, W.J.; Müller, M.J.; Hartmann, E.; Voigt, K.I. Development of a Risk Framework for Industry 4.0 in the Context of Sustainability for Established Manufacturers. *Sustainability* **2019**, *11*, 384. [CrossRef]
39. Takeda, H. *LCIA—Low Cost Intelligent Automation*, 3rd ed.; Finanzbuch Verlag GmbH: Munich, Germany, 2011.
40. Davis, J.; Edgar, T.; Porter, J.; Bernaden, J.; Sarli, M. Smart manufacturing, manufacturing intelligence and demand-dynamic performance. *Comput. Chem. Eng.* **2012**, *47*, 145–156. [CrossRef]
41. Gómez, A.; Cuiñas, D.; Catalá, P.; Xin, L.; Li, W.; Conway, S.; Lack, D. Use of Single Board Computers as Smart Sensors in the Manufacturing Industry. *MESIC Manuf. Eng. Soc. Int. Conf.* **2015**, *132*, 153–159. [CrossRef]
42. Culot, G.; Orzes, G.; Sartor, M. Integration and Scale in the Context of Industry 4.0: The Evolving Shapes of Manufacturing Value Chains. *IEEE Eng. Manag. Rev.* **2019**, *47*, 45–51. [CrossRef]
43. Jiménez, P.; Villalba-Díez, J.; Ordieres-Meré, J. HOSHIN KANRI Visualization with Neo4j. Empowering Leaders to Operationalize Lean Structural Networks. *Procedia CIRP* **2016**, *55*, 284–289.
44. Wang, J.; Ma, Y.; Zhang, L.; Gao, R.; Wu, D. Deep learning for smart manufacturing: Methods and applications. *J. Manuf. Syst.* **2018**. [CrossRef]
45. Jang, S.H.; Guejong, J.; Jeong, J.; Sangmin, B. *Fog Computing Architecture Based Blockchain for Industrial IoT. Computational Science—ICCS 2019*; Rodrigues, J.M.F., Cardoso, P.J.S., Monteiro, J., Lam, R., Krzhizhanovskaya, V.V., Lees, M.H., Dongarra, J.J., Sloot, P.M., Eds.; Springer International Publishing: Cham, Switzerland, 2019; pp. 593–606.
46. Ordieres-Meré, J.; Villalba-Diez, J.; Zheng, X. *Challenges and Opportunities for Publishing IIoT Data in Manufacturing as a Service Business*; Cyber Physical Manufacturing; Procedia Manufacturing; Elsevier: Chicago, IL, USA, 2019.
47. Villalba-Diez, J.; DeSanctis, I.; Ordieres-Meré, J.; Ciarapica, F. Lean Structural Network Resilience. In *Complex Networks and Its Applications VI: Proceedings of Complex Networks 2017 (The Sixth International Conference on Complex Networks and Their Applications)*; Cherifi, C., Cherifi, H., Karsai, M., Musolesi, M., Eds.; Number 689 in Studies in Computational Intelligence; Springer International Publishing: Lyon, France, 2017; pp. 609–619.
48. Davies, R.; Coole, T.; Smith, A. Review of Socio-technical Considerations to Ensure Successful Implementation of Industry 4.0. *Procedia Manuf.* **2017**, *11*, 1288–1295. [CrossRef]
49. Kumar, K.; Zindani, D.; Davim, J.P. Socio-technical Considerations. In *Industry 4.0: Developments towards the Fourth Industrial Revolution*; Kumar, K., Zindani, D., Davim, J.P., Eds.; Springer: Singapore, 2019; pp. 43–51. [CrossRef]
50. Womack, J.P.; Jones, D.T. Introduction. In *Lean Thinking*, 2nd ed.; Simon and Schuster: New York, NY, USA, 2003; pp. 15–28.
51. Toyota Motor Corporation. *Toyota Motor Corporation. Sustainability Report 2013*; Sustainability Report; Toyota Motor Corporation: Tokyo, Jaoan, 2014.
52. Burton, R.M.; Øbel, B.; Håkonsson, D.D. *Organizational Design: A Step-by-Step Approach*, 3rd ed.; Cambridge University Press: Cambridge, UK, 2015.
53. Covey, S.R. *The 8th Habit. From Effectiveness to Greatness*; Free Press: New York, NY, USA, 2004.

54. Rabelo, R.J.; Zambiasi, S.P.; Romero, D. Collaborative Softbots: Enhancing Operational Excellence in Systems of Cyber-Physical Systems. In *Collaborative Networks and Digital Transformation*; Camarinha-Matos, L.M., Afsarmanesh, H., Antonelli, D., Eds.; Springer International Publishing: Cham, Switzerland, 2019; pp. 55–68.
55. Romero, D.; Wuest, T.; Stahre, J.; Gorecky, D. Social Factory Architecture: Social Networking Services and Production Scenarios Through the Social Internet of Things, Services and People for the Social Operator 4.0. In *Advances in Production Management Systems. The Path to Intelligent, Collaborative and Sustainable Manufacturing*; Lödding, H., Riedel, R., Thoben, K.D., von Cieminski, G., Kiritsis, D., Eds.; Springer International Publishing: Cham, Switzerland, 2017; pp. 265–273.
56. Wang, F.; Shang, X.; Qin, R.; Xiong, G.; Nyberg, T.R. Social Manufacturing: A Paradigm Shift for Smart Prosumers in the Era of Societies 5.0. *IEEE Trans. Comp. Social Syst.* **2019**, *6*, 822–829. [CrossRef]
57. Guo, W.; Jiang, P. Product Service Systems for Social Manufacturing: A new service system with multi-provider. *IFAC-PapersOnLine* **2019**, *52*, 749–754. [CrossRef]
58. Lee, J.; Bagheri, B.; Kao, H.A. A Cyber-Physical Systems architecture for Industry 4.0-based manufacturing systems. *Manuf. Lett.* **2015**, *3*, 18–23. [CrossRef]
59. Wang, L.; Toerngren, M.; Onori, M. Current status and advancement of cyber-physical systems in manufacturing. *J. Manuf. Syst.* **2015**, *37*, 517–527. [CrossRef]
60. Sisinni, E.; Saifullah, A.; Han, S.; Jennehag, U.; Gidlund, M. Industrial Internet of Things: Challenges, Opportunities, and Directions. *IEEE Trans. Ind. Inform.* **2018**, *14*, 4724–4734. [CrossRef]
61. Zheng, P.; Wang, H.; Sang, Z.; Zhong, R.Y.; Liu, Y.; Liu, C.; Mubarok, K.; Yu, S.; Xu, X. Smart manufacturing systems for Industry 4.0: Conceptual framework, scenarios, and future perspectives. *Front. Mech. Eng.* **2018**, *13*, 137–150. [CrossRef]
62. Lu, Y.; Xu, X. Cloud-based manufacturing equipment and big data analytics to enable on-demand manufacturing services. *Robot. Comput. Integr. Manuf.* **2019**, *57*, 92–102. [CrossRef]
63. Kiel, D.; MÜller, J.M.; Arnold, C.; Voigt, K.I. Sustainable Industrial Value Creation: Benefits and Challenges of Industry 4.0. *Int. J. Innov. Manag.* **2017**, *21*, 1740015. [CrossRef]
64. Stock, T.; Obenaus, M.; Kunz, S.; Kohl, H. Industry 4.0 as enabler for a sustainable development: A qualitative assessment of its ecological and social potential. *Process Saf. Environ. Prot.* **2018**, *118*, 254–267. [CrossRef]
65. Shang, X.; Shen, Z.; Xiong, G.; Wang, F.Y.; Liu, S.; Nyberg, T.R.; Wu, H.; Guo, C. Moving from mass customization to social manufacturing: A footwear industry case study. *Int. J. Comput. Integr. Manuf.* **2019**, *32*, 194–205. [CrossRef]
66. Leng, J.; Jiang, P. A deep learning approach for relationship extraction from interaction context in social manufacturing paradigm. *Knowl. Based Syst.* **2016**, *100*, 188–199. [CrossRef]
67. Leng, J.; Chen, Q.; Mao, N.; Jiang, P. Combining granular computing technique with deep learning for service planning under social manufacturing contexts. *Knowl. Based Syst.* **2018**, *143*, 295–306. [CrossRef]
68. Subakti, H.; Jiang, J.-R. Indoor Augmented Reality Using Deep Learning for Industry 4.0 Smart Factories. In Proceedings of the 2018 IEEE 42nd Annual Computer Software and Applications Conference (COMPSAC), Tokyo, Japan, 23–27 July 2018; Volume 2, pp. 63–68. [CrossRef]
69. Tao, F.; Qi, Q.; Wang, L.; Nee, A.Y.C. Digital Twins and Cyber–Physical Systems toward Smart Manufacturing and Industry 4.0: Correlation and Comparison. *Engineering* **2019**, *5*, 653–661. [CrossRef]
70. Bronstein, M.M.; Bruna, J.; LeCun, Y.; Szlam, A.; Vandergheynst, P. Geometric Deep Learning: Going beyond Euclidean data. *IEEE Signal Process. Mag.* **2017**, *34*, 18–42. [CrossRef]
71. Ma, Y.; Fu, Y. *Manifold Learning Theory and Applications*; CRC Press: Boca Raton, FL, USA, 2011.
72. Keller, M. Curvature, Geometry and Spectral Properties of Planar Graphs. *Discret. Comput. Geom.* **2011**, *46*, 500–525. [CrossRef]
73. Wu, Z.; Menichetti, G.; Rahmede, C.; Bianconi, G. Emergent complex network geometry. *Sci. Rep.* **2015**, *5*, 10073. [CrossRef]
74. Bianconi, G.; Rahmede, C.; Wu, Z. Complex quantum network geometries: Evolution and phase transitions. *Phys. Rev. E Stat. Nonlinear Soft Matter Phys.* **2015**, *92*, 022815. [CrossRef]
75. Bianconi, G.; Rahmede, C. Complex Quantum Network Manifolds in Dimension d > 2 are Scale-Free. *Sci. Rep.* **2015**, *5*, 13979. [CrossRef]
76. Zhang, Z.; Cui, P.; Zhu, W. Deep Learning on Graphs: A Survey. *arXiv* **2018**, arXiv:1812.04202.

77. Duvenaud, D.; Maclaurin, D.; Aguilera-Iparraguirre, J.; Gómez-Bombarelli, R.; Hirzel, T.; Aspuru-Guzik, A.; Adams, R.P. Convolutional Networks on Graphs for Learning Molecular Fingerprints. *arXiv* **2015**, arXiv:1509.09292.
78. Krizhevsky, A.; Sutskever, L.; Hinton, G. Imagenet classification with deep convolutional neural networks. In Proceedings of the 25th International Conference on Neural Information Processing Systems, Lake Tahoe, CA, USA, 3–8 December 2012; pp. 1106–1114.
79. Chen, L.C.; Barron, J.T.; Papandreou, G.; Murphy, K.; Yuille, A.L. Semantic Image Segmentation with Task-Specific Edge Detection Using CNNs and a Discriminatively Trained Domain Transform. *arXiv* **2015**, arXiv:1511.03328.
80. Cao, S.; Lu, W.; Xu, Q. Deep Neural Networks for Learning Graph Representations. In Proceedings of the Thirtieth AAAI Conference on Artificial Intelligence, Phoenix, AZ, USA, 12–17 February 2016; pp. 1145–1152.
81. Shuman, D.; Narang, S.; Frossard, P.; Ortega, A.; Vandergheynst, P. The emerging field of signal processing on graphs: Extending high-dimensional data analysis to networks and other irregular domains. *IEEE Signal Process. Mag.* **2013**, *30*, 83–98. [CrossRef]
82. Henaff, M.; Bruna, J.; LeCun, Y. Deep convolutional networks on graph-structured data. *arXiv* **2015**, arXiv:1506.05163.
83. Defferrard, M.; Bresson, X.; Vandergheynst, P. Convolutional Neural Networks on Graphs with Fast Localized Spectral Filtering. *arXiv* **2016**, arXiv:1606.09375.
84. Kipf, T.N.; Welling, M. Semi-Supervised Classification with Graph Convolutional Networks. *arXiv* **2016**, arXiv:1609.02907.
85. Qiu, J.; Tang, J.; Ma, H.; Dong, Y.; Wang, K.; Tang, J. DeepInf: Social Influence Prediction with Deep Learning. In Proceedings of the 24th ACM SIGKDD International Conference on Knowledge Discovery and Data Mining, London, UK, 19–23 August 2018; ACM: New York, NY, USA, 2018; pp. 2110–2119. [CrossRef]
86. Garcia, V.; Bruna, J. Few-Shot Learning with Graph Neural Networks. *arXiv* **2017**, arXiv:1711.04043.
87. Jain, A.; Zamir, A.R.; Savarese, S.; Saxena, A. Structural-RNN: Deep Learning on Spatio-Temporal Graphs. *arXiv* **2015**, arXiv:1511.05298.
88. Marino, K.; Salakhutdinov, R.; Gupta, A. The More You Know: Using Knowledge Graphs for Image Classification. *arXiv* **2016**, arXiv:1612.04844.
89. Sandryhaila, A.; Moura, J.M.F. Discrete Signal Processing on Graphs. *IEEE Trans. Signal Process.* **2013**, *61*, 1644–1656. [CrossRef]
90. Harris, K.D.; Aravkin, A.; Rao, R.; Brunton, B.W. Time-varying Autoregression with Low Rank Tensors. *arXiv* **2019**, arXiv:1905.08389.
91. Sciriha, I. A characterization of singular graphs. *Electron. J. Linear Algebra* **2007**, *16*, 451–462. [CrossRef]
92. Ortega, A.; Frossard, P.; Kovačević, J.; Moura, J.M.; Vandergheynst, P. Graph Signal Processing: Overview, Challenges, and Applications. *Proc. IEEE* **2018**, *106*, 808–828. [CrossRef]
93. Zhou, Y.T.; Chellappa, R. Computation of optical flow using a neural network. In Proceedings of the IEEE 1988 International Conference on Neural Networks, San Diego, CA, USA, 24–27 July 1988; Volume 2, pp. 71–78. [CrossRef]
94. Ying, Z.; You, J.; Morris, C.; Ren, X.; Hamilton, W.; Leskovec, J. Hierarchical Graph Representation Learning with Differentiable Pooling. In *Advances in Neural Information Processing Systems 31*; Bengio, S., Wallach, H., Larochelle, H., Grauman, K., Cesa-Bianchi, N., Garnett, R., Eds.; Curran Associates, Inc.: Red Hook, NY, USA, 2018; pp. 4800–4810.
95. Wu, Z.; Pan, S.; Chen, F.; Long, G.; Zhang, C.; Yu, P.S. A Comprehensive Survey on Graph Neural Networks. *arXiv* **2019**, arXiv:1901.00596.
96. Lee, J.; Lee, I.; Kang, J. Self-Attention Graph Pooling. In Proceedings of the 36th International Conference on Machine Learning, Long Beach, CA, USA, 9–15 June 2019; Chaudhuri, K., Salakhutdinov, R., Eds.; PMLR: Long Beach, CA, USA, 2019; Volume 97, pp. 3734–3743.

sensors

MDPI

Article

# Deep Learning for Industrial Computer Vision Quality Control in the Printing Industry 4.0

**Javier Villalba-Diez [1,2,†,*], Daniel Schmidt [3,4,†], Roman Gevers [3], Joaquín Ordieres-Meré [4], Martin Buchwitz [5] and Wanja Wellbrock [1]**

1. Hochschule Heilbronn, Fakultät Management und Vertrieb, Campus Schwäbisch Hall, 74523 Schwäbisch Hall, Germany; Wanja.wellbrock@hs-heilbronn.de
2. Department of Artificial Intelligence, Escuela Técnica Superior de Ingenieros Informáticos, Universidad Politécnica de Madrid, 28660 Madrid, Spain
3. Matthews International GmbH, Gutenbergstraße 1-3, 48691 Vreden, Germany; Daniel.Schmidt@saueressig.de (D.S.); roman.gevers@saueressig.de (R.G.)
4. Departament of Business Intelligence, Escuela Técnica Superior de Ingenieros Industriales, Universidad Politécnica de Madrid, 28006 Madrid, Spain; j.ordieres@upm.es
5. InspectOnline, Wiley-VCH Verlag GmbH & Co. KGaA, 69469 Weinheim, Germany; mbuchwitz@wiley.com

* Correspondence: javier.villalba-diez@hs-heilbronn.de

† These authors contributed equally to this work.

Received: 9 July 2019; Accepted: 13 September 2019; Published: 15 September 2019

**Abstract:** Rapid and accurate industrial inspection to ensure the highest quality standards at a competitive price is one of the biggest challenges in the manufacturing industry. This paper shows an application of how a Deep Learning soft sensor application can be combined with a high-resolution optical quality control camera to increase the accuracy and reduce the cost of an industrial visual inspection process in the Printing Industry 4.0. During the process of producing gravure cylinders, mistakes like holes in the printing cylinder are inevitable. In order to improve the defect detection performance and reduce quality inspection costs by process automation, this paper proposes a deep neural network (DNN) soft sensor that compares the scanned surface to the used engraving file and performs an automatic quality control process by learning features through exposure to training data. The DNN sensor developed achieved a fully ***automated classification accuracy rate of 98.4%***. Further research aims to use these results to three ends. Firstly, to predict the amount of errors a cylinder has, to further support the human operation by showing the error probability to the operator, and finally to decide autonomously about product quality without human involvement.

**Keywords:** soft sensors; industrial optical quality inspection; deep learning; artificial vision

## 1. Introduction

Countries aspiring to lead these technological changes and remain in industrial leadership positions have strategically positioned themselves for the new type of cyber–physical infrastructure that will emerge from the Industrial Internet of Things (IIoT) and data science. Germany's Industry 4.0 framework has evolved into a pan-European collaborative effort to perform intelligent automation at scale [1]. In a similar move, the United States launched the Manufacturing Leadership Coalition (SMLC) [2] in 2011. Other notable examples include "China Manufacturing 2025" [3] that seeks to elevate advanced manufacturing technology, or Japanese's "Society 5.0" [4] with a holistic focus on the safety and well-being of humans through cyber–physical systems. As a paradigmatic example, the Japanese manufacturer has consistently gained a competitive edge towards its competition by providing its value stream elements with the ability not to pass defects to the next step in the manufacturing process [5].

A prime example of this is the remarkable success of Toyota's implementation of intelligent autonomation, or JIDOKA -自働化- [6–8], alongside other strategic Lean manufacturing system characteristics [9–14]. Thanks to the availability of sufficient data from virtually any element of the production process (through IIoT for example), and the development of computational elements powerful enough to perform real time calculations on the state of the value stream, the systematic extension of JIDOKA in the industry has been made possible [15]. In fact, there is great potential for other industries to increase the ability of machines to recognize their own state through intelligent sensors capable of ***sensing*** the specific needs of customers and ***responding*** flexibly and accordingly. This would improve the level of automation and increase product quality and customization while increasing related value stream performance [16–18] .

Within this framework, Optical Quality Control (OQC) is crucial to many manufacturing processes in an effort to meet customer requirements [19]. On the one hand, the performance of human-centered OQC does not meet the necessary requirements: it is limited by ergonomics and cost, as humans get tired with repetitive OQC tasks and these tasks are usually very labor-intensive. For this reason, automatic detection of visual defects, which aims to segment possible defective areas of a product image and subsequently classify them into defect categories, emerges as a necessary solution to the problem. On the other hand, simple threshold techniques are often insufficient to segment background defects when not applied to a controlled environment characterized by stable lighting conditions. Xie [20] provides a classification of existing methods, but the common practice in industrial environments is that each new feature has to be described manually by experts when a new type of problem occurs: surface defects in industrially manufactured products can have all kinds of sizes, shapes or orientations. These methods are often not valid when applied to real surfaces with rough textures, complex, or noisy sensor data. This has the immediate consequence that classifications are almost always insufficient and cannot be generalized to unknown problems [21]. For these reasons, more robust and reliable results are needed in the detection of defects by more sophisticated methods.

The printing industry underwent an enormous transformation through the digital revolution when inkjet reached a mature era. Inkjet printing is based on the formation of small liquid droplets to transfer precise amounts of material to a substrate under digital control. Inkjet technology is becoming relatively mature and is of great industrial interest due to its flexibility for graphic printing and its potential use in less conventional applications such as additive manufacturing and the manufacture of printed electronics and other functional devices. Its advantages over conventional printing processes are numerous. For instance, it produces little or not waste, it versatile thanks to different processes, it is non-contact, and does not require a master template which means printing patterns can be easily changed. However, the technology needs to be developed in order to be used in new applications such as additive manufacturing (3D printing).

Laser engraving of gravure cylinders (Figure 1) is the latest and most exciting development in gravure printing. Laser technology makes it possible to produce cells with variable shapes, which is not possible with electromechanical engraving. These new shapes actually provide a higher print density and it is possible to use inks with a higher viscosity than conventional electromechanically engraved cylinders. Laser engraved cylinders also reduce the influence of print speed on print quality and keep the highlight tone values stable.

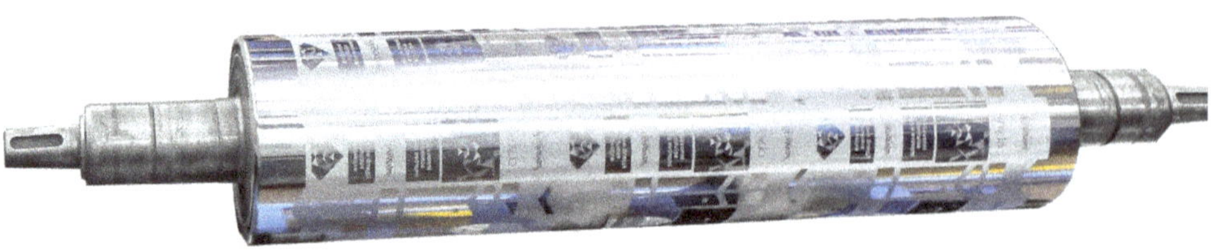

**Figure 1.** Printing Cylinder.

Although laser engraving of rotogravure cylinders is a new variant of etching rotogravure cylinders in the rotogravure market, today's systems are still susceptible to errors. Possible errors or optical detectable defects include dents, scratches, inclusions, spray, curves, offset, smearing and excessive, pale or missing printing or color errors (i.e., incorrect colors, gradients and color deviations from the desired pattern). The most common errors is dents, 32%, while the least common error is smearing, 3%. Due to the different errors and noise levels typical of industrial settings, an automatic error detection based on classical computer vision algorithms was not possible [22]. Most systems aim to select potential faults and present them to the human expert responsible for deciding the presence or severity of faults. Practice shows that about 30% of the possible errors that need to be checked are not relevant. This fact increases both the costs associated with the OQC and the lead time of the overall process. Both factors are crucial to achieving customer confidence and must be systematically optimized.

Bearing these issues in mind, this research delves into an alternative solution to overcome the problem of the need of manual predetermination of the specific characteristics for each new inspection problem: deep learning-based deep neural networks (DNN). Deep learning is a paradigm of machine learning that enables computational models consisting of multiple processing layers to learn representations of data with multiple levels of abstraction [23,24]. DNN are constructions created by combining a series of hierarchically superimposed and arbitrarily initialized filters that are capable of automatically learning the best features for a given classification problem due to exposure to training data [25,26]. Several DNN architectures have been successfully used to extract statistical information from physical sensors in the context of Industry 4.0 in several applications such as classification problems [27], visual object recognition [23], human activity recognition through wearables [28,29], predictive maintenance [30,31], or computer vision [32] among others. More specifically, DNN have recently proved useful for industrial computer OQC defect detection purposes with promising results by automatically extracting useful features with little to no prior knowledge about the images [33,34].

The goal of this paper is to present a soft sensor DNN that performs a ***classification*** of images from high-resolution cameras towards a fully computer vision OQC of the printing cylinder of a global leading player in the Printing Industry 4.0. As shown in detail in Section 3, this aims to increase the accuracy of the quality inspection process by first supporting the human expert final decision making, thereby reducing the cost of quality inspection process through automatization of the visual processing. This ought to be contextualized in a hostile industrial context in which the complexity of error detection is very high due both to the extraordinary variability of possible errors, as well as the changing environmental conditions of light, moisture, dirt, and pollution - all of which can confuse the best algorithms developed thus far.

The rest of the paper is structured to ensure clarity in the presentation, replication of the results obtained, and a proper framing in the ongoing global context of the fourth industrial revolution. Firstly, Section 2 briefly shows the continuous improvement of the manufacturing value stream of an Industry 4.0 leader that made the integration of deep learning technology possible. Secondly, Section 3 outlines the ***materials and methods*** used to design and implement a better performing OQC integrated DNN soft sensor. Additionally, DNN computer Code is made available on an Open Access Repository. Next, the ***results*** obtained are briefly discussed from a technical point of view in Section 4. Finally, in Section 5 the short, medium and long term ***consequences*** of these findings for the printing industry are discussed and highlighted in a broader manufacturing Industry 4.0 context.

## 2. Evolution towards Automatic Deep Learning-Based OQC

In order to frame this research in a more general context and allow its replication in other value streams, it is important to describe the constant process of continuous improvement [35] that a leading player in the printing industry has followed in recent years to reach the level that has allowed the implementation of the presented Deep Learning-based OQC research.

For the purpose of making it easier for interested readers to recognize the fundamental phases of this OQC evolutional continuous improvement process that paved the road for a fully automatized computer vision OQC process have been summarized in Table 1 and is depicted in Figure 2.

**Table 1.** State of the Art.

| Stage | Description of Improvement |
|---|---|
| Manual Inspection of Printed Product (Figure 2a) | In the first stage all cylinders of an order were printed together. Due to the processes used producing gravure cylinders, mistakes like holes in the cylinder are almost inevitable. To check the quality of the gravure cylinders, all the cylinders of one order are generally printed together and the resulting print checked manually with the help of a magnifying glass. To do this the approximate color of each individual cylinder must be mixed and all cylinders are printed one after the other on one substrate. On average this can be 5–10 cylinders or colours in one job. The big disadvantage is that all cylinders of a job must already be present. Thus, a one-piece flow is not possible. In addition, a lot of time is spent mixing the colours. As a direct comparison with the expected data was very difficult, the search for errors was focused on the most common errors that can happen during the production of an engraved printing cylinder. The coppering of the cylinder is a galvanic process, therefore it is possible that the cylinder has holes that also print. Another common mistake in the production of engraved printing cylinders is that parts that should print do not print. This can have different causes. Most of them can be traced back to problems during the engraving of the cylinder. To find these errors without a comparison to the expected data a search for irregularities in the carried out. As there are a lot of issues that had to be checked it was quite an ergonomically-challenging job, where some mistakes were not caught during the check. |
| Manual Inspection of Individual Color Printed Product (Figure 2b) | In the second stage the cylinders were all printed individually in the same (green) colour. In an attempt to further improve the quality control of each individual cylinder, the cylinder can also be printed itself. This impression was also checked manually with a magnifying glass by process experts. This has the advantage that there is no need to wait for the other cylinders of a job and no need to mix colours. However, the manual reading of the prints takes longer because there is one print for every cylinder of an order (5–10 cylinders) and not only one print for one order. Although this increased process reliability because process mistakes were directly tested on the product, the ergonomic weaknesses of the OQC process based on human experts could not be eliminated with this new improvement. |
| Evaluation of Errors by an Expert with aid of patented Software cLynx (Figure 2c) | This was then solved by the third stage: the digital scanning of the cylinder supported by the patented cLynx software (DE102017105704B3) [36]. To improve the quality and automate the process, a software named cLynx was developed to automatically compare the scanned file with the engraving file. The invention relates to a method for checking a printing form, in particular a gravure cylinder, for errors in an engraving printing form. A press proof of a cylinder gets printed and scanned using a high-resolution scanner. To compare the scans with the engraving file, a sequence of registration steps are performed. As a result the scans are matched with the engraving file. The differences between the two files are subject to a threshold in order to present the operator with a series of possible errors. As a result, the complexity of checking the entire print is reduced to a few possible errors that are checked by the operator. Since most of the work of troubleshooting was done by scanning + software, only the most conspicuous spots found by the software had to be evaluated by an expert. |
| Machine scans the cylinder and integrates the software cLynx (Figure 2d) | In the fourth stage, the entire printing process is omitted, as the cylinder surface is recorded directly with a camera within a cylinder scanning machine. To further reduce the cost of quality inspection, there is a need to check the cylinder without having to print it. To scan the surface of the cylinder a machine was built with a high-resolution line camera that scans the rotating cylinder at an approximate current speed of 1 meter/second. Because the scanning itself takes a minor portion of the processing time, this speed could actually be increased with a brighter LED lamp. After every movement a picture is taken, resulting in a flat image of the cylinder (Figure 3a). The main principles stay the same as with the scanned prints, as two complete recordings of the cylinder are made. These get matched to the engraving file and possible errors are presented to the operator using fixed thresholds (Figure 3b). This is done by automatically selecting areas around possible errors and calculating the absolute difference between the cylinder scan and the layout engraving file as shown in Figure 4. This significantly shortens the inspection time. However, the most prominent areas still have to be evaluated manually by the employee. For this reason, another fifth step towards a fully automated process is desired. |

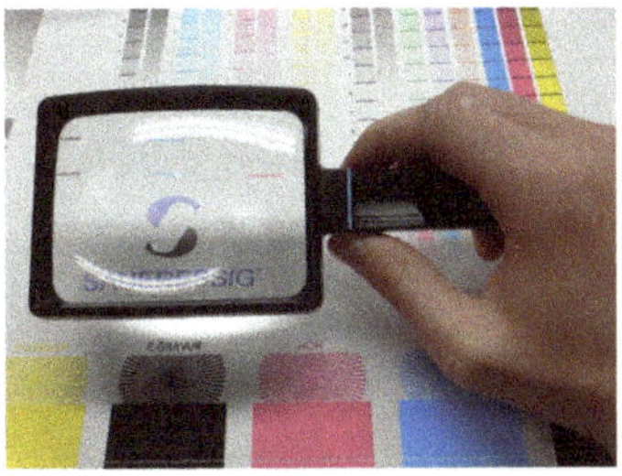

(**a**) Manual Inspection of Printed Product

(**b**) Manual Inspection of Monochrome Printed Product

(**c**) Expert Evaluation and software cLynx

(**d**) Machine scans and software cLynx

**Figure 2.** OQC evolutional continuous improvement process.

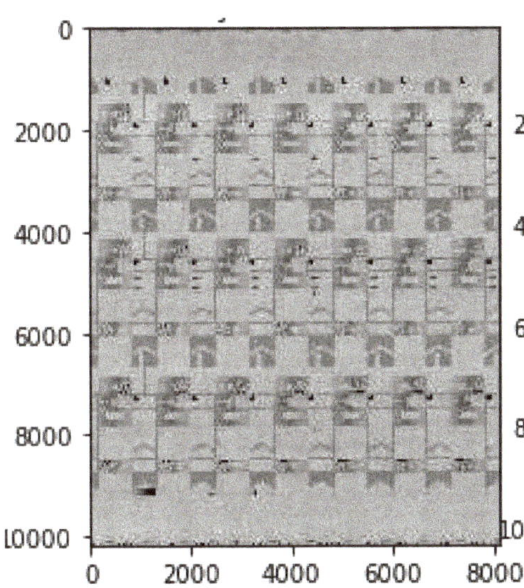


(**a**) Cylinder Scan

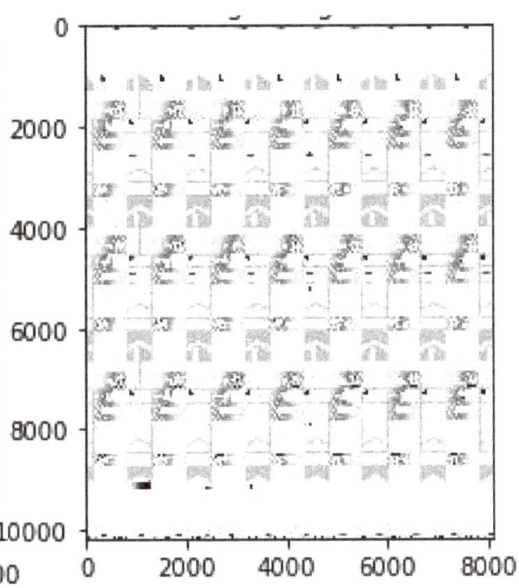


(**b**) Cylinder Engraving File

**Figure 3.** Cylinder Scan and Layout Engraving File.

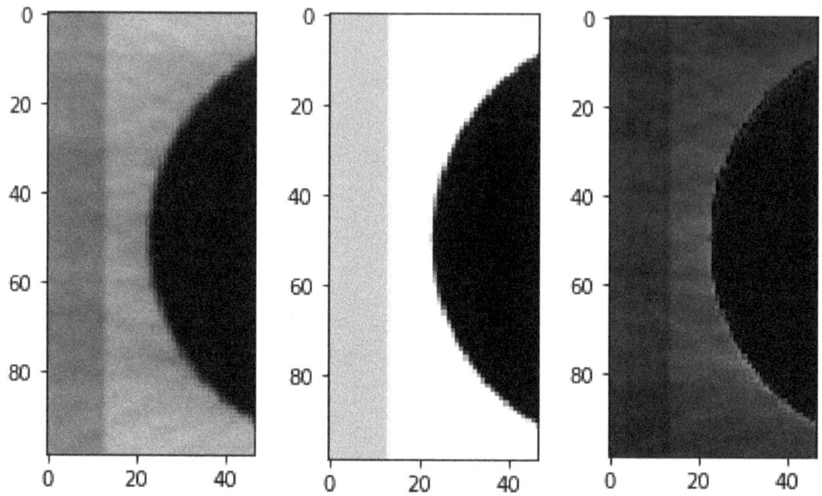


(**a**) Detail Cylinder Scan (**b**) Detail Engraving Layout (**c**) Absolute Difference

**Figure 4.** Example 1 of automatic selection of areas around possible errors.

## 3. Deep Learning for Industrial Computer Vision Quality Control

In order to reduce time checking possible mistakes on the cylinder, and further reduce OQC cost and value stream-related lead time, an automatic pre-selection of the errors using artificial intelligence is desired. Due to intensive research investment and strategic focus on quality control throughout the value stream process, real noisy industrial data has been classified and properly labelled. This is how the idea was born to design a DNN that would learn from the statistical information embedded within the previously classified data to perform a fully automated computer vision quality control.

Due to intensive research investment and strategic focus on quality control throughout the value stream process, there were previously numerous classified and properly labeled data aggregated through fourth stage. Possible errors were selected using thresholds between the original file and the scanned cylinder. These were then shown to the operator, who judged them as if they were real errors. These judgements were then saved comprising the labeled data-set.

In the fifth stage the process is taken over by a fully automated DNN architecture, as shown in Figure 5, and as proposed in this paper (see Section 3.1.3), after an intensive experimental program, which has tested different architectures (DNN, restricted boltzmann machines, deep belief networks, etc.) and configurations of different filter sizes, abstraction layers, etc. [37].

***The DNN soft sensor presented achieves an accuracy of 98.4% in fully automatic recognition of production errors.*** More details are provided in the following subsections. This contribution makes it possible to decide immediately after scanning whether the cylinder can be delivered or whether errors need to be corrected. It was decided not to use specific denoising treatments as specific filters before classification [38,39]. This is because of the intrinsic capabilities found in the adopted CNN architecture.

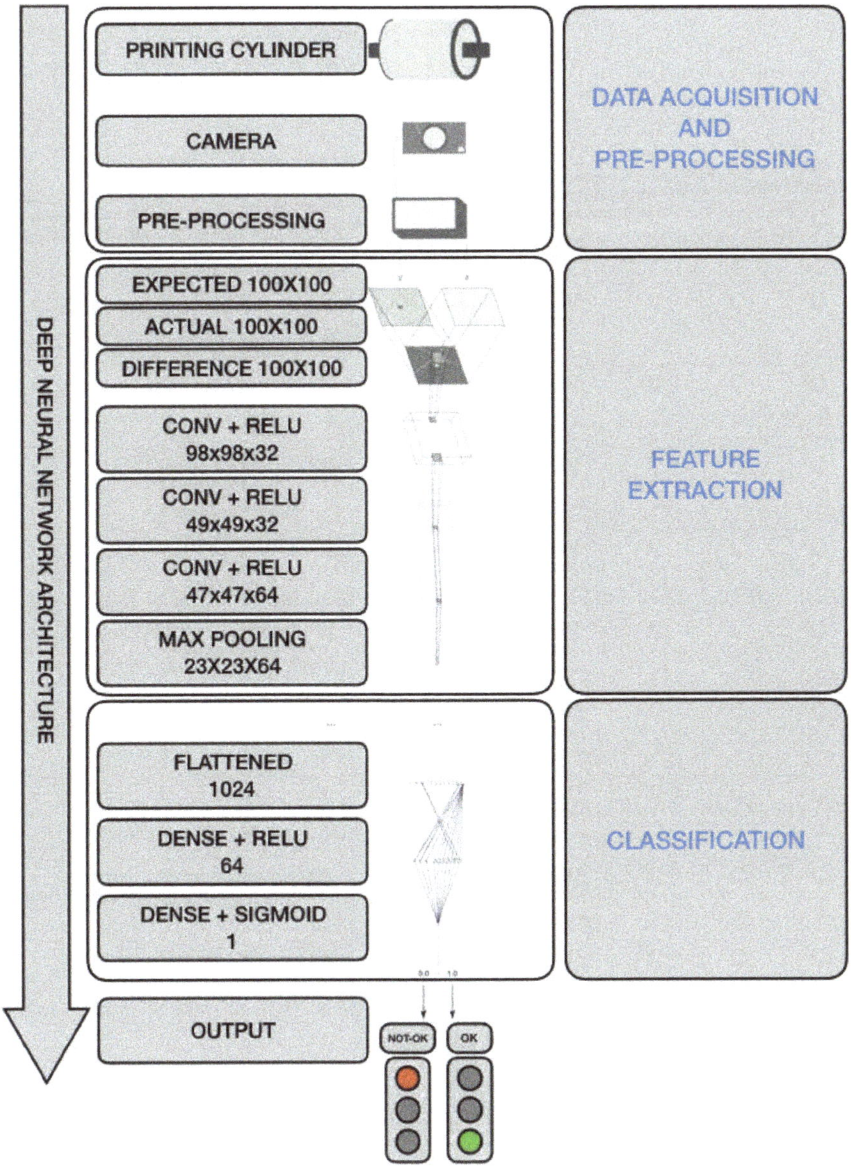


**Figure 5.** Deep Learning Architecture for Industrial Computer Vision OQC in the Printing Industry 4.0.

### *3.1. Deep Neural Network Architecture for Computer Vision in Industrial Quality Control in the Printing Industry 4.0*

#### 3.1.1. Experimental Setup

The experiments in this study were implemented with a computer equipped with an Intel(R) Xeon(R) Gold 6154 3.00GHz CPU and an NVIDIA Quadro P4000 Graphic Process Unit (GPU) with 96 GB of random-access memory (RAM). The operating system was ***Red Hat Linux*** 16.04 64-bit version.

The deep learning model training and testing were conducted with ***Keras*** which is an interface for ***TensorFlow*** (Version 1.8), and the model was built in ***Python*** (Version 2.7) language [40]. TensorFlow is an interface for expressing machine learning algorithms, and an application for executing such algorithms, including training and inference algorithms for DNN models. More specifically, the TF.Learn module of TensorFlow was adopted for creating, configuring, training, and evaluating the DNN. TF.Learn is a high-level Python module for distributed machine learning inside TensorFlow. It integrates a wide range of state-of-the-art machine learning algorithms built on top of TensorFlow's low-level APIs for small- to large-scale supervised and unsupervised problems. Additional Python interfaces were used: ***OpenCV*** for computer vision algorithms and image processing, ***Numpy*** for scientific computing and array calculation, and ***Matplotlib*** for displaying plots. The details of building the DNN model for OQC with Python are provided online at Open Access Repository and were created with ***Jupyter Notebook***.

#### 3.1.2. Data Pre-processing

In order to train the DNN, standardized classified input data is needed. For this reason, the Data pre-processing is divided in three steps: (1) decision of which is the size of the image that serves as input for the DNN and what the size of the convolutional window used by the DNN should be, (2) brightness adjustment through a histogram stretching, and (3) automatize the selection and labelling of the file structure to be fed to the DNN.

1. Image Size for DNN Input and Convolutional Window Size

   Due to the need for standardized input data, a decision needs to be made about which dimensions the input images should have. The first decision is the aspect ratio. The following decision should be how many pixels wide and high the input images should be. In order to get a first impression of the existing sizes, a short analysis of the previous manually confirmed errors is made. According to the data, the mean value of the width is slightly higher than that of the height. In the mean aspect ratio this gets even clearer with a mean aspect ratio of about 1.5. This is probably a result of some errors that are elongated by the rotation of the cylinder. The median aspect ratio is exactly at 1.0. Because the median describes a higher percentage of errors better this should also be the aspect ratio of the neural network input. As shown in the representation of the width and height of error in pixel against the LOG of the amount of errors Figure 6.

   As the size of the error also plays a role in the judgment of the errors, scaling operations should be reduced to a minimum. Due to the range of the sizes this is not always possible. The training time of the neural network would increase dramatically with large input sizes and small errors would mostly consist of *OK*-cylinder surface. Therefore a middle ground is needed so that most input images can be shown without much scaling or added *OK*-cylinder surface. A size in the middle would be 100 pixels. We therefore calculate the percentage of errors with the width smaller or equal to 100. The results show that about 90% of all errors have both the height and width below or equal to 100 and almost 74% have both the height and width below or equal to 10. One option would be to use an input size of $100 \times 100$.

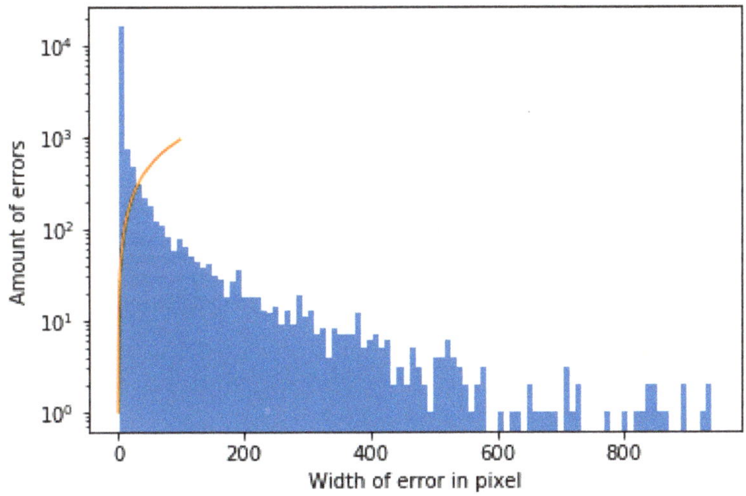


(a) Width of errors vs. LOG Number of errors

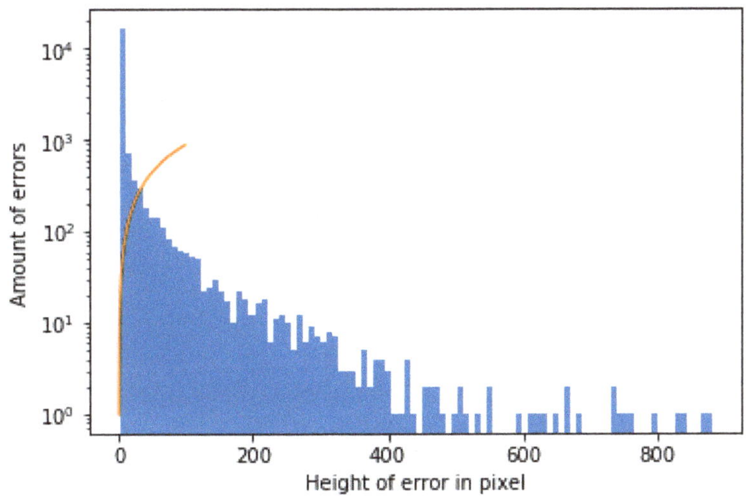


(b) Height of errors vs. LOG Number of errors

**Figure 6.** Aspect Ratio Inspection.

2. Brightness Adjustment

To get comparable data for all cylinder images, pre-processing is needed and is performed on the complete scan of a cylinder. From this scan multiple examples are taken. Because there can be slight deviations due to many influences during the recording of the cylinder surface, this can only be achieved by having a similar brightness for the cylinder surface and engraved parts. Another important point is that no essential information gets lost from the images and, that the brightness between the engraved and not engraved parts are comparable for all cylinder scans. Therefore a brightness stretch is needed but only few pixels are allowed to become the darkest or brightest pixels. Notwithstanding, the amount of pixel that become the darkest and brightest pixels ca not be set to a very low value because noise in the image data would result in big differences.

In conclusion a low percentage of the pixels should be set as darkest and brightest. For example, the lowest and the highest percentage should each have a maximum of 0.5%. Figure 7 shows a stretching example for brightness adjustment for one image so that 0.5% of all pixels will have a value of 0 and 0.5% of all pixels will have the value of 255.

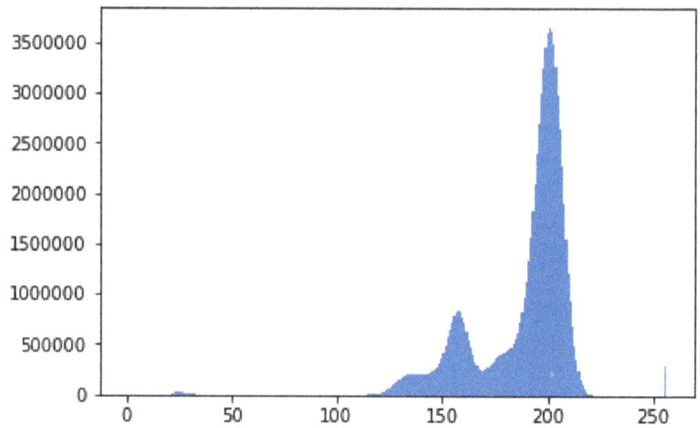


(**a**) Histogram before stretching

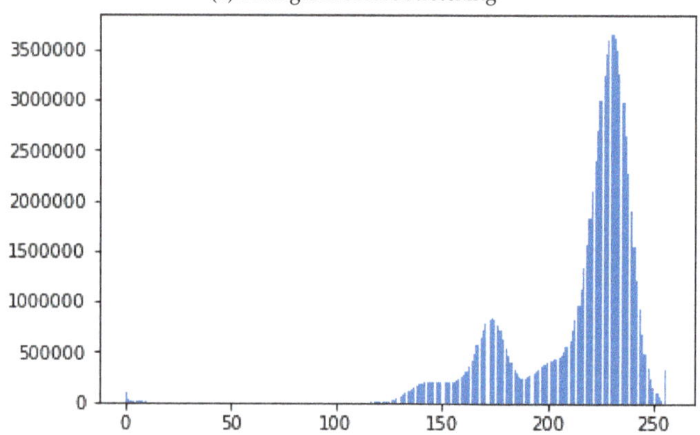


(**b**) Histogram after stretching

**Figure 7.** Pre-processing Histogram for brightness adjustment.

3. Automatic selection and Dataset Labelling

   To simplify the later steps, the images need to be cut from the original file and saved into two folders with examples that are ***OK***-cylinder (Figure 8a) and examples that are ***not-OK***-cylinder (Figure 8b). The great variety of patterns presented in the spectrum can be observed in the figures. The very nature of the process implies that each new product represents a new challenge for DNN, as it has probably never before been confronted with these images. For this reason, the errors may be of a very different nature. This implies a high complexity of solving the challenge of training and testing the DNN. Likewise, the different shades of black and grey, very difficult to appreciate with the naked eye when manually sorting the images, represent an added difficulty that must be resolved by DNN architecture.

   If errors are smaller in width or height than 100, the ROI gets increased to 100. If any size is bigger than 100 pixels is ignored. For the purpose of checking later on, the big input data is split into

$100 \times 100$ parts. If any one of these is detected as an error, all are marked as an error. As shown in the Open Access Repository, there are multiple possible ways to handle the bigger data. Every example also has the actual and target data. There are different ways of using this data as input. One way is just using the actual data. A different option is to use the difference between the actual and expected data. The problem in both cases is that information gets lost. Better results have been achieved by using the differences. These get adjusted, so that the input data is in a range from $[-1,1]$. Once this is performed, and because a balanced dataset is important to train the neural network and the ***OK***-cylinder examples far outnumber the ***not-OK***-cylinder examples, an ***OK***-cylinder example is only saved if a ***not-OK***-cylinder example has been found previously.

#### 3.1.3. Automatic Detection of Cylinder ErrorsUsing a DNN Soft Sensor

The DNN soft sensor architecture design is performed with two main goals in mind: classification and performance:

- *Classification* The first goal of this architecture is not to identify different objects inside of part of the images but to separate two classes (***not-OK*** and ***OK*** images), where the main source of noise came from the illumination factor from the scanner lectures. Therefore, neither the so deep architectures nor the identity transference, which was the key for the ResNet [41] is needed in our case, and just few convolutions shall help identify convenient structural features to rely on.
- *Performance*. The proposed architecture is even more simplistic than the AlexNet [42] one, as we do not use five convolution layers but just three. The main reason is to look for a compromise between the number of parameters and the available dataset of images. Our architecture was always looking to be *frugal* in terms of resources, as it is expected to be a soft sensor, running in real time and having the inherent capability of retrain for reinforced learning, close to such real time constraint.

After data acquisition and pre-processing, the input data of the DNN are figures represented as tensors. A type of network that performs well on the classification problem of such data is usually divided in two main parts: feature extractors and classifiers as shown in Figure 5:

- *Feature Extraction*. The feature extraction is performed by a deep stack of alternatively fully connected convolutional and sub-sampling max pooling layers, the even numbered layers are for convolutions and the odd numbered layers are for max-pooling operations.
  - *Convolution and ReLu (rectified linear unit) activated convolutional layers*. Convolution operations, by means of activation functions, extract the features from the input information which are propagated to deeper level layers. A *ReLu* activation function is a function meant to zero out negative values. The *ReLu* activation function was first presented in AlexNet [42] and solves the vanishing gradient problem for training DNN.
  - *Max pooling*. Consists of extracting windows from the input feature maps and outputting the max value of each channel. It's conceptually similar to convolution, except that instead of transforming local patches via a learned linear transformation (the convolution kernel), they are transformed via a max tensor operation.
- *Classification*. The classification is performed by fully connected activation layers [43]. Some examples of such models are LeNet [44], AlexNet [42], Network in Network [45], GoogLeNet [46–48], DenseNet [49].
  - Fully connected activation layers output a probability distribution over the output classes [25]. Because we are facing a binary classification problem and the output of our network is a probability, it is best to use the binary-crossentropy loss function. Crossentropy is a

quantity from the field of Information Theory that measures the distance between probability distributions or, in this case, between the ground-truth distribution and the predictions. It is not the only viable choice: we could use, for instance, mean-squared-error. However, crossentropy is usually the best choice when dealing with models that output probabilities. Because we are *attacking* a binary-classification problem, we end the network with a single unit (a Dense layer of size 1) and a sigmoid activation. This unit will encode the probability that the network is looking at one class or the other [25].

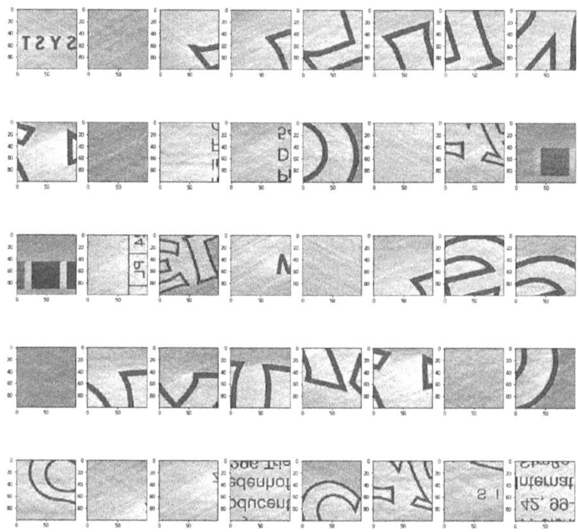

(**a**) OK cylinder Images

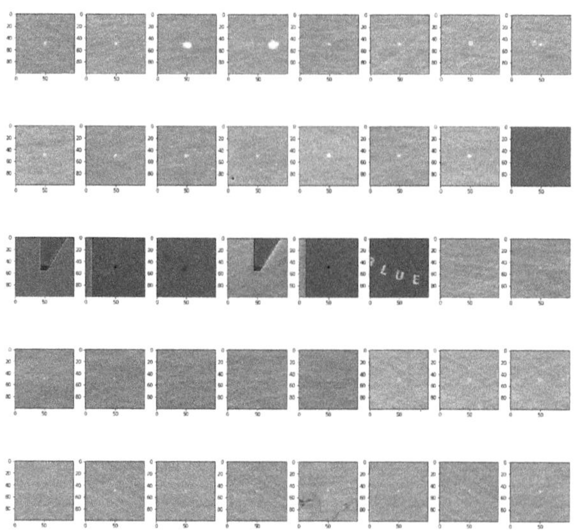

(**b**) not-OK cylinder Images

**Figure 8.** Examples of OK cylinder and not-OK cylinder Images.

As shown in the Open Access Repository, using Keras, Tensorflow backend for the DNN and OpenCV/Numpy for the image manipulation, a balanced dataset of 13,335 ***not-OK***- and 13335 ***OK***-cylinder examples is used, giving a total of 26,670. These were collected over a period of 14 months from almost 4000 cylinder scans. The training part is mirrored vertically and horizontally resulting in 85,344 training samples in total. All ***not-OK***- cylinder examples are labeled ***0*** and all Ok examples are labeled ***1***. As a standard procedure, the data is split into ***training dataset*** (80%), ***testing dataset*** (10%) and ***validation dataset*** (10%). The ***training dataset*** is used to train the DNN throughout an number of epochs as shown in Figure 9. It can be observed that both accuracy and loss do not increase or decrease significantly after epoch number 10.

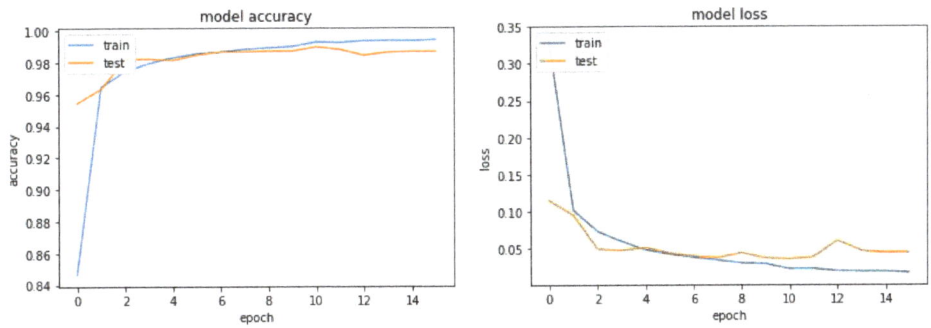


(**a**) DNN Model Training Accuracy (**b**) DNN Model Training Loss

**Figure 9.** DNN Training and Testing Results.

The ***testing dataset*** is subsequently used to test DNN performance. The confusion matrix is a standard procedure to summarize the results of such a training by typically combining contingency classes (*TRUE*, *FALSE*) and (*OK*, *not-OK*), hence building four categories: (1) True Negative (*TN*), which is an error and has been predicted as an error; (2) False Positive (*FP*), which is an error but has not been predicted as an error, and is by far the most damaging category; False Negative (*FN*) which is not an error but has been predicted as an error; and (4), True Positive (*TP*) which is not an error and has not been predicted as an error. Specifically, given the balanced dataset chosen, the accuracy (ACC) delivered by the DNN soft sensor, defined by the expression $ACC = (TP + TN)/(TP + TN + FP + FN)$, is 98.4%. The *TN* rate is 97.85%, the *TP* rate is 99.01%, the *FN* rate is 2.15% and the *FP* rate is 0.99%. These levels of *ACC* can be considered acceptable for such a complicated industrial classification problem. The results are summarized in Figure 10.

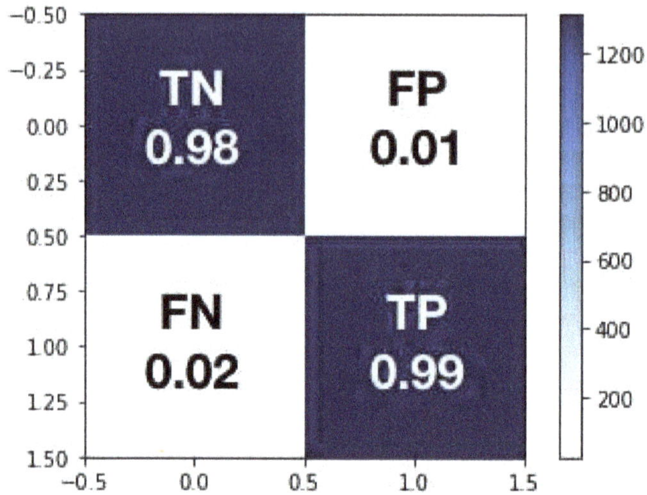


**Figure 10.** DNN Model Testing Confusion Matrix.

In Table 2 the DNN architecture shown in Figure 5 is described layer by layer by outlining the rationale behind the choice of a layer rather than another. Going even further, to compare the performance of the proposed soft DNN sensor, it has been compared with three similar architectures. The result of this comparison is shown in Open Access Repository and summarized in Figure 11 in which it is clearly shown that the proposed DNN soft sensor has superior performance to other alternative architectures.

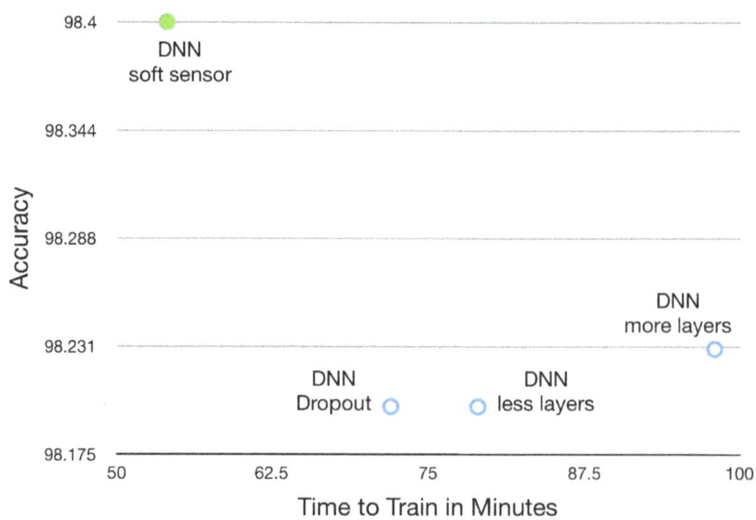


**Figure 11.** Deep Learning Architecture Comparison. Time to Train vs. Accuracy.

Two parameters, accuracy and computational time, have been measured consistently with the same training and test set, and then compared. First, it has been tested with an identical architecture by adding a dropout, then it has been tested with a deeper architecture and finally with a more shallow

DNN with fewer layers. The accuracy should be as high as possible in order to generate the lowest possible error in data characterization, and the computation time should be as low as possible in order to ensure that the soft DNN sensor can be effectively integrated into an Industry 4.0 environment, thus ensuring maximum effectiveness and efficiency respectively. A smooth DNN sensor must be not only accurate but also fast to ensure, among other things, a minimum Lead Time impact on the value creation process and low $CO_2$ emissions derived from the energy consumption associated with the computation.

**Table 2.** DNN Architecture Detailed Description.

| Layer Size | Layer Name | Layer Description and Rationale behind the Choice |
|---|---|---|
| (98, 98, 32) | conv2d 1<br>activation 1 (relu) | This is the first convolutional layer of the network. As observed in Figure 12 this layer mainly finds edges in the input image. In order to keep the values in check, an activation function is needed after each convolutional layer. |
| (49, 49, 32) | max pooling2d 1 | In order to reduce the complexity of the convoluted result a max pooling layer is used. Only the maximum in this case of a 2 × 2 pixel window is chosen. |
| (47, 47, 64) | conv2d 2<br>activation 2 (relu) | In the second convolutional layer the results describe more complex forms as is visible in Figure 12. In order to keep the values in check, an activation function is needed after each convolutional layer. |
| (23, 23, 64) | max pooling2d 2 | As with the previous max pooling layer this layer is used to reduce the complexity of the convoluted result. |
| (21, 21, 64) | conv2d 3<br>activation 3 (relu) | In the third convolutional layer resulting features are even more complex. In order to keep the values in check, an activation function is needed after each convolutional layer. |
| (10, 10, 64) | max pooling2d 3 | As with the previous max pooling layer this layer is used to reduce the complexity of the convoluted result. |
| (8, 8, 32) | conv2d 4<br>activation 4 (relu) | This is the final convolutional layer with the most complex features. In order to keep the values in check, an activation function is needed after each convolutional layer. |
| (4, 4, 32) | max pooling2d 4 | As with the previous max pooling layer this layer is used to reduce the complexity of the convoluted result. |
| (512) | flatten 1 | The flatten layer is used to flatten the previous 3 dimensional tensor to 1 dimension. |
| (64) | dense 1<br>activation 5 (relu) | To further reduce the complexity we use a fully connected layer. Before the final connection takes place the relu function is used to zero out the negative results. |
| (1) | dense 2<br>activation 6 (sigmoid) | As the probability of the input image being an error is wanted, the sigmoid function is needed to transform the input value into a probability [0–1]. |

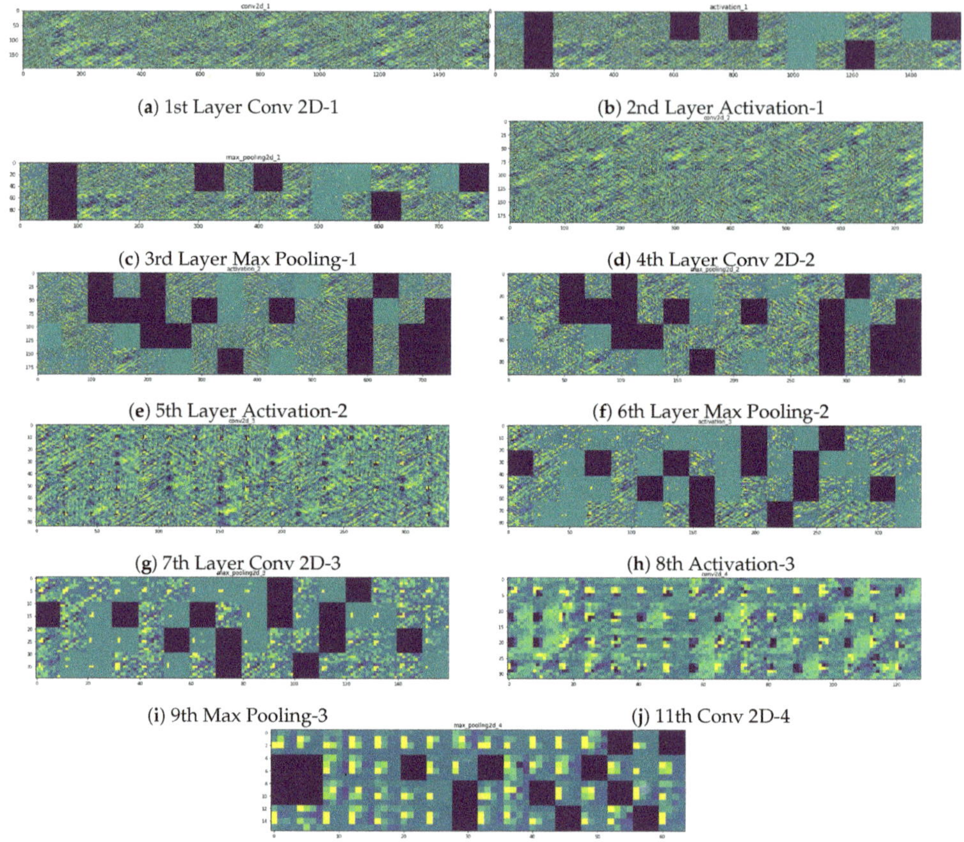

(**a**) 1st Layer Conv 2D-1 (**b**) 2nd Layer Activation-1 (**c**) 3rd Layer Max Pooling-1 (**d**) 4th Layer Conv 2D-2 (**e**) 5th Layer Activation-2 (**f**) 6th Layer Max Pooling-2 (**g**) 7th Layer Conv 2D-3 (**h**) 8th Activation-3 (**i**) 9th Max Pooling-3 (**j**) 11th Conv 2D-4 (**k**) 12th Max Pooling-4

**Figure 12.** Visualization of all DNN layers as color-coded images of a *TN* image.

### 3.1.4. Visualizing the Learned Features

Experience has shown that visualizing what each of the DNN layers learns can help deep architecture designers improve their understanding of the learning of the DNN hidden layers and thus support an appropriate fine tuning of their design for improvement purposes. This is because visualizing what the DNN has learned can help in the understanding of the decision making process. There are different ways of visualizing what has been learned by showing different parts. These can make it easier to understand why some things do not work as expected. For example why some pictures with errors were not categorized as errors (FP).

This visualization can be performed in different ways. For instance, given an example image of a ***not-OK*** cylinder shown in Figure 13a, an option is to visualize what the DNN captures using class activation heatmaps. A class activation heatmap is a 2D grid of scores associated with a specific output class, computed for every location in any input image, indicating how important each location is with respect to the class under consideration. An example is shown in Figure 13b.

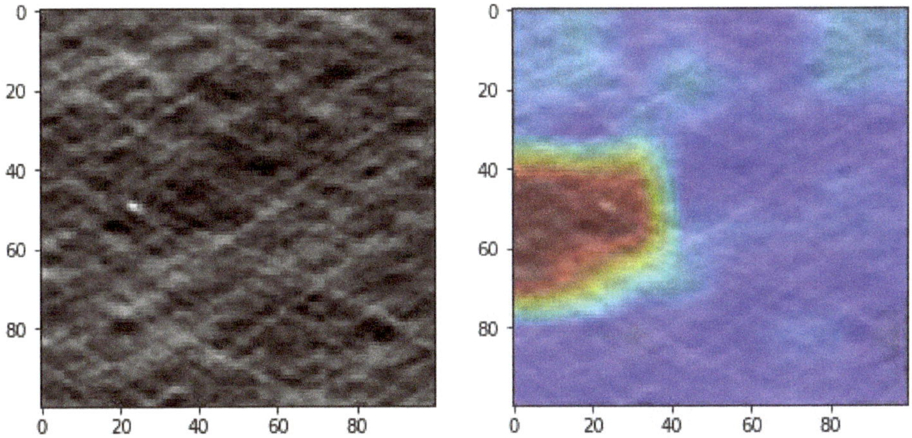


(**a**) Example Image of Error in ***not-OK*** cylinder (**b**) Activation Heatmap of Error in ***not-OK*** cylinder

**Figure 13.** Example Image ***not-OK***-cylinder and Activation Heatmap

Another option is to calculate an input image that gets the highest response from a layer. This is done by displaying the visual pattern that each filter is meant to respond to. This can be done with gradient ascent in input space: applying gradient descent to the value of the input image of a convolutional network so as to maximize the response of a specific filter, starting from a blank input image. The resulting input image will be one that the chosen filter is maximally responsive to. An example is shown in Figure 14.

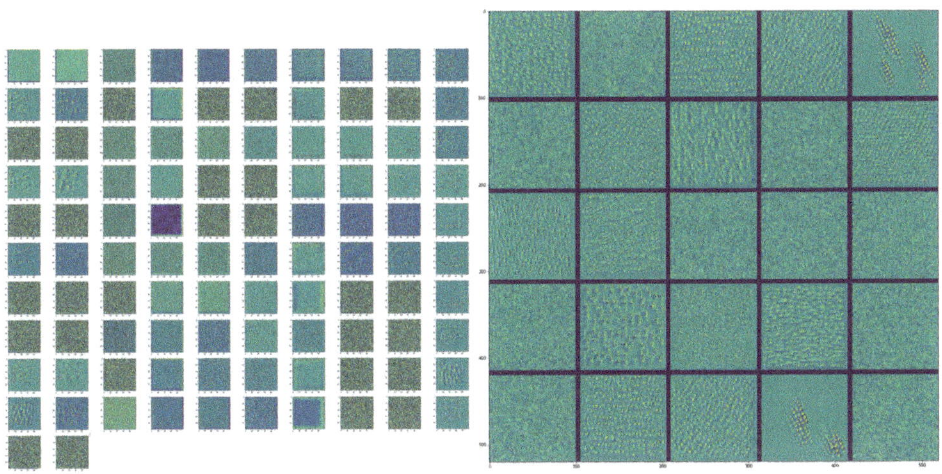

(**a**) Most Responding Input (**b**) Most Responding Input Detail

**Figure 14.** Most Responding Input.

Finally, an alternative approach would be to show the outputs of all DNN layers as color-coded images. Visualizing intermediate activations consists of displaying the feature maps that are output by various convolution and pooling layers in a network, given a certain input (the output of a layer is often called its activation, the output of the activation function). This gives a view into how an input is decomposed into the different filters learned by the network. We want to visualize feature maps with three dimensions: width, height, and depth (channels). Each channel encodes relatively independent features, so the proper way to visualize these feature maps is by independently plotting the contents of every channel as a 2D image. For explanatory purposes, on the Open Access Repository, four different examples, *TP-TN-FP-FN*, of such feature maps are depicted. These shall help the reader better understand what the DNN *sees* and how it *responds* in different circumstances. One of these examples, *TN*, is visualized in Figure 12.

## 4. Results and Discussion

Due to the automation by means of the soft DNN sensor, the costs associated with OQC could be drastically reduced. Also, the accuracy of error detection increased considerably. The results can be therefore considered *very promising* and allow for different ways of further industrial implementation. However, these results have to be interpreted in a broad context of Industry 4.0. This section provides some essential aspects that will help to understand and contextualize the contributed results through a meta-discussion at various organizational levels. This will help to present in the next section a possible future strategic development of these ***deep technologies*** in the short, medium and long term.

There are different steps that have to be taken until the full potential can be used in the production without taking a too high risk of missing an error.

1. Using the DNN fully automate OQC classification to predict the amount of errors a cylinder has.

   The DNN *only* provides a successful result 98.4% of the time. To be sure that the wrongly classified images are not big mistakes, human experts will review all possible errors. DNN has already had a positive influence on the workflow, as we know how many errors are very likely an error: DNN helps significantly in the planning of the next workflow step because it is known with a high probability if the cylinder needs to go to the correction department or if it is very likely that the product is an ***OK***-cylinder.
2. Showing the error probability to the operator that is currently deciding if it is an error or if it is not.

   This gives a hint to the operator, who can give feedback if there are relevant mistakes that were not predicted as mistakes. This can also help the operator to reduce the likelihood of missing an error. Once this soft sensor was integrated in production, OQC productivity, measured in hours per unit - time an operator spends in the OQC -, dramatically increased by ***210%*** as decision about defects is made in an automatic way.
3. Only showing possible errors that have been predicted by the DNN.

   In the last step, the DNN could completely filter out errors that are not relevant. This can also be used in multiple steps because it is possible to increase the threshold error probability for the possible error to be shown. At some point a threshold will have to be chosen taking into consideration the cost of checking a possible error and the cost of missing a error. This would completely eliminate the step of checking the errors and the confirmed errors would only be checked by the correction department.

## 5. Conclusions and Future Steps of Deep Learning in a Printing Industry 4.0 Context.

Although there has been an immediate performance increase in OQC error detection accuracy and cost effectiveness, larger scope for improvement is down to the managerial dimension of such a sensor. This is because it can be expanded to not only detect defects but also to classify them in categories. Although this requires additional effort, it will enable the cause-effect analysis regarding manufacturing conditions and defect frequencies.

Some of these efforts can be specifically targeted to achieve an improvement in the accuracy of the model. For example learning from the false predictions: to further improve the correct prediction

**Conflicts of Interest:** The authors declare no conflict of interest.

## Abbreviations

The following abbreviations are used in this manuscript:

| | |
|---|---|
| IIoT | Industrial Internet of Things |
| OQC | Optical Quality Control |
| DNN | Deep Neural Networks |
| GPU | Graphic Process Unit |
| RAM | Random Access Memory |

## References


1. Ustundag, A.; Cevikcan, E. *Industry 4.0: Managing The Digital Transformation*; Springer Series in Advanced Manufacturing, Springer: Cham, Switzerland, 2018.
2. Davis, J.; Edgar, T.; Porter, J.; Bernaden, J.; Sarli, M. Smart manufacturing, manufacturing intelligence and demand-dynamic performance. *Comput. Chem. Eng.* **2012**, *47*, 145–156. [CrossRef]
3. Li, L. China's manufacturing locus in 2025: With a comparison of 'Made-in-China 2025' and 'Industry 4.0'. *Technol. Forecasting Social Change* **2018**, *135*, 66–74. [CrossRef]
4. Shiroishi, Y.; Uchiyama, K.; Suzuki, N. Society 5.0: For Human Security and Well-Being. *Computer* **2018**, *51*, 91–95, [CrossRef]
5. Womack, J.; Roos, D. *The Machine That Changed the World*; Harper Perennial: New York, NY, USA, 1990.
6. Takeda, H. *Intelligent Automation Textbook*; Nikkan Kogyo Shimbun: Tokyo, Japan, 2009.
7. Nakabo, Y. Considering the competition and cooperation areas surrounding Industry 4.0. What will IoT automate. *J-Stage Top. Meas. Contr.* **2015**, *54*, 912–917, [CrossRef]
8. Kuwahara, S. About factory automation and IoT, AI utilization by intelligent robot. *J-Stage Top. Syst. Contr. Inf.* **2017**, *61*, 101–106, [CrossRef]
9. Villalba-Diez, J.; Ordieres-Mere, J. Improving manufacturing operational performance by standardizing process management. *IEEE Trans. Eng. Manage.* **2015**, *62*, 351–360. [CrossRef]
10. Villalba-Diez, J.; Ordieres-Mere, J.; Chudzick, H.; Lopez-Rojo, P. NEMAWASHI: Attaining Value Stream alignment within Complex Organizational Networks. *Procedia CIRP* **2015**, *7*, 134–139, [CrossRef]
11. Jimenez, P.; Villalba-Diez, J.; Ordieres.Mere, J. HOSHIN KANRI Visualization with Neo4j. Empowering Leaders to Operationalize Lean Structural Networks. *PROCEDIA CIRP* **2016**, *55*, 284–289. [CrossRef]
12. Villalba-Diez, J. *The HOSHIN KANRI FOREST. Lean Strategic Organizational Design*, 1st ed.; CRC Press. Taylor and Francis Group LLC: Boca Raton, FL, USA, 2017.
13. Villalba-Diez, J. *The Lean Brain Theory. Complex Networked Lean Strategic Organizational Design*; CRC Press, Taylor and Francis Group LLC: Boca Raton, FL, USA, 2017.
14. Womack, J.; Jones, D. Introduction. In *Lean Thinking*, 2 ed.; Simon & Schuster: New York, NY, USA, 2003; p. 4.
15. Arai, T.; Osumi, H.; Ohashi, K.; Makino, H. Production Automation Committee Report: 50 years of automation technology. *J-Stage Top. Precis. Eng. J.* **2018**, *84*, 817–820, [CrossRef]
16. Manikandan, V.S.; Sidhureddy, B.; Thiruppathi, A.R.; Chen, A. Sensitive Electrochemical Detection of Caffeic Acid in Wine Based on Fluorine-Doped Graphene Oxide. *Sensors* **2019**, *19*, [CrossRef]
17. Garcia Plaza, E.; Nunez Lopez, P.J.; Beamud Gonzalez, E.M. Multi-Sensor Data Fusion for Real-Time Surface Quality Control in Automated Machining Systems. *Sensors* **2018**, *18*, [CrossRef] [PubMed]
18. Han, L.; Cheng, X.; Li, Z.; Zhong, K.; Shi, Y.; Jiang, H. A Robot-Driven 3D Shape Measurement System for Automatic Quality Inspection of Thermal Objects on a Forging Production Line. *Sensors* **2018**, *18*, [CrossRef] [PubMed]
19. Weimer, D.; Scholz-Reiter, B.; Shpitalni, M. Design of deep convolutional neural network architectures for automated feature extraction in industrial inspection. *CIRP Annals* **2016**, *65*, 417–420, [CrossRef]
20. Xie, X. A Review of Recent Advances in Surface Defect Detection Using Texture Analysis Techniques. *Electron. Lett. Comput. Vision Image Ana.* **2008**, *7*, 1–22. [CrossRef]
21. Scholz-Reiter, B.; Weimer, D.; Thamer, H. Automated Surface Inspection of Cold-Formed MicroPart. *CIRP Ann. Manuf. Technol.* **2012**, *61*, 531–534. [CrossRef]

22. Rani, S.; Baral, A.; Bijender, K.; Saini, M. Quality control during laser cut rotogravure cylinder manufacturing processes. *Int. J. Sci. Eng. Comput. Technol.* **2015**, *5*, 70–73.
23. LeCun, Y.; Bengio, Y.; Hinton, G. Deep learning. *Nature* **2015**, *521*, 436–444. [CrossRef] [PubMed]
24. Jia, Y.; Shelhamer, E.; Donahue, J.; Karayev, S.; Long, J.; Girshick, R.; Guadarrama, S.; Darrell, T. Caffe: Convolutional Architecture for Fast Feature Embedding. *ACM Multimedia* **2014**, 675–678.
25. Chollet, F. *Deep Learning with Python*; Manning Publications Co.: Shelter Island, NY, USA, 2018.
26. Lin, T.; RoyChowdhury, A.; Maji, S. Bilinear CNN Models for Fine-Grained Visual Recognition. In Proceedings of the 2015 IEEE International Conference on Computer Vision (ICCV), Santiago, Chile, 7–13 December 2015; pp. 1449–1457, [CrossRef]
27. Miskuf, M.; Zolotova, I. Comparison between multi-class classifiers and deep learning with focus on industry 4.0. In Proceedings of the 2016 Cybernetics & Informatics (K&I), Levoca, Slovakia, 2–5 February 2016.
28. Zheng, X.; Wang, M.; Ordieres-Mere, J. Comparison of Data Preprocessing Approaches for Applying Deep Learning to Human Activity Recognition in the Context of Industry 4.0. *Sensors* **2018**, *2146*, 1–13, [CrossRef]
29. Aviles-Cruz, C.; Ferreyra-Ramirez, A.; Zuniga-Lopez, A.; Villegas-Cortez, J. Coarse-Fine Convolutional Deep-Learning Strategy for Human Activity Recognition. *Sensors* **2019**, *19*, [CrossRef]
30. Zhe, L.; Wang, K.S. Intelligent predictive maintenance for fault diagnosis and prognosis in machine centers: Industry 4.0 scenario. *Adv. Manuf.* **2017**, *5*, 377–387.
31. Deutsch, J.; He, D. Using Deep Learning-Based Approach to Predict Remaining Useful Life of Rotating Components. *IEEE Trans. Syst. Man Cybern. Syst.* **2018**, *48*, 11–20. [CrossRef]
32. Shanmugamani, R., Ed. *Deep Learning for Computer Vision*; Packt Publishing-ebooks Account: Birmingham, UK, 2018.
33. Wang, T.; Chen, Y.; Qiao, M.; Snoussi, H. A fast and robust convolutional neural network-based defect detection model in product quality control. *Int. J. Adv. Manuf. Technol.* **2018**, *94*, 3465–3471. [CrossRef]
34. He, M.; He, D. Deep Learning Based Approach for Bearing Fault Diagnosis. *IEEE Trans. Ind. App.* **2017**, *53*, 3057–3065. [CrossRef]
35. Imai, M. *KAIZEN: The Key to Japan's Competitive Success*; McGraw-Hill Higher Education: New York, NY, USA, 1986.
36. Schmidt, D. Available online: https://patentscope.wipo.int/search/de/detail.jsf;jsessionid=F4DFD8F2D86BB91896D53B4AB97E84A1.wapp1nC?docId=WO2018166551&recNum=871&office=&queryString=&prevFilter=&sortOption=Ver%C3%B6ffentlichungsdatum+ab&maxRec=70951352 (accessed on 15 September 2019).
37. Hinton, G.; Osindero, S.; Teh, Y. A fast learning algorithm for deep belief nets. *Neural Comput.* **2006**, *18*, 1527–1554. [CrossRef]
38. Zhang, K.; Zuo, W.; Gu, S.; Zhang, L. Learning Deep CNN Denoiser Prior for Image Restoration. In Proceedings of the 2017 IEEE Conference on Computer Vision and Pattern Recognition (CVPR), Honolulu, HI, USA, 21–26 July 2017; pp. 2808–2817, [CrossRef]
39. Zhang, K.; Zuo, W.; Chen, Y.; Meng, D.; Zhang, L. Beyond a Gaussian Denoiser: Residual Learning of Deep CNN for Image Denoising. *IEEE Trans. Image Process.* **2017**, *26*, 3142–3155, [CrossRef] [PubMed]
40. van Rossum, G. *Python Tutorial*; Technical Report CS-R9526; Computer Science/Department of Algorithmics and Architecture: Amsterdam, The Netherlands, 1995.
41. He, K.; Zhang, X.; Ren, S.; Sun, J. Deep Residual Learning for Image Recognition. *arXiv* **2015**, arXiv:1512.03385.
42. Krizhevsky, A.; Sutskever, L.; Hinton, G. Imagenet classification with deep convolutional neural networks. In Proceedings of the 25th International Conference on Neural Information Processing Systems, Lake Tahoe, Nevada, 3–6 December 2012; pp. 1106–1114.
43. Alom, M.Z.; Taha, T.M.; Yakopcic, C.; Westberg, S.; Sidike, P.; Nasrin, M.S.; Hasan, M.; Van Essen, B.C.; Awwal, A.A.S.; Asari, V.K. A State-of-the-Art Survey on Deep Learning Theory and Architectures. *Electronics* **2019**, *8*, [CrossRef]
44. Lecun, Y.; Bottou, L.; Bengio, Y.; Haffner, P. Gradient-based learning applied to document recognition. *Proc. IEEE* **1998**, *86*, 2278–2324, [CrossRef]
45. Lin, M.; Chen, Q.; Yan, S. Network In Network. *arXiv* **2013**, arXiv:1312.4400.

46. Szegedy, C.; Liu, W.; Jia, Y.; Sermanet, P.; Reed, S.; D. Anguelov.; D. Erhan.; V. Vanhoucke.; A. Rabinovich. Going deeper with convolutions. In Proceedings of the 2015 IEEE Conference on Computer Vision and Pattern Recognition (CVPR), Bosto, MA, USA, 7–12 June 2015; pp. 1–9, [CrossRef]
47. Szegedy, C.; Vanhoucke, V.; Ioffe, S.; Shlens, J.; Wojna, Z. Rethinking the Inception Architecture for Computer Vision. *arXiv* **2015**, arXiv:1512.00567.
48. Szegedy, C.; Ioffe, S.; Vanhoucke, C.; Alemi, A. Inception-v4, Inception-ResNet and the Impact of Residual Connections on Learning. *arXiv* **2016**, arXiv:1602.07261.
49. Huang, G.; Liu, Z.; Maaten, L.v.d.; Weinberger, K.Q. Densely Connected Convolutional Networks. In Proceedings of the 2017 IEEE Conference on Computer Vision and Pattern Recognition (CVPR), Honolulu, HI, USA, 21–26 July 2017; pp. 2261–2269.

*sensors*

MDPI

*Article*

# Characterization of Industry 4.0 Lean Management Problem-Solving Behavioral Patterns Using EEG Sensors and Deep Learning

**Javier Villalba-Diez [1,2,*], Xiaochen Zheng [3], Daniel Schmidt [4] and Martin Molina [2]**

1 Fakultät Management und Vertrieb, Hochschule Heilbronn Campus Schwäbisch Hall, 74523 Schwäbisch Hall, Germany
2 Departament of Artificial Intelligence, Escuela Técnica Superior de Ingenieros Informáticos, Universidad Politécnica de Madrid, 28660 Madrid, Spain
3 Departament of Business Intelligence, Escuela Técnica Superior de Ingenieros Industriales, Universidad Politécnica de Madrid, 2006 Madrid, Spain
4 Saueressig GmbH + Co. KG, Gutenbergstr. 1-3, 48691 Vreden, Germany
* Correspondence: javier.villalba-diez@hs-heilbronn.de

Received: 20 May 2019; Accepted: 21 June 2019; Published: 26 June 2019

**Abstract:** Industry 4.0 leaders solve problems all of the time. Successful problem-solving behavioral pattern choice determines organizational and personal success, therefore a proper understanding of the problem-solving-related neurological dynamics is sure to help increase business performance. The purpose of this paper is two-fold: first, to discover relevant neurological characteristics of problem-solving behavioral patterns, and second, to conduct a characterization of two problem-solving behavioral patterns with the aid of deep-learning architectures. This is done by combining electroencephalographic non-invasive sensors that capture process owners' brain activity signals and a deep-learning soft sensor that performs an accurate characterization of such signals with an accuracy rate of over 99% in the presented case-study dataset. As a result, the deep-learning characterization of lean management (LM) problem-solving behavioral patterns is expected to help Industry 4.0 leaders in their choice of adequate manufacturing systems and their related problem-solving methods in their future pursuit of strategic organizational goals.

**Keywords:** EEG sensors; manufacturing systems; problem-solving; deep learning

## 1. Introduction

In the search of operational excellence in an Industry 4.0 context, manufacturing leaders constantly face a myriad of ever-changing challenges. They make thousands of choices, often under pressure, between alternatives with different overall value outcomes, and thereby exercise their ability to make adequate decisions. This ultimately determines their individual and organizational success. Operational excellence is a business discipline whose original main driver is the continuous improvement of processes [1] while encompassing other disciplines such as lean management (LM) [2], its combination with six sigma [3], scientific management [4], and organizational design [5]. Specifically, LM is a management discipline that supports the operational excellence effort by focusing on maximizing the value [2] of complex networked value streams [4] by systematically reducing internal process variability [6,7]. The LM system is based on different variations of the Shewart–Deming problem-solving quality control loop [8]. LM thus enables organizational leaders to attain operational excellence and cope with the socio-technical challenges that environmental complexity poses by applying a set of problem-solving behavioral patterns to several challenges—such as just-in-time production, total quality management [9], or service quality level increase [10], for instance. For these reasons, LM was chosen as a preferable framework to try to better understand problem-solving behavioral patterns of individuals within complex manufacturing contexts.

Although many LM problem-solving behavioral patterns are reported to have been implemented with value-stream performance increase [11–15], there is still much controversy as to which discriminating characteristics make some of these problem-solving behavioral patterns better than others and why [16]. The reason for this might be that scholars have not provided quantifiable evidence yet of the process owners' real brain activity when performing such tasks. This could help to provide an understanding of the similarities and differences between the different proposed behavioral patterns. In the absence of such an analysis, the discussion remains subject at best to inference and at worst to trends or opinion. Such awareness is of utmost importance to facilitate the decision of which behavioral patterns should potentially be used during the implementation of different manufacturing systems.

This work aims to use modern sensor technology located on the human brain to capture signals that help characterize the cortical activity of individuals performing problem-solving tasks in Industry 4.0 environments. The technology based on non-invasive low-cost sensors that offer neuroimaging in real environments such as industrial ones is not sufficiently developed [17,18]. The sensors used in real environments must guarantee the necessary comfort, low invasiveness, and high reliability. For this reason, not all devices available on the market are suitable for these applications [19]. On the other hand, the combination of this hardware with soft sensors based on artificial intelligence that allow increase of the low signal-to-noise ratio (SNR), is a promising line of research when combining brain–computer interface algorithms with biosignal acquisition technologies [20]. This represents undoubtedly a strength of the work presented. The overarching goal of this research is to offer Industry 4.0 leaders a better understanding of the brain processes underlying problem-solving behavioral patterns, as well as to highlight possible management implications when choosing the most appropriate manufacturing systems to achieve their strategic objectives.

As the graphical abstract shows in Figure 1, this is achieved by means of a case study within an Industry 4.0 automotive Japanese manufacturing facility in which several LM process owners are asked to solve value-stream-related problems with two specific LM behavioral patterns while being subject to non-invasive low-cost sensors electroencephalographic (EEG) measures. Subsequently, two methods are used to perform a characterization of the tasks. One is based on expert neurophysiological hypotheses. Other is based on a deep-learning (DL) soft sensor that performs the classification of pre-processed labelled EEG signals with a 99% accuracy rate.

After placing the study in a broad context, exploring the importance of the problem, outlining the purpose and its significance, as well as highlighting the relevance of the achieved results, the structure of the paper hereinafter is structured in order to ensure clarity in the presentation, replication of the results obtained, and a proper framing in the ongoing global research context. First, Section 2 starts by providing a brief framework through key publications on neurological goal-directed decision-making, on LM methodologies and outlining the research hypotheses. Second, the Materials and Methods Section 3 describes in detail how field research was conducted with aid of a case study. Additionally, the dataset of the case study, and notebook code is made available on an Open Access Repository to allow for verification and ensure replicability. Third, the Results and Discussion Section 4 summarizes and discusses the results obtained. Finally, Section 5 outlines several managerial conclusions, and future expected management implications from a broad operational excellence endeavor perspective.

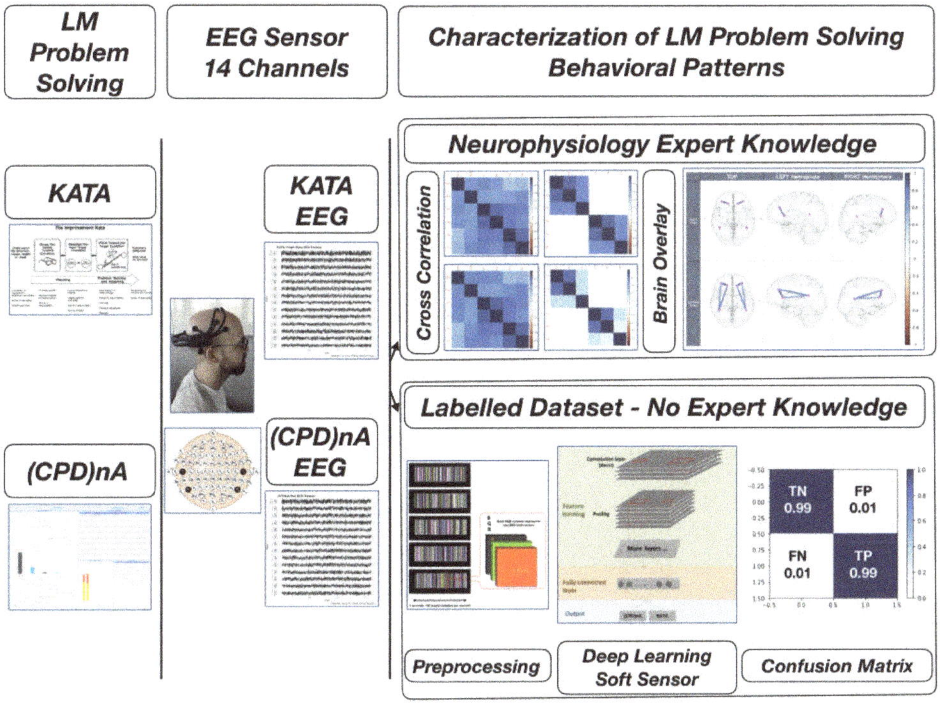


**Figure 1.** Graphical Abstract.

## 2. Literature Review

Industry 4.0 leaders make decisions in an ever-changing environment and in order to choose between value outcomes of their LM oriented actions they need to be aware that optimal decision-making requires three main characteristics [21]: self-control, active working memory, and adaptive modulation of this value signal. In neurological terms, such functions are understood as ***executive goal-directed decision-making*** and are neurologically managed by the prefrontal cortex (PFC). Neuroscientists such as Miyake [22] have shown that some skills crucial for Industry 4.0 decision-making constitute the PFC function:

1. Inhibition

   A capacity to resist to distraction. While solving problems in industrial shopfloors with high levels of potential distractions [23], it is important to focus on the most important root-causes of value-stream variability and discard less relevant information.
2. Shift

   A capacity to shift smoothly from one task, routine, or context to another. When dealing with highly interdependent complex processes, typical for instance of re-configurable manufacturing systems [24], it is important to shift within several levels of complexity to flexibly conduct an analysis in a multidimensional complex environment.
3. Working Memory

   A capacity to hold and manipulate multiple ideas. Within a manufacturing environment with multiple interconnected processes, it is necessary to accurately hold a significant amount of relevant information when realizing problem-solving tasks [25].

The PFC is a complex region of the brain that allows us to adapt to an ever-changing environment [26]. It seems, therefore, more than plausible to hypothesize that the brains of those industrial process owners who practice LM should present a high level of PFC activity. However, do they? The fact of the matter is that this is not really known with any certainty. Therefore, it is imperative to explore the unique PFC features in the LM context to better understand LM problem-solving behavioral patterns. This is the main motivation of this paper. To date there have been several systematical studies on the relationship of brain activity to high-level complex cognitive tasks [27,28] and our aim is to deepen this body of knowledge.

Decades of neuropsychological research has related the PFC of the brain processes that guide goal-directed and purposeful behavior: goal-directed spatial navigation [29,30], goal-directed food choice in obesity [31], cognitive rehabilitation [32], reward-based learning [33,34], decision-making impairment [35], response inhibition to stimuli [36,37], etc. PFC guided top-down modulation underlies our capacity to attend to significant and discard other less relevant stimuli [38]. This implies a hierarchical guidance of our thoughts, actions, and emotions. There are several organizational principles to distinguish between functions of the lateral and medial areas of the PFC:

1. Outer/Inner World Representation

   One of the first of these approaches in primates considers that the lateral PFC area represents the outer world related cognition and that the medial and ventral PFC represent our inner emotional world [39].
2. Abstract/Social Cognition

   Another approach considers that the PFC has an anterior-posterior organization in which anterior areas are involved in abstract information processing [40], such as metacognition, whereas more posterior regions are involved in social cognition [41].
3. Inhibition/Generative

   Aron [42] suggest that the PFC presents a hemispheric lateralization in which the right hemisphere inhibits improper emotions or actions, whereas the left hemisphere concentrates on generative processes. These results are in the same line of those exposed in the avoidance (BIS) vs. approach (BAS) resting state and personality component theory [43]. They explain how high levels of BAS explain high levels of cortical activity in the right hemisphere while in the resting state and in experimental conditions with positive stimuli. In contrast, high BIS levels indicate cortical activity in the right hemisphere while in the resting state and under experimental conditions with negative stimuli.
4. Context-Dependent Goal Modulation

   More recently, researchers have recognized that context-dependent, goal-directed behavioral control and decision-making 'involves constant reciprocal and dynamic communication between PFC cortices and posterior brain regions' [44]. Specifically, the ventromedial PFC supplies the basis for goal-directed decision-making [45] and the context-dependent functionality originates in a modulation of the ventromedial PFC by the dorsolateral PFC [46]. Correlative interaction between such brain regions, 'enable goal modulation of brain activity based on goal states' [47,48].

Subsequently, malfunctioning connectivity between the ventromedial PFC and dorsolateral PFC regions has been associated with 'poor context-dependent, goal-directed modulation and distorted problem-solving behavioral patterns' when aging [49]. Two relevant examples for organizational leaders and decision makers in the context of operational excellence of this can be found in transient (stress) or permanent (psychopathy) neural conditions:

1. Stress

   Manufacturing leaders are constantly under environmental pressure. It has been proven by that 'exposure to uncontrollable stress, acute, or chronic, causes temporal loss of PFC cognitive functions' [50], which leads to poor decision-making. The fact that even mildly 'acute uncontrollable stress induces a rapid and dramatic loss of PFC cognitive abilities' is particularly relevant for organizational leaders and decision-making when dealing with subordinates [51].

2. Psychopathy

   Psychopaths present a demonstrated, reduced neural synchronization between ventromedial PFC and dorsolateral PFC while engaged in cognitive tasks with an emotional component [52]. Such cerebral functional configuration seems to (1) suppress decentralized information that is a-priori irrelevant to the goal at hand [53] and (2) lead to a predisposition of moral judgement impairment [54]. This might be why there is a disturbingly high number of individuals with such a personality trait who assume leadership roles [55].

However, shifting attention between different perspectives or behavioral flexibility, depending on the context, is the key aspect to consider here. According to [56], behavioral flexibility is subserved by the dorsolateral PFC, but these scholars demonstrate that the temporoparietal junction (TPJ) plays a coordinated role with dorsolateral PFC in stimulus-driven attention shifting. A combined activity of dorsolateral PFC and TPJ predicts flexible context-dependent cognitive shifting. As such, changes in the reciprocal coordinated functional connectivity of these brain regions may provide a powerful marker with which to assess brains' ability to perform flexible context-dependent mapping from sensory evidence. Furthermore, the cost and limitations, depending on the task complexity of the ventromedial PFC-dorsolateral PFC [57] of goal-directed modulation and dorsolateral PFC-TPJ [56] context-dependent cognitive flexibility support the hypothesis that its engagement is only activated if the behavioral task at hand requires it.

The fundamental behavioral task of LM is the systematic implementation of the Shewart–Deming cycle or PDCA (Plan-Do-Check-Act) [2,4]. However, there are numerous interpretations of such a core common denominator, as shown in [14]. In behavioral terms, all of them are, by definition, goal-directed. They can be qualitatively categorized in one of two main classes, depending on their context-dependent valuation:

1. Context-Independent

   These typically present a fixed target-state condition or future-state that is to be achieved by the subject. Some examples are [11,15,58,59].

2. Context-Dependent

   This provides a direction (HOSHIN) of improvement, but does not set any specific goal. Examples include some Japanese interpretations of PDCA [14,23,60,61].

Within this frame, the scope can be narrowed now by seeking to determine which neural processes present a high correlation, while performing two specific LM problem-solving behavioral patterns, *KATA* [11] and *(CPD)nA (Check-Plan-Do-...n-times-...-Act)* [14], as shown in Figure 2:

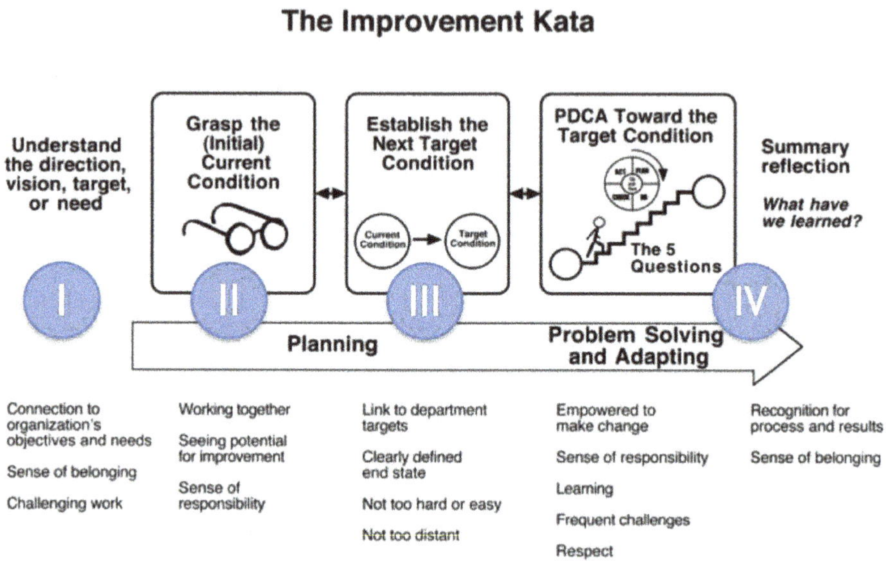


(a)

(b)

**Figure 2.** LM Goal-Directed problem-solving behavioral patterns [16]. (**a**) KATA [11]. (**b**) (CPD)nA [14] by Norbert Rosenfeld. Saueressig GmbH. Vreden. Germany. Reproduced with permission.

1. *KATA* [11] is a standardized behavioral pattern that can be summarized in four steps:

   I Set direction. Decide in which direction there can be improvement.

   II Understand the current state. Create a common understanding of the factual reality of the value stream at hand.

III Establish target condition. Fix a target state for the subject to achieve.
IV Perform PDCA towards the target condition. Systematically and iteratively approach the target state.

*KATA* fixes the subject's attention to a certain set of target-state conditions (Step 3) and does not permit these to be changed until they are achieved (through Step 4). This does not permit the subject to shift between contexts, for his/her mind is concentrated on target-state achievement.

2. *(CPD)nA* [14] derives from Japanese interpretations of continuous improvement [61] and its standardized behavioral pattern can be summarized in four steps:

I Check. Decide how to measure success.
II Plan.

i. Plan-Process. Separate what is known from what is unknown in the value stream.
ii. Plan-Priority. Understand the main sources of value-stream variability.
iii. Plan-Root Cause Analysis. Analyze the main source of internal process variability in search of its root cause.

III Do. Define an action to eliminate the source of internal process variability.
IV Act. Standardization of the best-known way to carry out the process.

*(CPD)nA* does not set any specific target state, and instead, encourages continuous improvement of the given success measurement (calculated from the Check) based solely on the knowledge of the current state of the value stream. This permits the subject to shift flexibly between contexts to adapt his/her behavior to the current state condition.

The use of non-invasive brain EEG signals through wearable technology has been previously proven helpful [62]. Some of the multiple applications of this technology can be found in task recognition [17], evaluation of driver vigilance [63–65], characterization of focused attention and working memory [66], emotional states [67] and stress [68,69] assessment, stimulus recognition [70], cognitive workload classification [71] or user's states assessment [72], and for the formulation of control commands [73]. Several electroencephalographic (EEG) standards exist in the sensor characterization on the human brain and in this paper the American Electroencephalography Society [74] standard was chosen, as shown in Figure 3.

To increase effectiveness of EEG brain signal processing, filters have been developed to remove noise on brain signals, as shown in [75–77]. This pre-processing is outlined in Section 3.4. In addition, various data analysis techniques have been used to extract relevant information from EEG data such as cross-correlation and DL:

1. Cross-Correlation Function

The most frequently used measure of interdependence between EEG signals in neuroscience is probably the cross-correlation function [78]. The cross-correlation function represents the inner product between two normalized signals and provides a measure of the linear synchronization or similarity between them [79]. Cross-correlation function combined with expert knowledge has been used, for example, in pattern recognition to correlate EEG frequency bands and other bodily signals, such as one's heart rate for sleep classification [80], in neurophysiology to detect the risk level of schizophrenia [81] or to analyze the relationship of brain activity and breathing [82], and even as a calibration method for brain–computer interfaces [83].

2. Deep Learning

Additionally, in the analysis of EEG signals, several approaches have been used that mostly consist of extracting features from the signals in several domains [84–86] that are selected by experts or by dimensional reduction algorithms, such as principal and independent component analysis [87] or more recently with differential entropy and linear discriminant analysis filters [88]. However, there is a fundamental inherent limitation in all these methods, as they require expert knowledge and manual expert manipulation of data is biased. Therefore, an automatic feature selection that is independent of human expertise is desirable.

DL can serve this purpose, as is an artificial intelligence method that can learn features purely from data [89]. This method presents two main advantages: first, it learns features directly from the raw data using several layers (deep) in a hierarchical manner [90], and second, it can be applied to unlabeled data by unsupervised methods, this is without the need for expert supervision [91]. In general, DL architectures such as deep neural networks, contain an input layer and an output layer of 'neurons'. In between, there are numerous layers of hidden units [92]. More specifically, deep neural networks use unsupervised learning to adjust the weights between hidden layers, enabling the network to identify the best internal features of the inputs [93].

Recent research has involved DL techniques to classify EEG datasets of subjects' executed movements [94–96] or motor imagery movements [97]. In addition, some contributions propose to use the EEG signals for DL biometric identification [98]. Also, there have been some results that are related to the identification of relevant sensors in emotion recognition EEG tests [99]. Recently scholars have used DL to perform human activity recognition from brain activity in Industry 4.0 environments [100] in which several transforms of raw data into images are depicted. Our research aims to expand this approach on the characterization of complex LM problem-solving behavioral patterns in an Industry 4.0 environment.

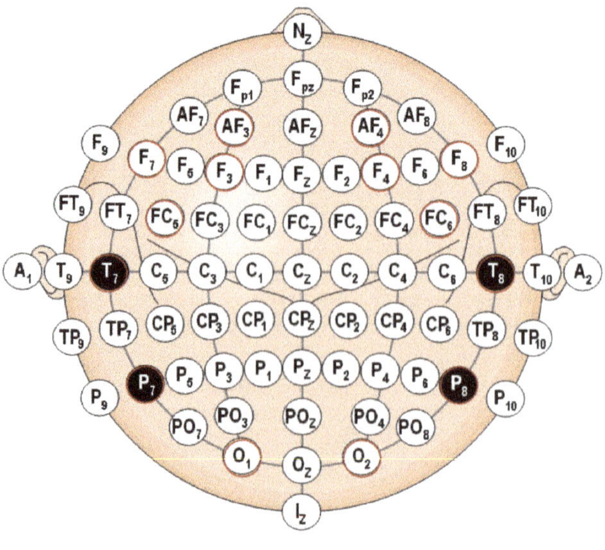


**Figure 3.** AES EEG electrode standardized nomenclature.

To achieve this, this study outlines the following four research hypotheses (H) and their related LM interpretation shown in Table 1. Furthermore, as these hypotheses are based on neurophysiological expert knowledge, management needs to be provided with tools that allow a proper discernment of which behavior is followed, based only on the data. For this reason, a DL-based soft sensor is developed that can perform this task.

**Table 1.** Research questions and related hypotheses.

| # | Hypotheses | LM Interpretation |
|---|---|---|
| 1 | *H1.* Subjects that engage in LM problem-solving behavioral patterns present a strong correlation in their PFC activity. In such a case, datasets from sensors *AF3-F7-F3-AF4-F4-F8* would present a strong correlation. | This would mean that LM problem-solving behavioral patterns can be understood in neurological terms as executive behavioral pattern. |
| 2 | *H2.* Subjects that engage in *KATA* and *(CPD)nA* present strong correlations of their dorsolateral PFC-ventromedial PFC combined activity. In such a case, datasets from sensors *F7* (ventromedial PFC Left Hemisphere) and *F3* (dorsolateral PFC Left Hemisphere), as well as *F4* (ventromedial PFC Right Hemisphere) and *F8* (dorsolateral PFC Right Hemisphere), would present a strong correlation. | This would mean that both *(CPD)nA* and *KATA* can be regarded in neurological terms as goal-oriented LM behavioral pattern. |
| 3 | *H3.* Subjects that engage in *KATA* present weakly dorsolateral PFC-TPJ correlated combined activity. In such a case, datasets from sensors *F7* (ventromedial PFC Left Hemisphere) and *F3* (dorsolateral PFC Left Hemisphere) would not correlate strongly with *P7* (TPJ Left Hemisphere), and sensors *F4* (ventromedial PFC Right Hemisphere) and *F8* (dorsolateral PFC Right Hemisphere) would not correlate strongly with *P8* (TPJ Right Hemisphere). | This would mean that *KATA* could be understood in neurological terms as a goal-oriented, context-independent LM behavioral pattern. |
| 4 | *H4.* Subjects that engage in *(CPD)nA* present a strong dorsolateral PFC-TPJ correlated combined activity. In such a case, datasets from sensors *F7* (ventromedial PFC Left Hemisphere) and *F3* (dorsolateral PFC Left Hemisphere) would correlate strongly with *P7* (TPJ Left Hemisphere), and sensors *F4* (ventromedial PFC Right Hemisphere) and *F8* (dorsolateral PFC Right Hemisphere) would correlate strongly with AF3 (dorsolateral PFC Left Hemisphere). | This would mean that *(CPD)nA* could be understood in neurological terms as a goal-oriented, context-dependent LM behavioral pattern. |

## 3. Materials and Methods

To quantitatively test these hypotheses, as a first step to evaluate brain activity while exhibiting LM problem-solving behavioral patterns, such as *KATA* [11] and *(CPD)nA* [14], when dealing with a complex value streams, a case study is used.

As argued by [101], a single case study can be seen as only a possible building block in the process of developing validity and reliability of the proposed hypothesis. Following the recommendations of [102], a clear case-study roadmap is followed. This roadmap has several phases: (1) scope establishment (2) specification of population and sampling (3) data collection (4) standardization procedure and (5) data analysis.

### 3.1. Scope Establishment

EEG signals that Lean Managers generate within an organization when performing complex process LM optimization tasks are sought to be recorded. The organization selected for this case study is a Japan-based automobile manufacturing facility, embedded within a multinational corporation, where one of the authors has accompanied a systematic implementation of LM methodologies. The factory in which the study is carried out has 30 leaders in four hierarchical levels, and consists of 800 blue collars and 150 white collars. The LM matrix organizational design structure becomes evident when the continuous improvement shopfloor management HOSHIN KANRI FOREST reporting structure [4] is visualized in Figure 4: a PDCA-based LM network with a "vertical" hierarchy responsible for the allocation of resources (engineering, logistic, production, sales,...) that is balanced by a "horizontal" structures that connects the process owners along the value stream. In this manner, the organization is aligned to jointly achieve the corporate strategic objectives through continuous improvement. This ensures the systematic weekly training of organizational leaders in LM continuous improvement problem-solving routines.

The socio-cultural context in which the data collection is carried out is that of an experienced LM staff, with a corporate culture oriented towards continuous improvement throughout decades. The economic context of the automotive group in question follows a strategy of pressing cost reduction.

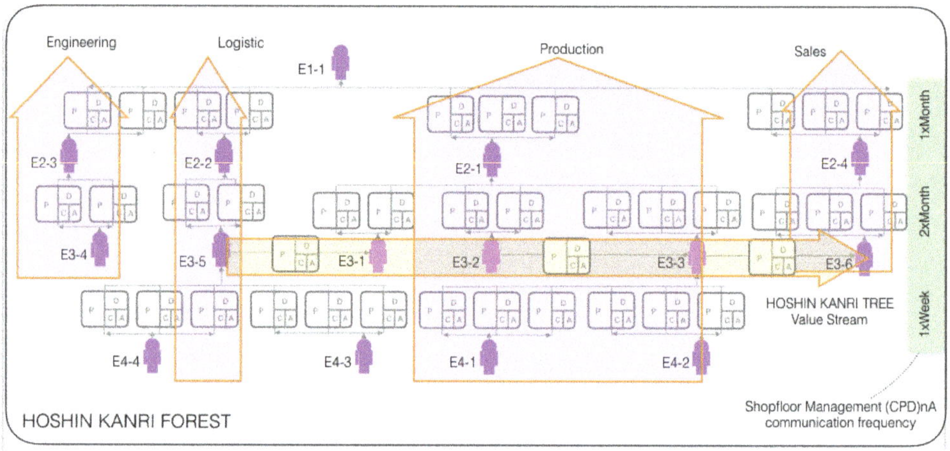


**Figure 4.** Part of the HOSHIN KANRI FOREST STRUCTURE [5].

### 3.2. Specifications of Population and Sampling

Data were collected from 26 healthy male adult leaders (20–60 years of age with a mean of 40 years). None of them had a history of neurological or psychiatric disorder or was on chronic medication. All subjects were fluent in Japanese and had learned the language before they were age seven. Significant differences in EEG activity is usually found between right-handed and left-handed groups of subjects irrespective of the side of the brain considered [103]. Handedness was determined by the Edinburgh Handedness Inventory [104]. The initial group included 24 left-hemisphere-dominant persons (lateralization index of 29.5 ± 100%), one right-hemisphere-dominant person (−78.59%) and one ambidextrous person (+6.25%). Right-hemisphere-dominant and ambidextrous participants were excluded. The final sample included 24 male subjects with no significant differences in years of education, LM problem-solving experience, or handedness scores.

### 3.3. Data Collection

As previously shown, location and nomenclature of the 14 EEG electrodes is chosen as standardized by the American Electroencephalographic Society (AES) [74], are depicted in Figure 3 and marked in red [AF3, F7, F3, FC5, T7, P7, O1, O2, P8, T8, FC6, F4, F8, AF4].

The technical specifications of the EEG low-cost portable sensor shown in Figure 5c can be summarized as follows:

- Sampling method: Sequential sampling. Single ADC.

- Sampling rate: 128 samples per second (2048 Hz internal).
- Resolution: 14 bits 1 least significant beat = 0.51 μV (16-bit ADC, 2 bits instrumental noise floor discarded), or 16 bits.
- Bandwidth: 0.2–43 Hz, digital notch filters at 50 Hz.
- Filtering: Built in digital 5th order Sinc filter.
- Dynamic range (input referred): 8400 μV.
- Coupling mode: AC coupled.

To ensure best data collection and reduce hardware-related noise, the hair of all subjects was cut to <1 mm in length prior to measurement.

### *3.4. Data Pre-Processing*

Initially, the raw data from the EEG is processed by applying a series of standard filters. Filtering such signals to remove artifacts is common in pre-processing these data, but may introduce temporary distortions in the signal [105]. The type of filter to choose depends essentially on the analysis of the dataset at hand. Filters can be causal, if they only include past and present information, while if they include past and future information, they are called non-causal. As in this case we are not interested in the timing of initial events it was decided to avoid non-causal filters at a price of introducing differences in the signal even before its onset at t=0, due to backward filtering. An open access ***MATLAB*** toolbox for EEG, ***Fieldtrip***, was used [106]. ***Fieldtrip*** performs an infinite impulse response as default. An impulse response basically represents how the filter uses the unitary information of the signal in time. Infinite response filters produce an irregular shift at different frequencies, but they have a fundamental advantage in this case and that is that they are computationally very efficient. Summarizing, there are multiple criteria and trade-offs to take into account when designing and choosing digital filters [107]. The specific filters chosen were the following:

- First, a high-pass filter is first performed to remove the DC components from the signal (a cut-off of 1 Hz is considered sufficient and consistently produced good results in terms of SNR). [108]. This is because large drifts in the data were observed.
- Next, as indicated in the EEG sensor specifications, a hardware embedded low pass filter was implemented to eliminate frequencies above 50 Hz. This reduced the noise is associated with higher frequencies.
- Finally, in order to ensure the maximum level of anonymity for the subjects and to be scrupulous with the compliance standards of the company in which the study is carried out, a normalization in the range *[0.1]* of the values is performed. This can only be done because this study will not make comparisons between subjects.

### *3.5. Standardization Procedure*

As exemplary shown in Figure 5c the subjects were placed individually in a room with 50 dBA artificially recreated large office noise and sat down to perform the tasks by writing down each step on an A3 sheet with paper and pencil. The tasks were completed without talking. The subjects sat in a reclining chair 20 cm away from the table so that the H-point, legs, and shoulders of the subject were fixed. This ensured that the position could be maintained in a defined replicable way and that only the arms, hands and the computer's mouse were movable.

Each subject performed *KATA* and *(CPD)nA* behavioral tasks in a value stream that they owned and were therefore familiar with. The length of time allocated for the both *KATA* and *(CPD)nA* tasks was limited to 300 s each. The subject was instructed to not return to previous parts of the task. Specifically, within each task, there were pre-determined time intervals for each sub task. They were: in *KATA*, 10 s for Step 1 (KATA-I), 40 s for Step 2 (KATA-II), and 250 s for Step 3 and Step 4 (KATA-III), and in *(CPD)nA*, 10 seconds for Check, 250 s for Plan and 40 s for Do. This was established to ease the tagging of tasks for the subsequent analysis. The control task consists of writing the katakana syllabic alphabet for 30 s after finishing the problem-solving task. For purpose of example, a 5-s recording time series multi-plot of the first subject performing (CPD)nA-Plan (a) and KATA-III (b) is shown in Figure 5c.

Since no distinction can be made between subjects in terms of sex, LM experience, handedness score or training, and because the data collection procedure has been standardized as described, the data can be considered balanced. The complicacy of these datasets makes the need for a cross-correlation function and DL technique apparent if we are to analyze and inspect the dataset for relevant features.

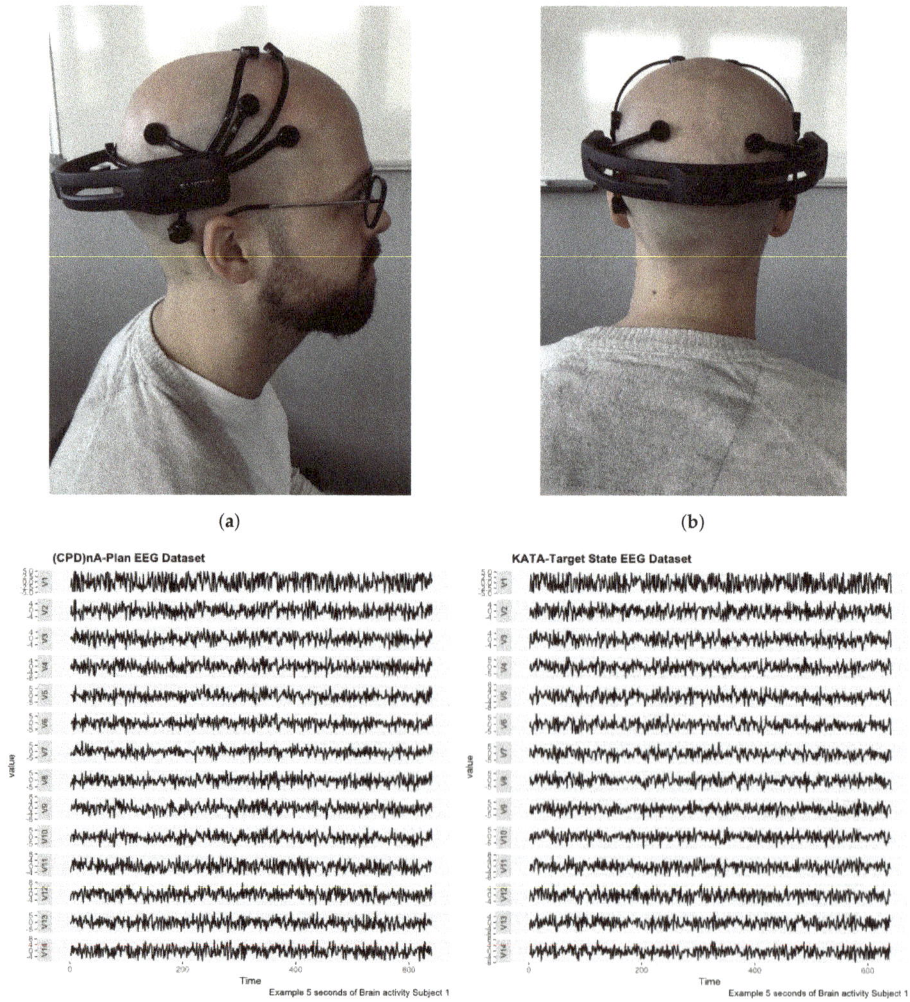


(a) (b) (c)

**Figure 5.** Data Collection. (**a**) EEG Low-Cost Portable Sensor. (**b**) EEG Low-Cost Portable Sensor. (**c**) 5 s recording time series multi-plot of first subject performing (CPD)nA-Plan (**a**) and KATA-III (**b**) of *Subject 1*.

### 3.6. Data Analysis

In this section, the soft sensors developed for the analysis is presented.

#### 3.6.1. Experimental Setup

The data analysis setup in this study were implemented with a computer equipped with an Intel(R) Xeon(R) Gold 6154 3.00 GHz CPU and an NVIDIA Quadro P4000 Graphic Process Unit (GPU) with 96 GB of random-access memory (RAM). The operating system was ***Red Hat Linux*** 16.04 64-bit version.

The training and testing of the DL model was carried out with ***Keras*** which is an interface to ***TensorFlow***. (Version 1.8), and the model was built in ***Python*** (Version 2.7) language [109]. TensorFlow is an interface for generating and executing machine learning algorithms, including training and inference algorithms for DNN models. Specifically, the TensorFlow TF.Learn module was adopted to create, configure, train, and evaluate the DNN. TF.Learn is a high-level Python module for distributed machine learning within TensorFlow and integrates a wide range of state-of-the-art machine learning algorithms. Additional Python interfaces were used: ***OpenCV*** for computer vision algorithms and image processing, ***Numpy*** for scientific computing and array calculation, and ***Matplotlib*** for displaying plots. The details of building the soft sensor model for problem-solving classification through EEG signals with Python are provided online at Open Access Repository and were created with ***Jupyter Notebook***.

#### 3.6.2. Deep Learning

1. Data Segmentation

   The time-dependent EEG data set is separated into 1-s segments during the data segmentation process. All subsequent operations, including feature extraction, classification, and validation, etc., are based on this previous segmentation. The nature of the segments depends on the application context and the sampling frequency of the EEG sensors. Increasing the length of the segments may improve the accuracy of the recognition, but the learning time will increase, and more time will be needed to obtain sufficient data. This could lead to delays in the response of applications in real time and restrict application scenarios [110].

2. Multichannel Method

   As described in [100], the multichannel data pre-processing method for DL treats data from three EEG channels as three superimposed color levels corresponding to red, green, and blue elements in the RGB color format. The EEG signal strength is projected to a corresponding color value in the [0.1] range. The three values of each point are represented as one pixel in the image. The resolution of the image is the same as the length of the segment (1 s/128 pixels because the sampling rate is 128 samples per second). The data collected from the different sensors are grouped in rows. The advantage of this method is that it greatly reduces the size of the image and results in a much shorter training time than that of the raw EEG time series analysis, and does not require expert knowledge. Figure 6 shows the principle of the application of this method and an example image. The data fragment used in this figure shows the first five seconds of the one used in Figure 5c.

3. Deep-Learning Soft Sensor Architecture

   After pre-processing and segmentation, the original data segments are transformed into images, to which the DL methods are applied. In this study, the deep convolutional neural network algorithm is used [111]. This model has its own parameters, such as the number of convolutional layers, the learning rate, pooling size, etc. Figure 7 shows the DL soft sensor architecture and workflow. The first layer to extract features from an input image is the convolution layer. It preserves the relationship between pixels by learning image features using small squares of input data.

The Rectified Linear Unit (ReLU) method is used for the non-linear operation to introduce non-linearity in the DL model. Following the convolution layer is the pooling layer which can reduce the dimensionality size. The max pooling method is used in our model, which takes the largest element from the rectified feature map. Multiple convolution layers and pooling layer can be added to the DL model to obtain the best performance. Finally, the feature map matrix produced by the convolution and pooling layers is flattened and fed into the fully connected layer to output the classes using the SoftMax activation function. Following the approach in [110], in order to classify between the LM behavioral patterns, the shallow features are merged with the deep-learned features on the last fully connected layer, as shown in Figure 7. More details of the DL models are available online at Open Access Repository.

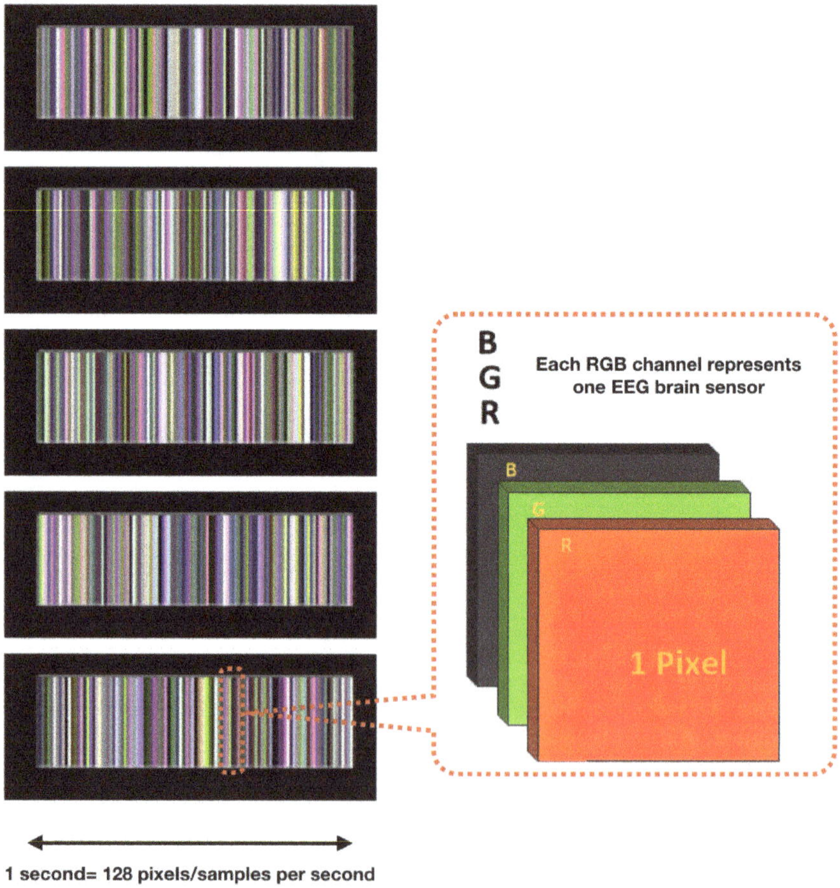


**Figure 6.** Multichannel Method [100].

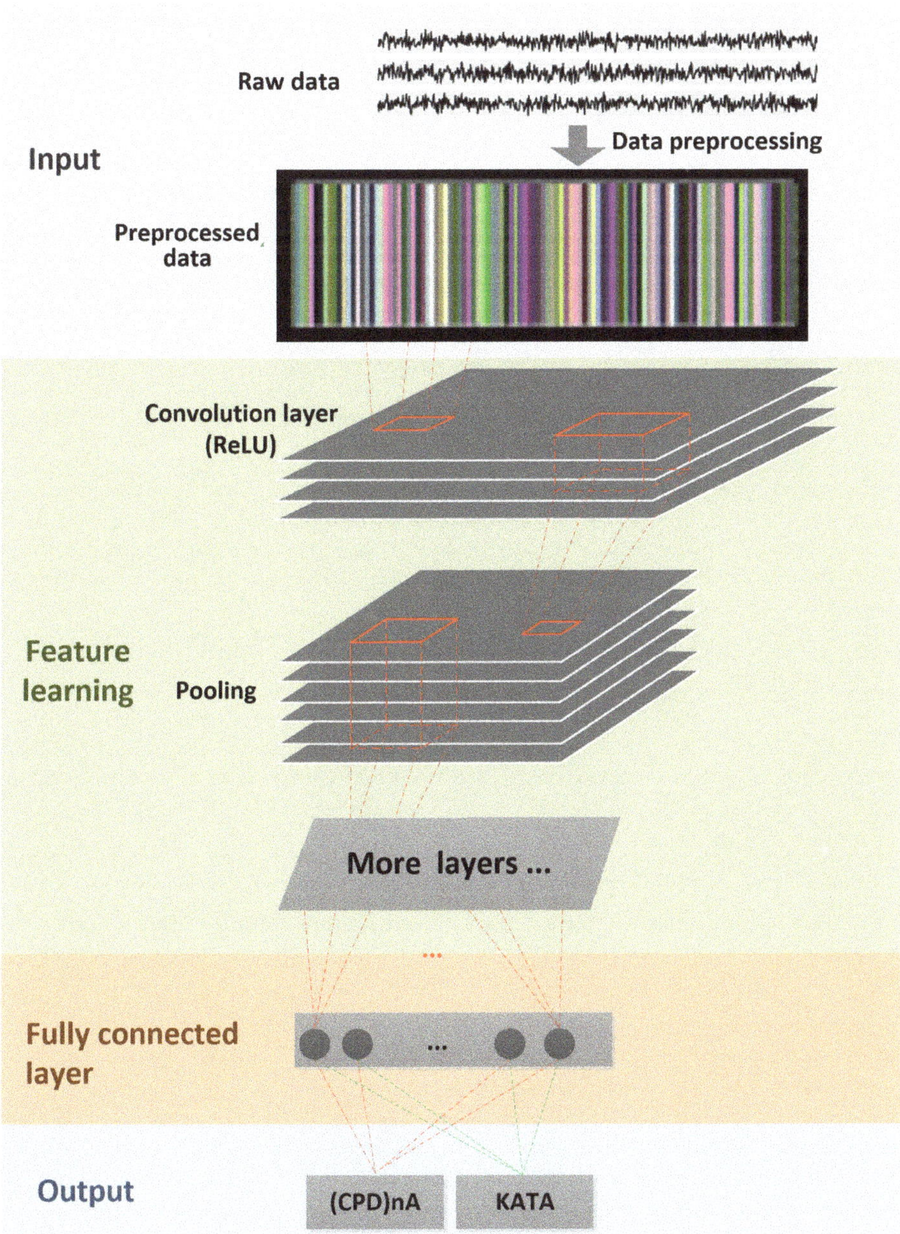


**Figure 7.** Deep-learning soft sensor for EEG classification.

## 4. Results and Discussion

In this section, the experimental results of the analysis are presented, their interpretation as well as the experimental conclusions that can be drawn from them. To do so, one by one on all the hypotheses presented in Table 1 are checked and commented by using the cross-correlation function, and the results of the automatic characterization of LM problem-solving behavioral patterns by means of the DL soft sensor are presented:

### 4.1. Results and Discussion of Cross-Correlation Function

1. Corresponding to *H1*

   All sensors *AF3-F7-F3-AF4-F4-F8* are expected to correlate with each other, although the strength of correlations may differ, which means that the task is *executive*.

   Figure 8a,b shows the cross-correlation among sensors *AF3-F7-F3-AF4-F4-F8* of *Subject 1*. These results show that for the same subject, all sensors *AF3-F7-F3-AF4-F4-F8* presented a correlation that exceeds 0.45. This supports *H1* which stated that subjects engaging in LM problem-solving behavioral patterns present a strong correlation in their PFC activity.
2. Corresponding to *H2*

   Sensors *F7* and *F3*, as well as sensors *F4* and *F8*, are expected to present stronger correlation, which means that the task is *goal driven*.

   Figure 8c,d shows that the correlations between sensors *F7* and *F3*, as well as sensors *F4* and *F8*, are stronger than others, which exceed 0.85. This supports *H2* which stated that subjects engaging in LM problem-solving behavioral patterns present a coordinated a dorsolateral- and ventromedial PFC activity.
3. Corresponding to *H3*

   Sensors *F7* and *P7*, as well as sensors *F8* and *P8*, are expected to present no correlation or a very weak correlation.

   The results show that for *KATA*, the correlations between sensor *P7* to sensors *F7* and *F3* (0.21–0.33), and sensor *P8* to sensors *F4* and *F8* between 0.21 and 0.34, are much weaker than *(CPD)nA*. This supports *H3* which stated that goal-oriented, context-independent LM problem-solving behavioral patterns would present a low correlation between the dorsolateral PFC and the TPJ.
4. Corresponding to *H4*

   Sensors *F7* and *P7*, as well as sensors *F8* and *P8*, are expected to present a strong correlation.

   The result shows that for *(CPD)nA*, sensor *P7* is correlated with sensors *F7* and *F3* between 0.69 and 0.73, sensor *P8* is correlated with sensors *F4* and *F8* between 0.68 and 0.73. This supports *H4* which stated that goal-directed, context-dependent LM problem-solving behavioral patterns would present a high correlation between the dorsolateral PFC and the TPJ.

Hypotheses *H1*, *H2*, *H3* and *H4* were verified by calculating the cross-correlation among sensors for both *KATA* and *(CPD)nA* LM behavioral patterns:

For clarity, Figure 9 depicts Figure 3b results on a brain layout. This shows how while performing both LM problem-solving behavioral patterns, the PFC shows a highly coordinated activity. When *KATA*, a goal-directed context-independent behavioral pattern is performed, the coordination between the dorso-lateral prefrontal cortex and the TPJ is non-existent. This changes when *(CPD)nA*, a goal-directed context-dependent behavioral pattern is performed.

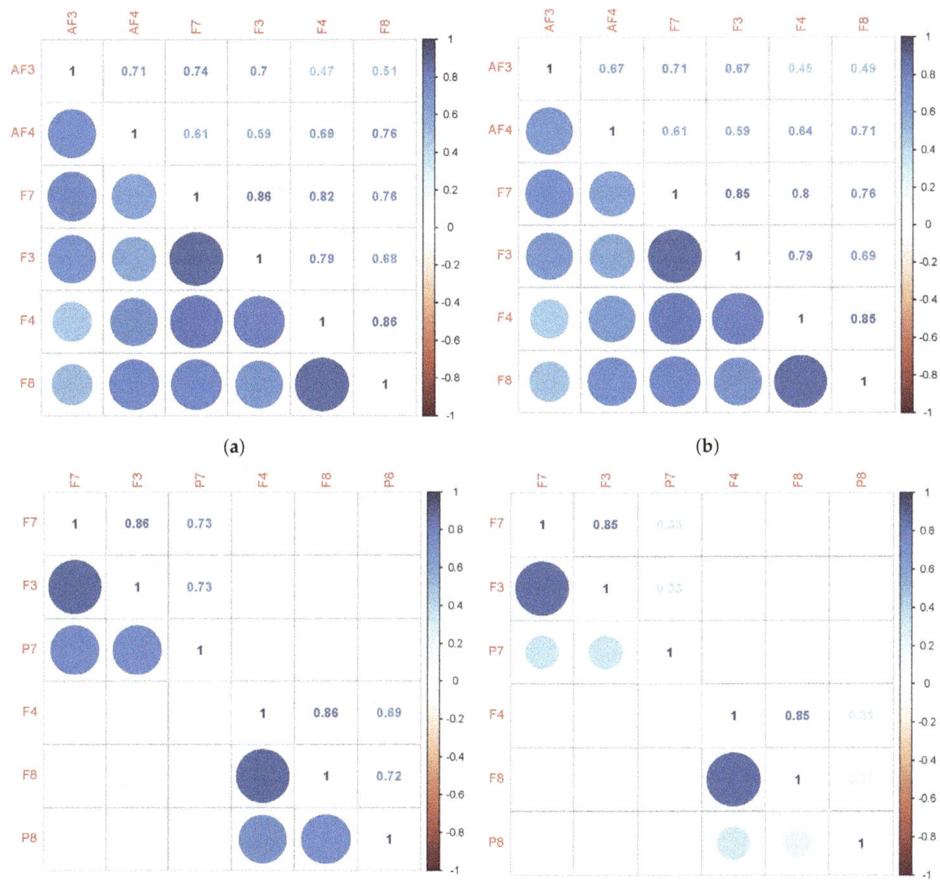


**Figure 8.** Graphical representation of Hypotheses confirmation with *Subject 1* results. (**a**) (CPD)nA Results. Sensors *AF3-F7-F3-AF4-F4-F8*. (**b**) KATA Results. Sensors *AF3-F7-F3-AF4-F4-F8*. (**c**) (CPD)nA Results. Sensors *F7-F3-P7-F4-F8-P8*. (**d**) KATA Results. Sensors *F7-F3-P7-F4-F8-P8*.

***In summary, all hypotheses were tested and verified.*** Subjects under scrutiny presented a high PFC activity and a high correlated dorsolateral PFC and vm-PFC activation. The combination of these factors enabled us to label such LM problem-solving behavioral patterns as executive and goal-oriented. Furthermore, *KATA* did not present a dl-PFC and TPJ modulation, whereas *(CPD)nA* did. This allows us to label *KATA* as context-independent and *(CPD)nA* as context-dependent behavioral pattern. These results were validated by a DL predictor algorithm at very high levels of accuracy.

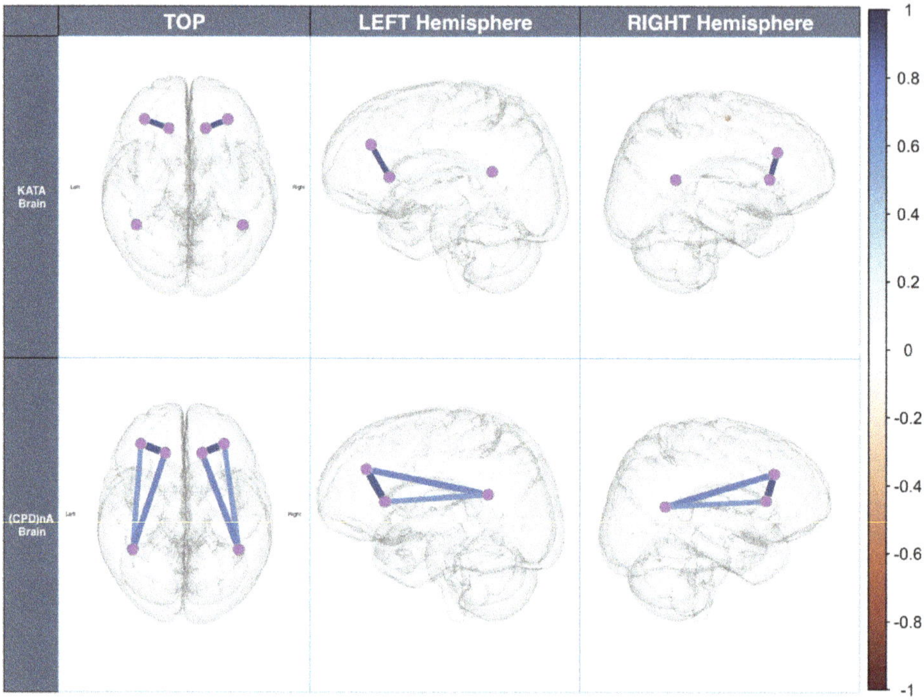


**Figure 9.** Brain Overlay of cross-correlation among sensors *F7*, *F3* and *P7*, as well as *F4*, *F8* and *P8* of Subject 1.

## 4.2. Results and Discussion of Deep-Learning Soft Sensor

After testing and verifying the hypotheses, the results of a ***DL soft sensor that can characterize the LM problem-solving behavioral task with a 99% of accuracy*** are presented. This is important, because it is not necessary to have an expert knowledge of neurophysiology to discern whether a certain LM problem-solving behavioral pattern is of one nature or another. The very nature of the DL soft sensor will determine it automatically.

As shown in the Open Access Repository, using Keras, TensorFlow backend for the DNN and OpenCV/Numpy for the image manipulation, a dataset of ***12,000 images*** is used. As a standard procedure, the data is split into ***training dataset*** of 20 Subjects (80%), ***testing dataset*** of 2 Subjects (10%) and ***validation dataset*** of 2 Subjects (10%). These subjects are chosen randomly between the sample of 24 Subjects.

The ***training dataset*** is used to train the DNN throughout several epochs as shown in Figure 10. It can be observed that both accuracy and loss do not increase or decrease significantly after epoch number 4.

The ***testing dataset*** is subsequently used to test DNN performance. The confusion matrix is a standard procedure to summarize the results of such a training by typically combining contingency classes (TRUE, FALSE) and (OK, not-OK), hence building four categories:

1. True Negative *(TN)*, which is an error and has been predicted as an error
2. False Positive *(FP)*, which is an error but has not been predicted as an error, and is by far the most damaging category
3. False Negative *(FN)* which is not an error but has been predicted as an error

4. True Positive *(TP)* which is not an error and has not been predicted as an error.

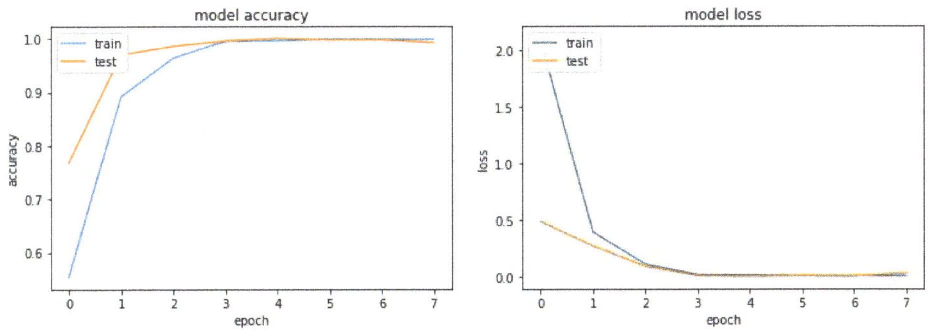


(**a**) (**b**)

**Figure 10.** DL Training and Testing Results. (**a**) DL Model Training Accuracy. (**b**) DL Model Training Loss.

The results are summarized in Figure 11. Specifically, given the balanced dataset chosen, the *accuracy* (ACC) delivered by the DNN soft sensor, defined by the expression $ACC = (TP + TN)/(TP + TN + FP + FN)$, is 99%. The $TN$ rate is 99%, the $TP$ rate is 99%, the $FN$ rate is 1% and the $FP$ rate is also 1%. These levels of $ACC$ can be considered acceptable for such a complicated industrial classification problem.

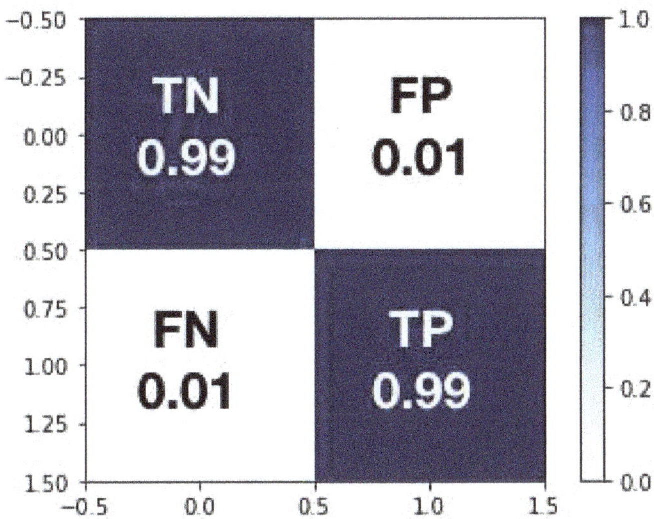


**Figure 11.** DL Model Testing Confusion Matrix.

## 5. Management Conclusions and Future Steps

These results allow for different ways of further industrial implementation. To do so, these results must be interpreted in a broad context of Industry 4.0. This section provides some essential aspects that will help to understand and contextualize the contributed results through a meta-discussion at various organizational levels.

To attain operational excellence, leaders need to better understand their people. At the verge of empirical psychological neuroscience, organizational behavioral theory, and artificial intelligence, this multidisciplinary paper seeks to help organizational leaders, LM practitioners and scholars to develop a better understanding of the brain's dynamics that are associated with certain standard LM problem-solving behavioral patterns that are commonly found in corporate settings.

The empirical results have provided evidence to assume that from a neurological perspective, it is possible to provide organizational leaders with certain conclusions and take-offs for future endeavors:

- The LM tasks studied can be regarded as goal-oriented tasks due to the highly coordinated activity of the dorsolateral and ventromedial PFC. This means that organizational leaders who exhibit such problem-solving behavioral patterns are intending to attain certain goals and perform a cerebral internal modulation of those goals. The immediate consequence is that strategic goals such as operational excellence are more likely to be achieved when implementing LM.
- LM tasks can be regarded as executive tasks that are guided mainly by the PFC. This means that organizational leaders, when dealing with such problem-solving behavioral patterns, consistently exercise decision-making, working memory, and self-control while performing LM. The consequence is that LM is provably a managerial conglomerate that induces and executive cerebral state and therefore, organizational leaders that decide to implement LM within their organizations and setting them in a systematic path of execution towards operational excellence.
- The LM problem-solving behavioral pattern, *KATA*, after definition of the target states apparently induces the subjects into a mental state in which information that is not relevant to the target-state achievement is not taken into consideration. This is shown by the lack of coordinated activity between PFC areas and the TPJ. This has powerful implications for the operations management community. It could mean that target-state setting would induce subjects into undesirable inflexible problem-solving behavioral patterns in which the decision-making process is not modulated by the complexity of ever-changing organizational value-stream settings. Individuals could make decisions independently of their context to serve their individual targets. This could potentially not serve a higher organizational alignment. In highly complex organizational settings where interdependent behavior is essential for organizational alignment, this could have dire consequences.
- In contrast, the LM problem-solving behavioral pattern (CPD)nA-Plan, which advocates only continuous improvement without target conditions, seems to enable cerebral modulation of the PFC activity by providing for coordination with the TPJ. In highly complex environments where interdependent value-stream constraints are to be simultaneously considered, such an LM behavioral trait seems to permit the flexibility that is necessary for a coordinated organizational effort towards the demands of alignment and, from a cerebral perspective, offers a better promise to ensure individual and organizational fitness.

In an Industry 4.0 context, EEG sensor signals placed on human process owners combined with DL soft sensor architectures within Industry 4.0 environments could have an impact at various levels of aggregation in value chains.

1. EEG combined with DL at a shoopfloor level shall impact quality, reliability, and cost.

   In an Industry 4.0 shopfloor environment, in which man and machine interact constantly to create value, it is essential that they communicate effectively and efficiently in real time. The creation of intelligent algorithms capable of characterizing the complex behaviors of the human brain and making them understandable to the machine seems of vital importance to ensure a symbiosis that increases machine efficiency and human effectiveness.

   Future lines of research should try to better understand how the human brain can integrate its work into the Industry 4.0 shopfloor by means of brain sensors, making possible the cerebral interface between man and machine without the need for low-bandwidth elements such as touch screens or verbal commands.

The DL-based algorithms based on process EEG signals presented in this paper can be a spearhead that allows the classification and training of Industry 4.0 intelligence systems that allow this integration. This intelligence integrated in the value streams will allow humans and machines to co-exist in a way in which artificial and human intelligence will complement each other, thus increasing the process capability of generating higher standards of quality, reliability, and ultimately reducing cost.

2. EEG combined with DL at a strategic manufacturing system level.

The DL characterization of LM problem-solving behavioral patterns is expected to help Industry 4.0 leaders in their choice of adequate manufacturing systems and their related problem-solving methods in their future pursuit of strategic organizational goals.

As demonstrated by the presented DL algorithms, no neurophysiological expert knowledge is necessary to discriminate between two different complex LM problem-solving behavioral patterns performed by Industry 4.0 process owners. This could help future industry leaders make better decisions about which manufacturing systems to choose from a neurological point of view. This bottom-up approach is novel in the field of management and represents in itself a breakthrough in the study of manufacturing systems in Industry 4.0 environments.

DL-based applications combined with multiple simultaneous EEG measurements to different actors during the performance of different complex tasks such as decision-making, data analysis, leadership interactions with subordinates, or other relevant actors, could lead to new revelations in the field of *neuroeconomics* among other fields. Likewise, by establishing a feedback loop to the leadership process of each individual, this knowledge could provide specific knowledge of each individual during their interaction with other stakeholders. This could mean a breakthrough towards a customization of leadership and towards a transformation of business culture from the neuroscientific knowledge of human behavior in an Industry 4.0 environment.

As a final note, a word of caution. Although the results are promising, no premature conclusions of causality should be drawn in any way. For several reasons: first, blinking and eye movement produce strong electrical impulses that can affect EEG measurement. Therefore, in future research, as subjects perform tasks with their eyes open in Industry 4.0 environments, pre-processing using an electro-oculogram as an adaptive noise canceller may be necessary. Second, subjects were asked to cut their hair to <1 mm in length prior to measurement to facilitate signal recording and consequently increase algorithm's performance. This is a rather unrealistic condition for an Industry 4.0 setting. Third, group analysis would have been desirable. However, in this study focus on inter-subject correlations was not possible mainly for one reason: compliance rules of the organization in which the study was carried out, did not allow the researchers to compare the results from different subjects in order to avoid labor-related conflicts. For this reason, only one subject was exemplary displayed in Figures 8 and 9. Fourth, the population used for the study was relatively small, quite homogeneous, focused on one technological set of problems and drawn from only one geographical region. Furthermore, the level of LM expertise, age, or gender could be aspects to be controlled for and/or used as a covariate or explanatory variable in future research.

**Author Contributions:** Conceptualization, J.V.-D. and X.Z.; methodology, J.V.-D. and X.Z.; software, J.V.-D., X.Z. and D.S.; validation, J.V.-D., X.Z. and M.M.; formal analysis, J.V.-D. and X.Z.; investigation, J.V.-D.; resources, X.Z.; data curation, X.Z. and D.S.; writing—original draft preparation, J.V.-D.; writing—review and editing, J.V.-D.; visualization, J.V.-D. and D.S.; supervision, J.V.-D. and X.Z.; project administration, J.V.-D.; funding acquisition, J.V.-D.

**Acknowledgments:** This research was partially supported by Hochschule Heilbronn, Fakultät Management und Vertrieb, Campus Schwäbisch Hall, 74523, Schwäbisch Hall, Germany. We thank Oliver Lenzen and Daniela Ludin, for their institutional support.

**Conflicts of Interest:** The authors declare no conflict of interest.

## Abbreviations

The following abbreviations are used in this manuscript:

| | |
|---|---|
| LM | Lean Management |
| SNR | Signal-to-Noise Ratio |
| PFC | Prefrontal Cortex |
| PDCA | Plan-Do-Check-Act |
| (CPD)nA | Check-Plan-Do-...-Act |
| EEG | Electroencephalography |
| DL | Deep Learning |
| H | Hypothesis |

## References


1. Imai, M. *KAIZEN: The Key to Japan's Competitive Success*; McGraw-Hill Higher Education: New York, NY, USA, 1986.
2. Womack, J.; Jones, D. Introduction. In *Lean Thinking*, 2nd ed.; Simon & Schuster: New York, NY, USA, 2003; p. 4.
3. Shah, R.; Chandrasekaran, A.; Lindeman, K. In pursuit of implementation patterns: The context of Lean and Six Sigma. *Int. J. Prod. Econ.* **2008**, *46*, 6679–6699. [CrossRef]
4. Villalba-Diez, J. *The HOSHIN KANRI FOREST. Lean Strategic Organizational Design*, 1st ed.; CRC Press/Taylor and Francis Group LLC: Boca Raton, FL, USA, 2017.
5. Villalba-Diez, J. *The Lean Brain Theory. Complex Networked Lean Strategic Organizational Design*; CRC Press/Taylor and Francis Group LLC: Boca Raton, FL, USA, 2017.
6. Shah, R.; Ward, P. Lean Manufacturing: Context, practice bundles and performance. *J. Oper. Manag.* **2003**, *21*, 129–149. [CrossRef]
7. Shah, R.; Ward, P. Defining and developing measures of lean production. *J. Oper. Manag.* **2007**, *25*, 785–805. [CrossRef]
8. Shewhart, W.; Deming, E. *Statistical Method. From the Viewpoint of Quality Control*; Department of Agriculture, The Graduate School: Washington, DC, USA, 1939.
9. Madanhire, I.; Mbohwa, C. Application of just in time as a total quality management tool: The case of an aluminium foundry manufacturing. *Total Qual. Manag. Bus. Excell.* **2016**, *27*, 184–197. [CrossRef]
10. Yang, C.C. The effectiveness analysis of the practices in five quality management stages for SMEs. *Total Qual. Manag. Bus. Excell.* **2018**. [CrossRef]
11. Rother, M. *Toyota Kata: Managing People for Improvement, Adaptiveness and Superior Results*, 1st ed.; McGraw-Hill: New York, NY, USA, 2009.
12. Sobek, D., II; Smalley, A. *Understanding A3 Thinking: A Critical Component of Toyota's PDCA Management System*, 1st ed.; Productivity Press: Boca Raton, FL, USA, 2008.
13. Balle, M.; Balle, F. *Lead with Respect: A Novel of Lean Practice*; Lean Enterprises Inst Inc.: Boston, MA, USA, 2014.
14. Villalba-Diez, J.; Ordieres-Mere, J. Improving manufacturing operational performance by standardizing process management. *Trans. Eng. Manag.* **2015**, *62*, 351–360. [CrossRef]
15. Rother, M.; Aulinger, G. *Toyota Kata Culture: Building Organizational Capability and Mindset through Kata Coaching*; McGraw-Hill Higher Education: New York, NY, USA, 2017.
16. Villalba-Diez, J.; Ordieres-Mere, J.; Rubio-Valdehita, S. Lean Learning Patterns. (CPD)nA vs. KATA. *Procedia CIRP* **2016**, *54*, 147–151. [CrossRef]
17. Di Flumeri, G.; Aricò, P.; Borghini, G.; Sciaraffa, N.; Di Florio, A.; Babiloni, F. The Dry Revolution: Evaluation of Three Different EEG Dry Electrode Types in Terms of Signal Spectral Features, Mental States Classification and Usability. *Sensors* **2019**, *19*, 1365. [CrossRef]
18. Lopez-Gordo, M.A.; Sanchez-Morillo, D.; Valle, F.P. Dry EEG Electrodes. *Sensors* **2014**, *14*, 12847–12870. [CrossRef]

19. Pathirana, S.; Asirvatham, D.; Johar, G. A Critical Evaluation on Low-Cost Consumer-Grade Electroencephalographic Devices. In Proceedings of the 2018 2nd International Conference on BioSignal Analysis, Processing and Systems (ICBAPS), Kuching, Malaysia, 24–26 July 2018; pp. 160–165. [CrossRef]
20. Aricò, P.; Borghini, G.; Flumeri, G.D.; Sciaraffa, N.; Babiloni, F. Passive BCI beyond the lab: Current trends and future directions. *Physiol. Meas.* **2018**, *39*, 08TR02. [CrossRef]
21. Goldberg, E. *The New Executive Brain. Frontal Lobes in a Complex World*; Oxford University Press: New York, NY, USA, 2009.
22. Miyake, A.; Friedman, N.; Emerson, M.; Witzki, A.; Howerter, A.; Wager, T. The unity and diversity of executive functions and their contributions to complex "Frontal Lobe" tasks: A latent variable analysis. *Cogn. Psychol.* **2000**, *41*, 49–100. [CrossRef] [PubMed]
23. Imai, M. *Gemba Kaizen: A Commonsense Approach to a Continuous Improvement Strategy*, 2nd ed.; McGraw-Hill Professional: New York, NY, USA, 2012.
24. Wang, W.; Koren, Y. Scalability planning for reconfigurable manufacturing systems. *J. Manuf. Syst.* **2012**, *31*, 83–91. [CrossRef]
25. Swanson, H.; Fung, W. Working memory components and problem-solving accuracy: Are there multiple pathways? *J. Educ. Psychol.* **2016**, *108*, 1153–1177. [CrossRef]
26. Fuster, J. *The Prefrontal Cortex*, 5th ed.; Academic Press: Cambridge, MA, USA, 2015.
27. Brümmer, V.; Schneider, S.; Abel, T.; Vogt, T.; Strüder, H. Brain cortical activity is influenced by exercise mode and intensity. *Med. Sci. Sports Exerc.* **2011**, *43*, 1863–1872. [CrossRef] [PubMed]
28. Leslie, G.; Ojeda, A.; Makeig, S. Measuring musical engagement using expressive movement and EEG brain dynamics. *Psychomusicol. Music Mind Brain* **2014**, *24*, 75–91. [CrossRef]
29. Ito, H.T.; Zhang, S.J.; Witter, M.P.; Moser, E.I.; Moser, M.B. A prefrontal–thalamo–hippocampal circuit for goal-directed spatial navigation. *Nature* **2015**, *522*, 50. [CrossRef] [PubMed]
30. Brown, T.I.; Carr, V.A.; LaRocque, K.F.; Favila, S.E.; Gordon, A.M.; Bowles, B.; Bailenson, J.N.; Wagner, A.D. Prospective representation of navigational goals in the human hippocampus. *Science* **2016**, *352*, 1323. [CrossRef] [PubMed]
31. Janssen, L.K.; Duif, I.; van Loon, I.; Wegman, J.; de Vries, J.H.; Cools, R.; Aarts, E. Loss of lateral prefrontal cortex control in food-directed attention and goal-directed food choice in obesity. *NeuroImage* **2017**, *146*, 148–156. [CrossRef] [PubMed]
32. Cicerone, K.; Dahlberg, C.; Malec, J.; Langenbahn, D.; Felicetti, T.; Kneipp, S.; Ellmo, W.; Kalmar, K.; Giacino, J.; Harley, P.; et al. Evidence-Based Cognitive Rehabilitation: Updated Review of the Literature From 1998 Through 2002. *Arch. Phys. Med. Rehabil.* **2011**, *92*, 519–530. [CrossRef] [PubMed]
33. Helfrich, R.F.; Knight, R.T. Oscillatory Dynamics of Prefrontal Cognitive Control. *Trends Cogn. Sci.* **2016**, *20*, 916–930. [CrossRef] [PubMed]
34. Merre, P.L.; Esmaeili, V.; Charrière, E.; Galan, K.; Salin, P.A.; Petersen, C.C.H.; Crochet, S. Reward-Based Learning Drives Rapid Sensory Signals in Medial Prefrontal Cortex and Dorsal Hippocampus Necessary for Goal-Directed Behavior. *Neuron* **2018**, *97*, 83–91.e5. [CrossRef] [PubMed]
35. Reber, J.; Feinstein, J.S.; O'Doherty, J.P.; Liljeholm, M.; Adolphs, R.; Tranel, D. Selective impairment of goal-directed decision-making following lesions to the human ventromedial prefrontal cortex. *Brain* **2017**, *140*, 1743–1756. [CrossRef] [PubMed]
36. Zhou, X.; Zhu, D.; King, S.G.; Lees, C.J.; Bennett, A.J.; Salinas, E.; Stanford, T.R.; Constantinidis, C. Behavioral response inhibition and maturation of goal representation in prefrontal cortex after puberty. *Proc. Natl. Acad. Sci. USA* **2016**, *113*, 3353–3358. [CrossRef] [PubMed]
37. Voytek, B.; Kayser, A.S.; Badre, D.; Fegen, D.; Chang, E.F.; Crone, N.E.; Parvizi, J.; Knight, R.T.; D'Esposito, M. Oscillatory dynamics coordinating human frontal networks in support of goal maintenance. *Nat. Neurosci.* **2015**, *18*, 1318. [CrossRef] [PubMed]
38. Gazzaley, A.; Cooney, J.; McEvoy, K.; Knight, R.; D'Esposito, M. Top-down Enhancement and Suppression of the Magnitude and Speed of Neural Activity. *J. Cogn. Neurosci.* **2005**, *17*, 507–517. [CrossRef]
39. Goldman-Rakic, P. Circuitry of primate prefrontal cortex and regulation of behavior by representational memory. In *Comprehensive Physiology, Supplement 5: Handbookof Physiology, the Nervous System, Higher Functions of the Brain*; John Wiley & Sons, Inc.: Hoboken, NJ, USA, 1987; pp. 373–417.
40. Badre, D.; D'Esposito, M. Functional magnetic resonance imaging evidence for a hierarchical organization of the prefrontal cortex. *J. Cogn. Neurosci.* **2007**, *19*, 2082–2099. [CrossRef]

41. Amodio, D.; Frith, C. Meeting ofminds: The medial frontal cortex and social cognition. *Nat. Rev. Neurosci.* **2006**, *88*, 615–626.
42. Aron, A. From reactive to proactive and selective control: Developing a richer model for stopping inappropriate responses. *Biol. Psychiatry* **2011**, *69*, e55–e68. [CrossRef]
43. Balconi, M.; Vanutelli, M.E.; Grippa, E. Resting state and personality component (BIS/BAS) predict the brain activity (EEG and fNIRS measure) in response to emotional cues. *Brain Behav.* **2017**, *7*, e00686. [CrossRef]
44. Waskom, M.; Frank, M.; Wagner, A. Adaptive Engagement of Cognitive Control in Context-Dependent Decision Making. *Cereb. Cortex* **2017**, *27*, 1270–1284. [CrossRef]
45. Hare, T.; Camerer, C.; Rangel, A. Self-Control in Decision-Maiking Involves Modulation of the vmPFC Valuation System. *Science* **2009**, *324*, 646–648. [CrossRef] [PubMed]
46. Rudort, S.; Hare, T. Interactions between Dorsolateral and Ventromedial Prefrontal Cortex Underlie Context-Dependent Stimulus Valuation in Goal-Directed Choice. *J. Neurosci.* **2014**, *34*, 15988–15996. [CrossRef] [PubMed]
47. Chao, L.; Knight, R. Human prefrontal lesions increase distractability to irrelevant sensory inputs. *Neuroreport* **1995**, *6*, 1605–1610. [CrossRef] [PubMed]
48. Lorenc, E.; Lee, T.; Chen, A.W.; D'Esposito, M. The Effect of Disruption of Prefrontal Cortical Function with Transcranial Magnetic Stimulation on Visual Working Memory. *Front. Syst. Neurosci.* **2015**, *9*, 1–11. [CrossRef] [PubMed]
49. Spreng, R.; Shoemaker, L.; Turner, G. Executive Functions and Neurocognitive Aging. In *Executive Functions in Health and Disease*, 1st ed.; Academic Press: Cambridge, MA, USA, 2017; pp. 169–196.
50. Arnsten, A.; Raskind, M.; Taylor, F.; Connor, D. The effects of stress exposure on prefrontal cortex: Translating absic research into successful treatments for post-traumatic stress disorder. *Neurobiol. Stress* **2015**, *1*, 89–99. [CrossRef] [PubMed]
51. Arnsten, A. Stress signalling pathways that impair prefrontal cortex structure and function. *Nat. Rev. Neurosci.* **2009**, *10*, 410–422. [CrossRef]
52. Birbaumer, N.; Veit, R.; Lotze, M.; Erb, M.; Hermann, C.; Grodd, W.; Flor, H. Deficient fear conditioning in psychopathy: a functional magnetic resonance imaging study. *Arch. Gen. Psychiatry* **2005**, *62*, 799–805. [CrossRef]
53. Contreras-Rodríguez, O.; Pujol, J.; Batalla, I.; Harrison, B.; Soriano-Mas, C.; Deus, J.; López-Solà, M.; Macià, D.; Pera, V.; Hernández-Ribas, R.; et al. Functional Connectivity Bias in the Prefrontal Cortex of Psychopaths. *Biol. Psychiatry* **2014**, *78*, 647–655. [CrossRef]
54. Pujol, J.; Batalla, I.; Contreras-Rodríguez, O.; Harrison, B.; Pera, V.; Hernández-Ribas, R.; Bosa, L.; Soriano-Mas, C.; Deus, J.; López-Solà, M.; et al. Breakdown in the brain network subserving moral judgment in criminal psychopathy. *Soc. Cogn. Affect. Neurosci.* **2012**, *7*, 917–923. [CrossRef]
55. Babiak, P.; Hare, R. *Snakes in Suits: When Psychopaths Go to Work*, Reprint edition ed.; HarperBusiness: New York, NY, USA, 2007.
56. Tei, S.; Fujino, J.; Kawada, R.; Jankowski, K.; Kauppi, J.P.; van den Bos, W.; Abe, N.; Sugihara, G.; Miyata, J.; Murai, T.; et al. Collaborative roles of Temporoparietal Junction and Dorsolateral Prefrontal Cortex in Different Types of Behavioural Flexibility. *Sci. Rep.* **2017**, *7*, 6415. [CrossRef]
57. Hearne, L.; Cocchi, L.; Zalesky, A.; Mattingley, J. Reconfiguration of brain network architectures between resting state and complexity-dependent cognitive reasoning. *J. Neurosci.* **2017**, *37*, 8399–8411. [CrossRef] [PubMed]
58. Rother, M.; Shook, J. *Learning to See: Value Stream Mapping to Add Value and Eliminate MUDA*, 1st ed.; Lean Enterprise Insititute: Cambridge, MA, USA, 1999.
59. Womack, J.; Jones, D. *Seeing the Whole Value Stream*, 2nd ed.; Lean Enterprise Institute: Boston, MA, USA, 2011.
60. Baba, F. Study on stable facility conservation activities based on PDCA cycle. *Yokohama Int. Soc. Sci. Res.* **2012**, *17*, 99.
61. Center, J.M.A.M. *PDCA Starting from C Works Faster!*; Japan Management Association Management Center: Tokyo, Japan, 2013.
62. Valentin, O.; Ducharme, M.; Crétot-Richert, G.; Monsarrat-Chanon, H.; Viallet, G.; Delnavaz, A.; Voix, J. Validation and Benchmarking of a Wearable EEG Acquisition Platform for Real-World Applications. *IEEE Trans. Biomed. Circuits Syst.* **2019**, *13*, 103–111. [CrossRef] [PubMed]

63. Lin, C.; Chuang, C.; Huang, C.; Tsai, S.; Lu, S.; Chen, Y.; Ko, L. Wireless and Wearable EEG System for Evaluating Driver Vigilance. *IEEE Trans. Biomed. Circuits Syst.* **2014**, *8*, 165–176. [CrossRef] [PubMed]
64. Zhang, Z.; Luo, D.; Rasim, Y.; Li, Y.; Meng, G.; Xu, J.; Wang, C. A Vehicle Active Safety Model: Vehicle Speed Control Based on Driver Vigilance Detection Using Wearable EEG and Sparse Representation. *Sensors* **2016**, *16*, 242. [CrossRef] [PubMed]
65. Zhang, X.; Li, J.; Liu, Y.; Zhang, Z.; Wang, Z.; Luo, D.; Zhou, X.; Zhu, M.; Salman, W.; Hu, G.; et al. Design of a Fatigue Detection System for High-Speed Trains Based on Driver Vigilance Using a Wireless Wearable EEG. *Sensors* **2017**, *17*, 486. [CrossRef] [PubMed]
66. Mohamed, Z.; El Halaby, M.; Said, T.; Shawky, D.; Badawi, A. Characterizing Focused Attention and Working Memory Using EEG. *Sensors* **2018**, *18*, 3743. [CrossRef] [PubMed]
67. Masood, N.; Farooq, H. Investigating EEG Patterns for Dual-Stimuli Induced Human Fear Emotional State. *Sensors* **2019**, *19*, 522. [CrossRef] [PubMed]
68. Ahn, J.W.; Ku, Y.; Kim, H.C. A Novel Wearable EEG and ECG Recording System for Stress Assessment. *Sensors* **2019**, *19*, 1991. [CrossRef]
69. Blanco, J.A.; Vanleer, A.C.; Calibo, T.K.; Firebaugh, S.L. Single-Trial Cognitive Stress Classification Using Portable Wireless Electroencephalography. *Sensors* **2019**, *19*, 499. [CrossRef]
70. Pérez-Vidal, A.F.; Garcia-Beltran, C.D.; Martínez-Sibaja, A.; Posada-Gómez, R. Use of the Stockwell Transform in the Detection of P300 Evoked Potentials with Low-Cost Brain Sensors. *Sensors* **2018**, *18*, 1483. [CrossRef] [PubMed]
71. Zhang, Y.; Shen, Y. Parallel Mechanism of Spectral Feature-Enhanced Maps in EEG-Based Cognitive Workload Classification. *Sensors* **2019**, *19*, 808. [CrossRef] [PubMed]
72. Borghini, G.; Aricò, P.; Di Flumeri, G.; Sciaraffa, N.; Babiloni, F. Correlation and Similarity between Cerebral and Non-Cerebral Electrical Activity for User's States Assessment. *Sensors* **2019**, *19*, 704. [CrossRef] [PubMed]
73. Khan, M.; Hong, M.; Hong, K. Decoding of four movement directions using hybrid NIRS-EEG brain-computer interface. *Front. Hum. Neurosci.* **2014**, *8*, 244. [CrossRef] [PubMed]
74. American Electroencephalographic Society guidelines in electroencephalography, evoked potentials, and polysomnography. *J. Clin. Neurophysiol.* **1994**, *11*, 147.
75. Li, J.; Struzik, Z.; Zhang, L.; Cichocki, A. Feature learning from incomplete EEG with denoising autoencoder. *Neurocomputing* **2015**, *165*, 23–31. [CrossRef]
76. Runnova, A.; Zhuravlev, M.; Koronovskiy, A.; Hramov, A. Mathematical approach to recover EEG brain signals with artifacts by means of Gram-Schmidt transform. *SPIE Proc.* **2017**, *10337*, 103370Y.
77. Elsayed, N.; Zaghloul, Z.; Bayoumi, M. Brain Computer Interface: EEG Signal Preprocessing Issues and Solutions. *Int. J. Comput. Appl.* **2017**, *169*, 12–16. [CrossRef]
78. Shanbao, T.; Thankor, N. Cross-Correlation Function. In *Quantitative EEG Analysis Methods and Applications (Engineering in Medicine & Biology)*; Artech House Publishers: Norwood, MA, USA, 2009; pp. 111–112.
79. Chandaka, S.; Chatterjee, A.; Munshi, S. Cross-correlation aided support vector machine classifier for classification of EEG signals. *Expert Syst. Appl.* **2009**, *36*, 1329–1336. [CrossRef]
80. Abdullah, H.; Maddage, N.; Cosic, I.; Cvetkovic, D. Cross-correlation of EEG frequency bands and heart rate variability for sleep apnoea classification. *Med. Biol. Eng. Comput.* **2010**, *48*, 1261–1269. [CrossRef]
81. Panischev, O.; Demin, S.; Kaplan, A.; Varaksina, N. Use of Cross-Correlation Analysis of EEG Signals for Detecting Risk Level for Development of Schizophrenia. *Biomed. Eng.* **2013**, *47*, 153–156. [CrossRef]
82. Morelli, M.; Giannoni, A.; Passino, C.; Landini, L.; Emdin, M.; Vanello, N. A Cross-Correlational Analysis between Electroencephalographic and End-Tidal Carbon Dioxide Signals: Methodological Issues in the Presence of Missing Data and Real Data Results. *Sensors* **2016**, *16*, 1828. [CrossRef] [PubMed]
83. Hermanto, B.; Mengko, T.; Prihatmanto, A.; Indrayanto, A. Signal reference selection and dimensionality reduction for crosscorrelation based feature extraction in EEG signals of brain computer interface. *Far East J. Electron. Commun.* **2017**, *17*, 185–207. [CrossRef]
84. Turner, J.; Page, A.; Mohsenin, T.; Oates, T. Deep Belief Networks used on High Resolution Multichannel Electroencephalography Data for Seizure Detection. In Proceedings of the 2014 AAAI Spring Symposium, Palo Alto, CA, USA, 24–26 March 2014; pp. 24–26.

85. Jia, X.; Li, K.; Li, X.; Zhang, A. A novel semi-supervised deep learning framework for affective state recognition on eeg signals. In Proceedings of the 2014 IEEE International Conference on Bioinformatics and Bioengineering (BIBE), Boca Raton, FL, USA, 10–12 November 2014; pp. 30–37.
86. Kasabov, N. From multilayer perceptrons and neurofuzzy systems to deep learning machines: Which method to use?—A survey. *Int. J. Inf. Technol. Secur.* **2017**, *9*, 3–24.
87. Subasi, A.; Gursoy, M. EEG signal classification using PCA, ICA, LDA and support vector machines. *Expert Syst. Appl.* **2010**, *37*, 8659–8666. [CrossRef]
88. Chen, D.W.; Miao, R.; Yang, W.Q.; Liang, Y.; Chen, H.H.; Huang, L.; Deng, C.J.; Han, N. A Feature Extraction Method Based on Differential Entropy and Linear Discriminant Analysis for Emotion Recognition. *Sensors* **2019**, *19*, 1631. [CrossRef]
89. Goodfellow, I.; Bengio, Y.; Courville, A. *Deep Learning*, 1st ed.; Adaptive Computation and Machine Learning Series; The MIT Press: Cambridge, MA, USA, 2016.
90. Glorot, X.; Bengio, Y. Understanding the difficulty of training deep feedforward neural networks. In *Artificial Intelligence and Statistics (AISTATS)*; W&CP: Sardinia, Italy, 2010; Volume 9, pp. 249–256.
91. Ngiam, J.; Khosla, A.; Kim, M.; Nam, J.; Lee, H.; Ng, A.Y. Multimodel deep learning. In Proceedings of the 28th International Conference on Machine Learning, Bellevue, WA, USA, 28 June–2 July 2011; pp. 689–696.
92. Bengio, Y. Learning deep architechtures for AI. *Found. Trends Mach. Learn.* **2009**, *2*, 1–127. [CrossRef]
93. Movahedi, F.; Coyle, J.; Sejdic, E. Deep belief networks for electroencephalography: A review of recent contributions and future outlooks. *IEEE J. Biomed. Health Inform.* **2018**, *22*, 642–652. [CrossRef]
94. Schirrmeister, R.; Springenberg, J.; Fiederer, L.; Glasstetter, M.; Eggensperger, K.; Tangermann, M. Deep learning with convolutional neural networks for brain mapping and decoding of movement-related information from the human EEG. *Hum. Brain Mapp.* **2017**, *38*, 5391–5420. [CrossRef]
95. Dai, M.; Zheng, D.; Na, R.; Wang, S.; Zhang, S. EEG Classification of Motor Imagery Using a Novel Deep Learning Framework. *Sensors* **2019**, *19*, 551. [CrossRef]
96. Majidov, I.; Whangbo, T. Efficient Classification of Motor Imagery Electroencephalography Signals Using Deep Learning Methods. *Sensors* **2019**, *19*, 1736. [CrossRef] [PubMed]
97. Tayeb, Z.; Fedjaev, J.; Ghaboosi, N.; Richter, C.; Everding, L.; Qu, X.; Wu, Y.; Cheng, G.; Conradt, J. Validating Deep Neural Networks for Online Decoding of Motor Imagery Movements from EEG Signals. *Sensors* **2019**, *19*, 210. [CrossRef] [PubMed]
98. Mao, Z.; Yao, W.; Huang, Y. EEG-based biometric identification with deep learning. In Proceedings of the Neural Engineering (NER), Shanghai, China, 25–28 May 2017; pp. 609–612. [CrossRef]
99. Zheng, W.L.; Lu, B.L. Investigating critical frequency bands and channels for EEG-based emotion recognition with deep neural networks. *IEEE Trans. Auton. Ment. Dev.* **2015**, *7*, 162–175. [CrossRef]
100. Zheng, X.; Wang, M.; Ordieres-Mere, J. Comparison of Data Preprocessing Approaches for Applying Deep Learning to Human Activity Recognition in the Context of Industry 4.0. *Sensors* **2018**, *18*, 2146. [CrossRef] [PubMed]
101. Byrd, T.; Turner, D. Measuring the flexibility of information technology infrastructure: Exploratory analysis of a construct. *J. Manag. Inf. Syst.* **2000**, *17*, 167–208.
102. Eisenhardt, K. Building theories from case study research. *Acad. Manag. Rev.* **1989**, *14*, 532–550. [CrossRef]
103. Provins, K.; Cunliffe, P. The Relationship Between E.E.G. Activity and Handedness. *Cortex* **1972**, *8*, 136–146. [CrossRef]
104. Oldfield, R. The assessment and analysis of handedness: The Edinburgh Inventory. *Neuropsychologia* **1971**, *9*, 97–113. [CrossRef]
105. Lyons, R. *Understanding Digital Signal Processing*, 2nd ed.; Prentice Hall PTR: Upper Saddle Rvier, NJ, USA, 2004.
106. Oostenveld, R.; Fries, P.; Maris, E.; Schoffelen, J.M. FieldTrip: Open Source Software for Advanced Analysis of MEG, EEG, and Invasive Electrophysiological Data. *Comput. Intell. Neurosci.* **2011**, *2011*, 9. [CrossRef]
107. Widmann, A.; Schröger, E. Filter effects and filter artifacts in the analysis of electrophysiological data. *Front. Psychol.* **2012**, *3*, 233–233. [CrossRef]
108. Winkler, I.; Debener, S.; Mueller, K.; Tangermann, M. On the influence of high-pass filtering on ICA-based artifact reduction in EEG-ERP. In Proceedings of the 2015 37th Annual International Conference of the IEEE Engineering in Medicine and Biology Society (EMBC), Milano, Italy, 25–29 August 2015; pp. 4101–4105. [CrossRef]

109. Van Rossum, G. *Python Tutorial*; Technical Report CS-R9526; Centrum voor Wikunde en Informatica (CWI): Amsterdam, The Netherlands, 1995.
110. Ravi, D.; Wong, C.; Lo, L.; Yang, B. A Deep Learning Approach to on-Node Sensor Data Analytics for Mobile or Wearable Devices. *IEEE J. Biomed. Health Inform.* **2017**, *21*, 56–64. [CrossRef] [PubMed]
111. LeCun, Y.; Bengio, Y.; Hinton, G. Deep learning. *Nature* **2015**, *521*, 436–444. [CrossRef] [PubMed]

sensors

MDPI

*Article*

# Indoor Air-Quality Data-Monitoring System: Long-Term Monitoring Benefits

**Shengjing Sun [1,2,*], Xiaochen Zheng [1,3], Javier Villalba-Díez [4,5] and Joaquín Ordieres-Meré [1]**

1 ETSII, Universidad Politécnica de Madrid, José Gutiérrez Abascal 2, 28006 Madrid, Spain; xiaochen.zheng@epfl.ch (X.Z.); j.ordieres@upm.es (J.O.-M.)
2 Exposure, Epidemiology, and Risk Program, Department of Environmental Health, Harvard T.H. Chan School of Public Health, Boston, MA 02115, USA
3 School of Engineering, Institute of Mechanical Engineering. École polytechnique fédérale de Lausanne, 1015 Lausanne, Switzerland
4 Fakultaet fuer Management und Vertrieb, Campus Schwäbisch-Hall, Hochschule Heilbronn, 74081 Heilbronn, Germany; javier.villalba-diez@hs-heilbronn.de
5 ETSIInformática, Department of Artificial Intelligence, Universidad Politécnica de Madrid, Calle de los Ciruelos, Boadilla del Monte, 28660 Madrid, Spain
* Correspondence: shengjing.sun@alumnos.upm.es or shengjingsun@hsph.harvard.edu

Received: 25 August 2019; Accepted: 20 September 2019; Published: 25 September 2019

**Abstract:** Indoor air pollution has been ranked among the top five environmental risks to public health. Indoor Air Quality (IAQ) is proven to have significant impacts on people's comfort, health, and performance. Through a systematic literature review in the area of IAQ, two gaps have been identified by this study: short-term monitoring bias and IAQ data-monitoring solution challenges. The study addresses those gaps by proposing an Internet of Things (IoT) and Distributed Ledger Technologies (DLT)-based IAQ data-monitoring system. The developed data-monitoring solution allows for the possibility of low-cost, long-term, real-time, and summarized IAQ information benefiting all stakeholders contributing to define a rich context for Industry 4.0. The solution helps the penetration of Industrial Internet of Things (IIoT)-based monitoring strategies in the specific case of Occupational Safety Health (OSH). The study discussed the corresponding benefits OSH regulation, IAQ managerial, and transparency perspectives based on two case studies conducted in Spain.

**Keywords:** long-term monitoring benefits; indoor air quality; low cost; occupational safety and health; industry 4.0; IOTA tangle

## 1. Introduction

Indoor air pollution is a leading environmental risk, which affects people's working performance, comfort, health, and well-being [1–3]. People spend around 90% of their time indoors, and human exposure to indoor air pollutants may occasionally be more than 100 times higher than outdoor pollutant levels [4]. Exposure to poor indoor air is a significant cause of productivity loss, for the U.S., as productivity decreases 0.5–5% per workplace, generating a loss of 20 to 200 billion US dollars annually [5].

Indeed, exposure to poor indoor air also increases numerous adverse health problems, such as nausea, headaches, skin irritation, sick building syndrome, kidney failure, and even cancer [1,3,6]. The World Health Organization (WHO) estimates that 700,000 people per year die from poor breathing conditions [7]. Therefore, IAQ, has a significant impact on people's comfort, health, and performance.

IAQ have been investigated by research community and practitioners. However, two important gaps are identified by a systematic literature review. Details of literature review method and results are presented in Appendix A. The first gap is that long-term data-monitoring is lacking in the IAQ research community and in practice. The second gap is that IAQ data monitoring solution is hard to operate, expensive, and lacks transparency in terms of Occupational Safety Health (OSH) management.

**Gap I.** In most research work, sampling time period is relatively short term, and even sometimes lasts for less than one hour. Measurements were made based on assumption the IAQ conditions are the same during the year [3,8,9]. Several studies have shown that seasonal variation or non-heating and heating time period differences [10–12], considering IAQ variation by season climate change and human heating behavior. However, those studies only took a short time sampling each season. As IAQ varies from time to time due to changes in working conditions, human activity, and weather conditions etc., short-term or seasonal sampling could not cover all kinds of variations. Therefore, long-term monitoring becomes a need in the research community.

In addition to the research dimension, the practical applications, it is increasingly becoming important to gather indoor working conditions to evaluate and minimize adverse health problems. To ensure OSH, environmental regulatory agencies, e.g., Occupational Safety and Health Administrations (OSHA) and local authorities have developed monitoring strategies to assess employee exposure to indoor pollutants. Generally, the monitoring reference period is a short-term basis. A Short-Term Exposure Limit (STEL) is a term used in occupational health, industrial hygiene, and toxicology, and it is regularly adopted to be 15 min.

Long-term monitoring is challenging for environmental regulatory agencies considering instrument calibration, labor time, and costs. In regular monitoring strategies, the professional determination method is used to measure indoor contaminant level. For measuring Volatile Organic Components (VOCs), is to collect air samples, either based on whole air samples in SUMMA passivated stainless steel canisters or on solid adsorbent tubes. Subsequently, the VOCs are separated by gas chromatography and measured by mass-selective detector or multidetector techniques in a remote laboratory basis [13,14]. Due to obstacles in sampling pump technology, professional particulate matter meters such as personal environmental monitor (PEM) with Leland Legacy pump and sioutas personal cascade impactor sampler, only allow maximal 24-hour sampling [15]. Therefore, although those determination methods are accurate, in practice, it will not be possible to have a long-term monitoring strategy with professional instruments.

There are specific measurements considering different episodes, such as an eight-hour working period, night and day cycles, and seasonal variations. However, indoor working conditions vary greatly over time, and on spot short-term sampling or measurement in specific episodes could fail to provide a holistic assessment of the working environment. Long-term monitoring becomes a demand in the workplace and real applications such as OSH management.

**Gap II.** IAQ data-monitoring solution challenges are presented into two aspects. One challenge is that IAQ data sampling/collection is expensive, complex to customize and operate, and professional expertise dependency. To measure multiple pollutants, various devices should be bought from different manufactures [3,10,12]. For example, Aeroqual 200 to measure nitrogen dioxide ($NO_2$) and Total Volatile Organic Components (TVOC); Extech VPC300 to measure particulate matter (PM); htV-M to measure formaldehyde (HCHO); Q-Trak to measure carbon monoxide (CO). In addition, diffusive or passive samplers should be prepared and analyzed by chemical domain experts, and frequently replaced with new ones due to limited equipment lifespan [8,11,12], which is complicated to operate and time and labor consuming. Moreover, since different pollutants are measured with different instruments, the various collected pollutant data is complex to manage and process. Another challenge is that IAQ data sampling/collection lacks data sharing in terms of IAQ transparency to all stakeholders. IAQ transparency is vital for managers to regulate working conditions, because IAQ affects employee's productivity, comfort, and health [2]. IAQ transparency is significant for employees to enhance worker empowerment. However, few data-monitoring solutions consider IAQ data- sharing from a transparent point of view.

As the graphical abstract shows in Figure 1, the research presented in this study will address those gaps by proposing an IoT and DLT based IAQ data-monitoring system. The system is a light, low-cost, long-term solution enabled by blooming development of IoT and sensor technology, and it does enable customization because of users can freely choose pollutant sensors by a simple plug-in. It supports multiple pollutants data-monitoring, which will facilitate research community and practitioners for long-term and integrated multiple pollutants data-monitoring solutions. The main contribution from the paper is not only the hardware layer involved, although it provides a solution ahead of what it is possible to find in the market these days, mainly because of the provided flexibility but also because of the data released over a public tangle in both ways, consolidated summaries as well as stream data flow, which overcomes the private clouds that providers used to adopt. Such approach is hard to handle in Europe regarding the General Data Protection Regulation (GDPR).

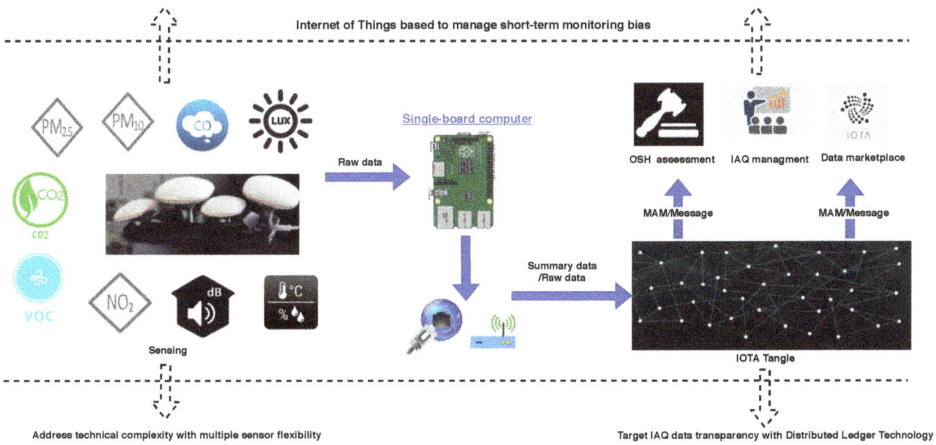


**Figure 1.** Graphical Abstract. IAQ: Indoor Air Quality; MAM: Masked Authenticated Messaging; OSH: Occupational Safety Health.

The paper promotes an open view of interaction from different layers of application, which enables different kinds of relationships and actually becomes kind of referential framework. The promoted system, which fits into the framework, applies IOTA distributed ledger techniques (concept introduced in Section 2.1) to enable data sharing, which benefits all stakeholders. It provides flexibility and low-cost, real-time, and summarized IAQ information to managers, aligns IAQ transparency to worker empowerment, and enables other benefits related to improving environments in the workplace. The relevant benefits are discussed and presented by two case studies conducted in Spain, from perspectives of OSH assessment, regulating working conditions, OSH transparency and data sharing with IOTA distributed ledger techniques.

A significant point highlighted by this paper is that although the paradigm of Industry 4.0 is being widely adopted by many industries in different sectors, there is a lack of penetration of these technologies in the specific case of the OSH [16]. Actually, the contribution from the IIoT can be considered as very significant because it can help in changing the implemented monitoring strategies. A contribution in this line is essentially the way adopted in in this paper.

## 2. Materials and Methods

### 2.1. Framework

The framework of the proposed data-monitoring architecture is presented in Figure 2. It is composed of five layers, including the sensing layer, network layer, IOTA-based data storage & sharing layer, data analysis layer, and application layer. (i) The sensing layer is the perception layer, which is the lowest layer of the conventional architecture of IoT. It contains different sensors for sensing and gathering IAQ information; (ii) The network layer is responsible for connecting to other smart things, network devices, and servers. It also facilitates transmitting and processing sensor data; (iii) The storage & sharing layer is based on DLT, the IOTA Tangle in this case, which supports secure and tamper-resistant data storage and sharing. The raw IAQ data can be shared through IOTA Tangle and in return the data publisher can receive monetary or other types of benefits. Moreover, the IAQ data analysis results, e.g., recommendation strategies, can also be shared through IOTA Tangle to help enhance regulation assessment; (iv) The analysis layer receives data from previous layers and use certain data processing techniques and machine learning models, to extract information and knowledge or even further means of wisdom; (v) The application layer is responsible for delivering specific services to corresponding users. It defines various scenarios in which the IoT and DLT can be deployed, for example, information transparency, IAQ management and assessment, gaining economic benefits for data providers. The proposed framework can also address low-cost sensor accuracy issue, as it supports persistently data aligning with OSH regulatory assessment conducted by high reliable professional instrument. The main enabling technologies involved in this framework are introduced as follows:

- **IoT**. The term "Internet of things" was coined by Kevin Ashton of Procter & Gamble in 1999, when he viewed Radio-frequency identification (RFID) as essential to the IoT, allowing computers to manage all individual things (all existing things). Presently, the IoT concept is that the pervasive presence of a variety of things or objects—such as RFID tags, sensors, actuators, mobile phones, etc.
- **Low-cost IoT-based sensing**. The low-cost IoT sensors enable the use of wireless communications and computing for interacting with the physical world. The relevant sensors could sense indoor environmental parameters such as IAQ, comfort, lighting, and acoustic conditions. Several systems [17–19] have been developed for monitoring indoor environmental conditions with low-cost sensors. The data quality generated by these sensors are often of questionable. The performance of different low-cost air-quality sensors vary from unit to unit, spatially and temporally, as it relies on different algorithms, the meteorological conditions and atmospheric composition [20]. The IAQ data-monitoring platform implemented in this study is low-cost sensor-based considering that high accuracy is not the top requirement for the targeted applications of this study. Instead, this platform is developed for purposes such as awareness raising and recommendation of sampling period selection for OSH legal compliance, which only demand the pollution level on a coarse scale. In addition, as shown in Figure 2 , the accuracy of the proposed platform can be improved through data adjustment with professional instrument at each OSH regulatory spot-check in long periods, just by observing potential bias or sensor saturation.
- **Network**. The network e.g., IoT gateway, bridges sensor networks with the traditional communication networks. It settles the heterogeneity between various sensor networks, mobile communication networks, and the Internet (all computer networks) [21,22]. A single-board computer (SBC), such as Raspberry Pi, could provide low-cost and efficient gateway services based on emerging IoT standards.
- **DLT**. Blockchain, as the first DLT, was invented by Satoshi Nakamoto in 2008 to serve as the public transaction ledger of the cryptocurrency Bitcoin [23]. The main component of DLT is a distributed ledger, which is used as a distributed database maintained by a consensus protocol run by nodes in a peer-to-peer network. This consensus protocol replaces a central administrator, since all peers contribute to maintaining the integrity of the database [24]. With a

decentralized and consensus-driven nature, DLT could provide reliable solutions, such as blockchain [23], Ethereum [25] and IOTA Tangle [26], to enable secure and tamper-resistant data storage and sharing.

- **IOTA and the Tangle**. IOTA is a tangle-based cryptocurrency designed specifically for the IoT industry. The IOTA tangle naturally succeeds the blockchain as its next evolutionary step by overcoming some of its fundamental limitations, such as scalability, high transaction fees, and vulnerability to quantum attack [26]. The main feature of the tangle is that it uses a Directed Acyclic Graph (DAG) for storing transactions instead of sequential blocks. In the Tangle, users need to perform a small amount of computational work to approve two previous transactions to issue a new transaction. This new transaction will be validated by subsequent transactions [27].
- **Masked Authenticated Messaging (MAM)**. The main data communication protocol used for data sharing in IOTA is MAM. It enables clients to emit and access an encrypted data streams over the IOTA Tangle, regardless of the size or cost of a device [28]. MAM uses channels (Public/Private/Restricted) for message spreading. IOTA users can create a channel and publish a message of any size, at any time. A small amount of proof-of-work is required to allow the data to propagate through the network and to prevent spamming. Other users can subscribe to this channel through its address, and receive a message that is published by the channel owner.

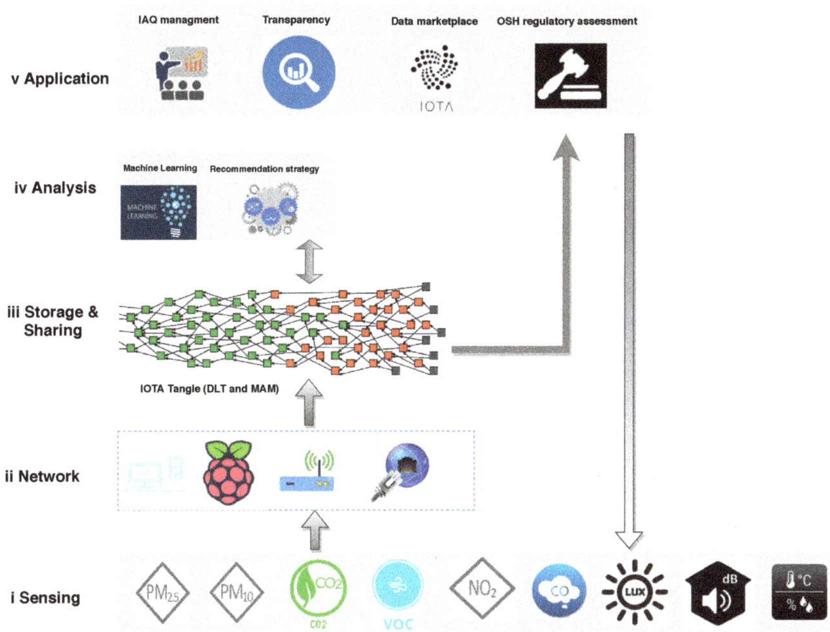


**Figure 2.** IAQ data-monitoring application framework supported by Internet of Things (IoT) and Distributed Ledger Technology (DLT). IAQ: Indoor Air Quality; MAM: Masked Authenticated Messaging; OSH: Occupational Safety Health.

The framework is also a functional guide following presented research work, for better understanding the IoT and DLT-based IAQ data-monitoring system and its long-term monitoring benefits.

### 2.2. Standards and Guidelines for OSH Assessment

The US National Institute for Occupational Safety and Health (NIOSH) defined a recommended exposure limit (REL) for hundreds of workplace chemical contaminants [29]. For NIOSH RELs, a time-weighted average (TWA) concentration was measured for up to a 10 h workday during a 40 h workweek. They also define STEL as a TWA exposure that should not be exceeded at any time during a workday. For a ceiling REL, it is the ceiling value which should not be exceeded at any time. The STEL is as a legal limit for the exposure of an employee to a chemical substance. For chemicals, STEL assessments last for 15 min and are expressed in parts per million (ppm), or sometimes in milligrams per cubic meter (mg/m$^3$). Table 1 lists a couple of indoor chemical pollutants and their STEL, presented in NIOSH. We also list an averaging period of 24 h Threshold Limit Value (TLV) for PM referencing from EPA [30] and European Union (EU) air-quality standards [31], because NIOSH only provides TLV for a total particulate 10 mg/m$^3$ 8 h TWA.

**Table 1.** TLV for pollutant based on NIOSH, EPA and EU air-quality standards. STEL: Short-Term Exposure Limit.

| Pollutant | STEL (15 min) | Average over 24 h |
|---|---|---|
| $CO_2$ | 30,000 ppm (54000 mg/m$^3$) STEL | |
| CO | 200 pm (229 mg/m$^3$) ceiling | |
| Benzene | 1 ppm (3.2 mg/m$^3$) ceiling (15 min) | |
| Formaldehyde | 0.1 ppm (0.12 mg/m$^3$) ceiling (15 min) | |
| $NO_2$ | 1 ppm (0.18 mg/m$^3$) STEL | |
| $O_3$ | 0.1 ppm (0.2 mg/m$^3$) ceiling | |
| PM2.5 | | 50 µg/m$^3$ (EPA) |
| PM10 | | 50 µg/m$^3$ from EU air-quality standards |

Considering the variations of workplace concentrations that originate from work patterns, processes (batch production or continuous process), human activity, and meteorological variations, several samples are required for the whole air-quality testing procedure. As shown in Table 2, the sampling duration and its related number of samples are presented, introduced by standard EU BS EN 689:1996.

**Table 2.** Minimum number of samples in relation to sampling duration:BS EN 689:1996.

| Sampling Duration Time | Number of Samples |
|---|---|
| 10 s | 30 |
| 1 min | 20 |
| 5 min | 12 |
| 15 min | 4 |
| 30 min | 3 |
| 1 h | 2 |
| 2 h | 1 |

### 2.3. *IoT and DLT-Based Data-Monitoring System*

The research, unifying the proposed framework, has designed an IoT and DLT-based IAQ data-monitoring system (Figure 3), which is developed using kagoo devices manufactured by Circulate (Figure 3a,b), Raspberry Pi (Figure 3c), and IOTA Tangle (Figure 3d).

The kagoo devices (Figure 3a,b were adopted as the sensing layer. Several indoor environmental conditions are measured with those devices, including air quality, acoustic conditions, lighting, and thermal comfort. Nine sensors, particulate matter (PM), formaldehyde (HCHO), TVOC, benzene ($C_6H_6$), carbon dioxide ($CO_2$), carbon monoxide (CO), ozone ($O_3$), nitrogen dioxide ($NO_2$), and T.H.I.N (Temperature & Humidity & Illumination & Noise), are used to measure indoor conditions. Those sensors can be freely selected and plugged into an island, where five maximal sensors are enabled. The list of mushroom sensors are presented in Table 3.

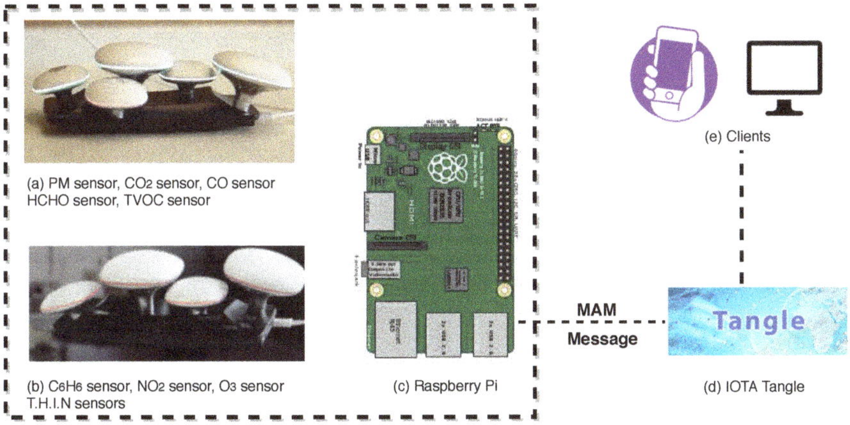


**Figure 3.** Deployment of Indoor Air-Quality (IAQ) data-monitoring system, enabling different type of clients. MAM: Masked Authenticated Messaging.

**Table 3.** Sensor specification.

| No. | Sensor Name | Model | Functions | Range |
|---|---|---|---|---|
| 1 | PM | KG-PM2 | PM2.5, PM10 Concentration Monitor | 0–1000 μg/m$^3$ |
| 2 | HCHO | KG-HO2 | HCHO Concentration Monitor | 0–7 mg/m$^3$ |
| 3 | TVOC | KG-TV2 | TVOC Concentration Monitor | 0–3 mg/m$^3$ |
| 4 | $C_6H_6$ | KG-C62 | $C_6H_6$ Concentration Monitor | 0–320 mg/m$^3$ |
| 5 | $CO_2$ | KG-C22 | $CO_2$ Concentration Monitor | 0–0.5% |
| 6 | CO | KG-C12 | CO Concentration Monitor | 0–500 ppm |
| 7 | $NO_2$ | KG-N22 | $NO_2$ Concentration Monitor | 0–20 ppm |
| 8 | $O_3$ | KG-O32 | $O_3$ Concentration Monitor | 0–20 ppm |
| 9 | T.H.I.N | KG-TN2 | Comfort Monitor (Temperature, humidity, illumination and noise) | T: –40–80°; H: 0–99.0% RH; I: 0–2000 Lux; N: 0–120 dB |

The SBC Raspberry Pi (Figure 3c) was used as the network layer. A python program was run at Raspberry Pi to collect data measurements from sensors, parse data measurements, and calculate raw data measurement and statistic summaries. The raw data is collected with a frequency of 1 min. Usually, data measurements are stored every 1 min or 5 min in most IAQ monitoring devices [32,33]. The study took 1 min since smaller granularity data could be collected for data analysis. The relevant source code could be found on GitLab [34].

The continuous collected raw data is transmitted to IOTA Tangle through MAM communication protocol. The transmitted data will be broadcast in a streaming channel. Any IOTA user who knows the address of the channel (and the private key in case the channel is restricted) can consume the IAQ data.

The periodical statistic summary, such as 15 min (STEL basis) average indoor pollutant concentration, is uploaded and stored to IOTA Tangle as a message. Through different clients, all the users can review or use the real-time and long-term periodic statistic summary results, which could be applied for OSH regular assessment, IAQ management, and employee transparency for worker empowerment. For instance, when the organization needs to be OSH assessed, they can share with the regulatory authorities the data access from a certain time. Afterward, the regulatory agencies will be able to fetch data streams (e.g., statistic summary data report) for further assessment. Considering low-cost sensor's accuracy constrains, as the initial application, those data streams could be taken as pre-assessment to ensure spot-checking is conducted efficiently and effectively.

Indeed, larger populations could assess the data as scalability was considered to be a capability in the system.

### 2.4. Case Studies

Two case studies were conducted in Spain. The choice of location selection was mainly based on availability of sites; however, the location of each industrial building was carefully examined regarding the influence of the surroundings, urban/rural area, and green zone/heave traffic. Regarding their building structure, the selected locations were representative of the building stock of the country in terms of typology, construction techniques, and age. Site 1 is an advertising workshop located at a warehouse area next to a highway. Site 2 is a steel processing plant located at a rural area near a busy road, where the office section is monitored. The office represents the most common working environment and the advertising workshop represents a less common but with possible higher pollution environment. The site characteristics are listed in Table 4.

The chemical and physical parameters measured were PM2.5, PM10, HCHO, TVOC, $C_6H_6$, $CO_2$, CO, $O_3$, $NO_2$, temperature, humidity, illumination, and noise. The data-monitoring system was placed near worker activity area, with a height of 1.5 m above the ground. On Site 1, the data-monitoring period was from 15 October 2018 to 15 November 2018. On Site 2, the office section is from 7 December 2018 to 11 January 2019. 24 h with granularity 1-minute data measurements were collected inside two sites. All collected data are open access for researchers in OSF (https://osf.io/t6rp8/) .

**Table 4.** Building site characteristics overview.

| Characteristic | Site 1 | Site 2 |
|---|---|---|
| Section | workshop section | office section |
| Year of construction | 35 | 46 |
| Floor | 1 | 1 |
| Number of occupants | 12 | 8 |
| Total area ($m^2$) | 200 | 100 |
| Heating | No | Yes |
| Ventilation | Natural | Ventilation System |
| Windows | Single Glazing | Single Glazing |
| Floor covering | Coating | Coating |
| Facilities | One solvent printing machine, two caving machine, computers, furniture | Computers, furniture |
| Cleaning schedule | Once a week | Everyday |
| Working schedule | Flexible, 24 h, including weekends | Two shifts: 06:00–14:00; 14:00–22:00, only business days |
| Smoking | Yes | No |
| Nearby potential pollutant sources | No | No |

## 3. Results and Discussion

### 3.1. Long-term Monitoring Benefits for OHS Assessment

The Occupational Safety and Health Act of 1970 (OSHAct) was passed to prevent workers from being harmed at work. The act created the OSHA, which enforces protective workplace safety and health standards. To fulfill legal compliance, employers used to contact accredited inspectors to perform air-quality testing. However, as presented in Table 2, some standards are defined to help regular short-term sampling. For example, the sampling duration time (15 min) is in relation to minimum 4 times samples established by statistical analysis and practical experience. However, it is still challenging for inspectors to select a sampling period. IAQ varies as working condition change such as different working process. As shown in Figure 4, heave printing work was done in afternoon in Site 1 leading to formaldehyde concentration rising and reaching to peak.

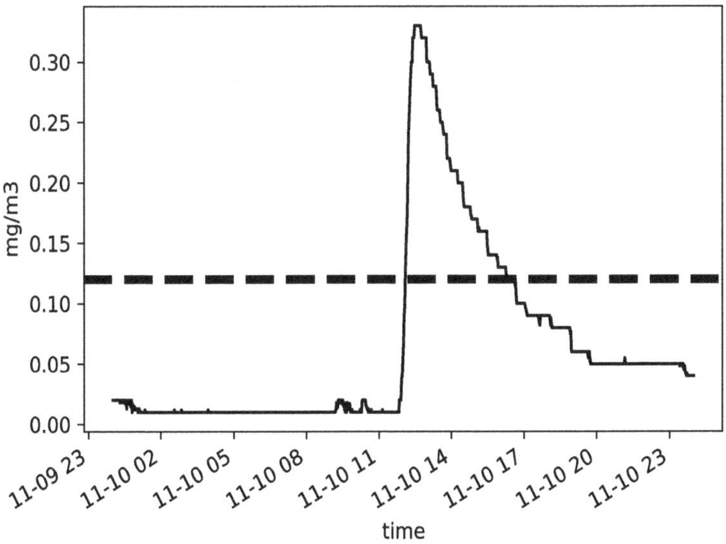


**Figure 4.** Time evolution of formaldehyde(HCHO) concentration in Site 1 during the day 2018-11-10. Dashed line refers to STEL threshold.

Practical research was conducted in Site 1, which has proved that regular spot checks are not sufficient to ensure employee health and safety. Suppose the inspector implemented a formaldehyde measuring path of 15 min sampling with stops of 30 min in between. If the inspector starts the testing by 09:00 a.m. considering that employee starts working at 08:00 a.m. the sampling period covers from 09:00 a.m. to 11:00 a.m. As depicted, formaldehyde evolution for the 10th of November in 2018 in Site 1, shown in Figure 4, there would not be any exceeding found. However, if the time span is expanded wider, exceedings appear continuously between 12:00 p.m. to 17:00 p.m. Therefore, it is proven that the inspector criteria, in full respect of regulation, still fails to guarantee employee health and safety. Although some surveys could be conducted, such as a review of work patterns, production processes, and exposure times that help select better sampling periods, they are always time-consuming and less accurate.

To address the sampling period selection bias, we designed a recommendation strategy which could give out a reasonable sampling period based on long-term measuring data and a statistical analysis approach. Considering all the historical data collected in the site for each indoor pollutant, a holistic statistical method was used to select better sampling periods. The recommendation strategy working flow is shown in Figure 5. The example of showing how the valid sampling duration for pollutant formaldehyde in Site 1 is selected based on the recommendation strategy is given. The data measurement from the whole data-monitoring period (15 October 2018–15 November 2018) are applied as input data. For each day in the monitoring period, all possible 15 min time intervals daily, with a time translation of 1 min are segmented, and the avg formaldehyde value during each segmentation is calculated. The 15 min segmentation with the max avg value is selected out in each day and the hour and two hours where the 15 min is located is marked and recorded, as shown in Figure 6b. Finally, based on a voting strategy of all monitoring days, those valid sampling durations could be recommended and selected out. Then, specific professional determination methods are used to measure indoor contaminant levels where the time windows are better selected.

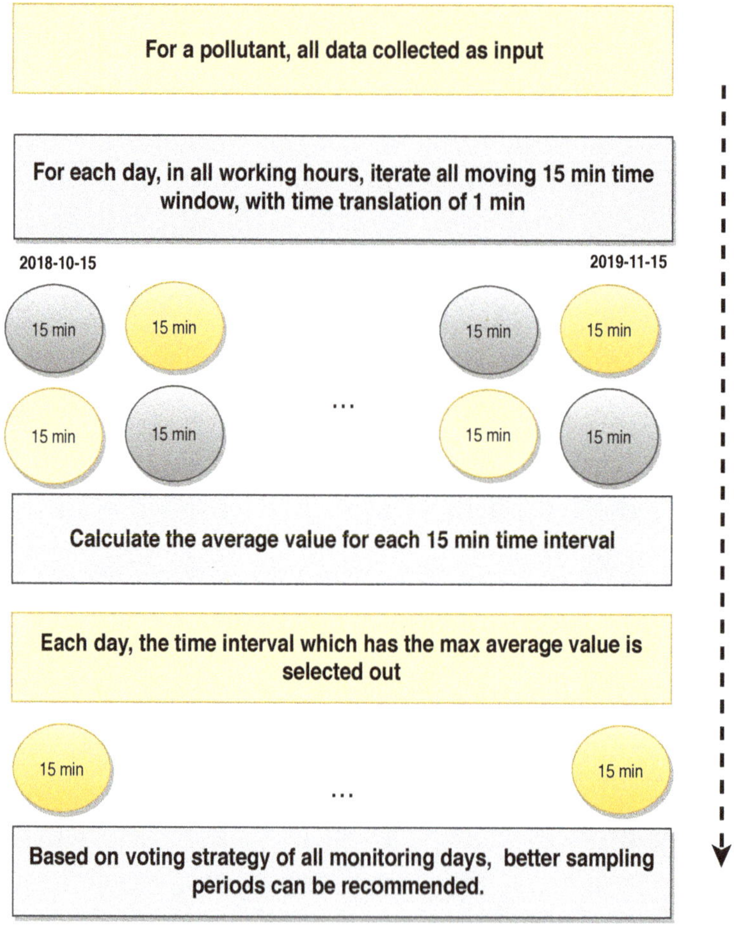


**Figure 5.** Recommendation strategy flow diagram.

The recommendation strategy is evaluated with the case studies conducted in Site 1 and Site 2. Taking PM2.5 in Site 2 as an example, our recommendation framework enables us to demonstrate a distribution of PM2.5 maximal average value occurrences (sampling time: 15 min) in site. The detail is shown in Figure 6a. Each point representing the hour where the better 15 min is located in and each line segment representing the 15 min sampling duration covering 2 h, e.g., from 18:50 to 19:05. As shown in Figure 6a, most high PM2.5 values appear in the morning, before 08:00 a.m. Therefore, based on long-term measuring data analysis, for a regular PM2.5 check in Site 2, the sampling time period is recommended for the morning, before 08:00 a.m. As shown in Figure 6b, most of high formaldehyde values in Site 1 appear in the morning, between 08:00 a.m. to 12:00 p.m. Similarly, as shown in Figure 6c, the recommendation sampling time for benzene in Site 1 would be in the afternoon, around 14:00 p.m. to 18:00 p.m. With the recommendation strategy, exceeding and significant variation could be caught up to ensure employee's health and safety.

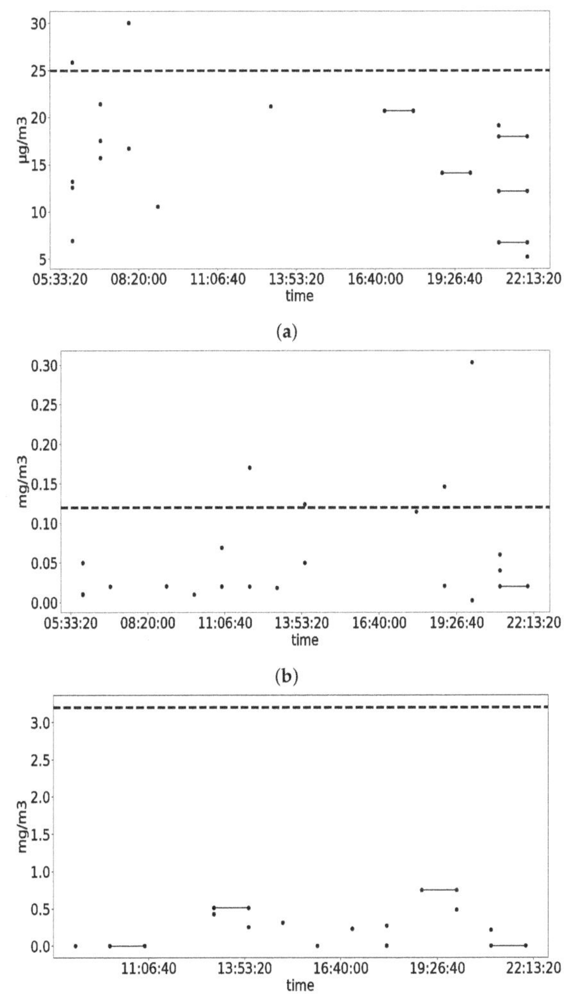


(c)

**Figure 6.** Distribution of indoor pollutant maximal average value occurrences (sampling time: 15 min) in site. (**a**) Distribution of PM2.5 maximal average value during monitoring period in Site 2. Dashed line refers to EPA TLV; (**b**) Distribution of HCHO maximal average value during monitoring period in Site 1. Dashed line refers to STEL threshold; (**c**) Distribution of $C_6H_6$ maximal average value during monitoring period in Site 1. Dashed line refers to STEL threshold.

### *3.2. Long-Term Monitoring Benefits for Regulating Working Conditions*

The employer is legally responsible for ensuring the good working conditions of employees. Long-term IAQ monitoring enables employers to understand IAQ data and IAQ patterns, so they can take appropriate measures to regularly improve working conditions. As shown in Figure 7a, in Site 2, $CO_2$ concentration is constantly higher than TLV(0.1%). The TLV(0.1%) is based on a daily average, which obtained references from Circulate App: EnvCon [35]. The Circulate company set TLVs, taking references from China's air-quality standards. Measures should be taken to reduce $CO_2$ concentration in Site 2. The corresponding measures could be opening windows, adapting heating, ventilation, and air conditioning (HVAC) systems or with plants [36,37] to reduce $CO_2$ concentration.

Thermal comfort normally refers to temperature and humidity, and is the condition of mind that expresses satisfaction with the thermal environment and subjective evaluation (ANSI/ASHRAE Standard 55). The temperature and humidity ranges are 16–28° and 30–80% respectively, according to WHO. It is also important not to over-design illumination, which can induce adverse health effects such as headache frequency, stress, and increased blood pressure. For the work requiring perception of details, such as offices, sheet metal work, and bookbinding, the minimal illuminance is 100 lux, which is defined by EU standard. On Site 2, as shown in Figure 7b,c, displays very low humidity and illumination levels. Therefore, measures should be taken to improve employee comfort.

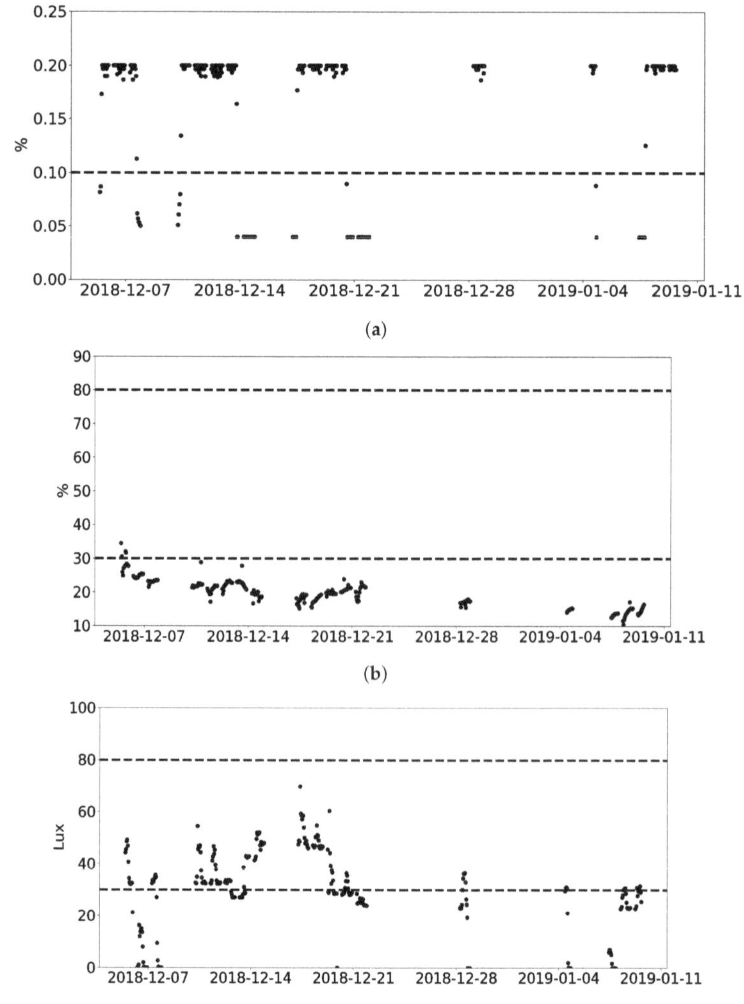


**Figure 7.** Working conditions demonstration in site 2. (**a**) Evolution of $CO_2$ hourly average concentration during monitoring period in site 2. Dashed line refers to Circulate TLV; (**b**) Evolution of humidity hourly average during monitoring period in site 2. Dashed line refers to WHO comfort recommendation; (**c**) Evolution of illumination hourly average during monitoring period in site 2. Dashed line refers to EU illuminance standard.

### 3.3. Long-Term Monitoring Benefits for OSH Transparency

Long-term IAQ monitoring ensures that OSH dimension is given the same emphasis as other business objectives. The economic benefits of high-quality indoor working conditions was demonstrated by [5]. The magnitude of productivity gains may be obtained by providing better indoor environments, a 20 to 50% reduction in sick building syndrome, saving between 10 and 100 billion US dollars. 8 to 25% fewer asthma-related absences save 1 to 4 billion US dollars. A 23 to 76% reduction in respiratory diseases saves 6 to 14 billion US dollars. The IAQ has a significant effect on economic benefits in enterprise management.

In building science studies, thermal comfort has been related to productivity and health. Office workers who are satisfied with their thermal environment are more productive [38]. For example, it is valuable to provide the correct light intensity for each task or environment. Otherwise, energy not only could be wasted, and over-illumination can lead to adverse health and psychological effects. Beyond the energy factors being considered, glare or excess light can decrease worker efficiency. The field of OSH comprises a variety of risks that need to be managed. Considering economic loss deriving from poor air quality, it is important to report IAQ daily and take it as a Key Performance Index (KPI) vector, along with other business objectives. Moreover, the relevance of the KPIs increases when they are based on real-time measurements.

To quantify how a workplace affects productivity, creativity, and well-being, CBRE, a real-estate services and investment company, designed a science-based tool to measure specific criteria [39]. The related experiments proved that information awareness also affects employee performance. That is to say, if an employee knows they are working in a good quality environment, it is helpful to improve their performance. The real-time long-term monitoring solution would provide IAQ transparent employee empowerment.

### 3.4. Long-Term Monitoring Benefits for Data Sharing by IOTA

Recently, with the tremendous development of Industry 4.0, DLT (e.g., IOTA) has attracted significant attention. With DLT, we will have the Internet of value. DLT has great potential to create new foundations for our economic and social systems by efficiently establishing trust among people and machines, reducing cost, and increasing the use of resources [40]. IOTA, as the most prominent distributed ledger project, whose goal is to become the very fundamental layer of such society, is challenging the looming paradigm shift.

Both continuous collected IAQ raw data and statistical summary data are transmitted to IOTA's Tangle through MAM or message. Different clients can register their interest to receive such data streams. According to relevant business models, different sharing mechanisms can be packaged to better serve all stakeholders [41]. For example, the calculated avg pollutant value during each 15 min, introduced in Section 3.1, can be uploaded and stored in the IOTA Tangle as the statistical summary data. Relevant accredited inspectors could assess this data in advance for better sampling period selections in OSH assessment.

The long-term IAQ monitoring solution could gain economic benefits for enterprises with the support of IOTA, with which enterprises could receive automatic, transparent, and frictionless payments from IAQ data consumers.

## 4. Conclusions

As proven by our study, long-term IAQ monitoring and data analytics have been lacking in the research community and in practice. Under this context, this research has contributed to address identified gaps by designing and testing a framework and a system, which is proven to be an effective solution for all stakeholder needs. For instance, through the monitoring system, managers can take measures to improve indoor working conditions. Some $CO_2$ exceeding values were found in Site 2. Managers could apply one basic green plant, an Areca palm (Chrysaidocarpus lutescens), which was discovered by NASA to efficiently remove $CO_2$. In addition, this paper proves the enormous potential of the IIoT in the context of Industry 4.0 to contribute in bringing new insight in worker's environment, both by consistently monitoring such environment and to easily disseminate the collected information with minimum cost and infrastructure requirements. Besides aligning IOTA, a long-term monitoring solution provides continuous values to OSH assessment agencies, supporting IAQ transparency to employee empowerment, and bringing continuous economic value to enterprises through paid data sharing services.

The limitation of this research study is that precision could issue IoT based measurements, but the data-monitoring system could be re-adapted by the conducted professional spot-check by an accredited inspector, as indicated in Figure 2. At each spot-check, more accurate data measurements could be obtained with the professional instruments. The data-monitoring system would calibrate itself with those accurate measurement, therefore, in the long-term, the precision of the data-monitoring solution would be better improved.

The carried-out research results would be applied in CBRE in future work to assess IAQ influences on employee productivity, health, and well-being.

**Author Contributions:** S.S. has been responsible for the development of the case studies, and she has shared the efforts of implementation of the dissemination with X.Z. J.O.-M. contributed with S.S. and J.V.-D. to provide the industrial dimension context for OHS application. The IOTA selection has been responsibility of J.O.-M. and X.Z.

**Funding:** This research was partially funded by the European Commission through the RFCS program, grant number with ID 793505 (WISEST project).

**Acknowledgments:** The authors thank China Scholarship Council (CSC) (No.201206730038) for the support they provided for this work. Also, the authors want to thank the EU RFCS research program for the support of this research through the grant with ID 793505 (WISEST project).

**Conflicts of Interest:** The authors declare no conflict of interest.

## Abbreviations

The following abbreviations are used in this manuscript:

| | |
|---|---|
| DLT | Distributed Ledger Technologies |
| GDPR | General Data Protection Regulation |
| IAQ | Indoor Air Quality |
| IoT | Internet of Things |
| IIoT | Industrial Internet of Things |
| OSH | Occupational Safety Health |
| TLV | Threshold Limit Value |
| TVOC | Total Volatile Organic Components |

## Appendix A

The literature review method is based on a guideline from [42]. The time span of the review is from Jan 1999 to Jan 2019. Only studies in English are considered. The IAQ monitoring and analytic are considered to be a whole, its sub-problems, such as the standalone monitoring system, exposure risk assessment, and micro-environment are not included in the literature review. The data sources include four digital libraries (ACM Digital Library, IEEE Xplore, Springer Link, and Science Direct), hand searching two conferences: the International Society of Indoor Air Quality and Climate (ISIAQ), the International Conference on Indoor Air Quality, Ventilation and Energy Conservation (IAQVEC) in Buildings. The search terms used are indoor (environmental/air), and quality (investigation/research/assessment/monitoring/analysis). After excluding irrelevant studies based on exclusion criteria and an analysis of their titles and abstracts, 65 studies were included based on full text screening, and 7 studies are selected from the reference lists. In the end, 72 studies were used as the final primary studies. Considering the objective of the research work is mainly from time and data-monitoring solution dimensions, the 23 most relevant studies were selected and listed in Table A1, from pollutant (P), time period (T), seasonal (S), data collection (D), and transparency (Tr) aspects, respectively.

**Table A1.** Systematic literature review of IAQ.

| Study | P | T | S | D | Tr |
|---|---|---|---|---|---|
| [3] | $NO_2$, TVOC, PM0.3-10 | 8h working time in five working days, September 2015 | No | Aeroqual 200 ($NO_2$, TVOC), Extech VPC300 (PM0.3-10) | No |
| [10] | PM2.5, HCHO, $CO_2$ | PM2.5 and $CO_2$ entire year, HCHO in four seasons (sampling time: 20 min) | Yes | A: on-line monitoring system with Ikair ($CO_2$) and Yun (PM2.5) sensors B: on-site measurement for HCHO by spectrophotometry | No |
| [43] | HCHO, $CO_2$ | 4 h between 08:00 AM and 12:00 AM | No | A real-time occupational exposure monitoring system with Grove-HCHO and T6613C ($CO_2$) | No |
| [8] | $NO_2$, $O_3$ and 29 VOCs | One week between 20 and 27 December 2012 | No | Diffusive samplers | No |
| [11] | 34 VOCs, $NO_2$,$O_3$ | Summer: 24 and 28 May 2010; Winter: February 21 and 25, 2011 | Yes | Passive samplers | No |
| [12] | Temperature, humidity, HCHO, $C_6H_6$, $C_2HCL_3$, Pinene, Limonene, $NO_2$, $CO_2$, CO, PM2.5, VOCs, Radon, $O_3$ | Monday to Friday, in both non-heating (26/09/2011-14/10/2011) and heating (23/01/2012-10/02/2012) | Yes | Diffusive samplers (HCHO, $C_6H_6$, $C_2HCl_3$, Pinene, Limonene, $NO_2$, $O_3$); Telair 7001 ($CO_2$), aeroQUAL (CO), PM2.5 (Derenda LVS3.1/PMS3.1-15) | No |
| [9] | PM2.5, PM10, $CO_2$, CO, HCHO, and VOCs, $O_3$ | 1 h | No | Lighthouse handheld 3016 (PM, temperature, humidity), WolfSense ($CO_2$, CO, VOC and $O_3$), htV-M (HCHO) | No |
| [44] | PAHs | One month in April | No | Passive sampler | No |
| [45] | VOCs, HCHO, acetone and $O_3$ | During 4 h with a 40-m frequency | No | PRO-EKOS AT. 401X (HCHO, $O_3$), gas chromatograph Voyager (VOCs and acetone) | No |
| [46] | temperature, humidity, CO, $CO_2$, PM10, $NO_2$, HCHO, $C_6H_6$ and toluene, bacteria and fungi | 3–10 December | No | Passive bubblers (HCHO), passive bubbler ($NO_2$), SKC passive sampler (VOCs) | No |
| [47] | PM, noise, temperature, humidity | May 2009 (hot season) and February 2010 (cold season) | Yes | - | No |
| [48] | Bacteria, fungi, dust, ammonia, and HCHO | 2 h | No | Passive sampler | No |
| [49] | Eighteen PAHs | 28 days (May–June 2014) | No | Passive sampler | No |
| [50] | PM | Pre-winter (November and early December 2013) and winter season (January and early February 2014) | Yes | MOUDI | No |
| [51] | 17 VOCs | May 2015 | No | Passive sampler | No |
| [52] | TVOC, 13 VOCs, PM2.5, NOx, $O_3$ | Two weeks (working and non-working days) which starts from early morning (08:00 a.m.) to late evening (20:00 p.m.)during winter season of 2014 | No | Model EC 9810 series ($O_3$), Model Ecotech Sernious 40 (NOx), Micro IV Single Gas Detector (CO), MiniVol™ TAS (PM2.5), PhoCheck 5000 photo-ionization detector (PID) (TVOC), NIOSH method (VOCs) | No |
| [53] | benzene, toluene, ethylbenzene m,p-xylene and o-xylene (BTEX) | Winter (from 9 December 2013 to 17 January 2014) and Spring (from 24 March to 17 April 2014 | Yes | Passive sampler | No |
| [54] | PM | Three weeks during the summer, autumn, and winter in 2014 and 2015 | Yes | OPS; TSI model 3330 | No |
| [55] | HCHO and $C_6H_6$ | 45 min | No | Passive samplers | No |
| [56] | HCHO | Second semester of 2010 and first semester of 2011 | No | Passive samplers | No |
| [57] | VOCs | 24 h | No | Passive sampling | No |
| [58] | Temperature, humidity, fungi, dust, endotoxins, CHO, VOCs, $CO_2$, $NO_2$ | Two seasons: October–Match; April–September | Yes | Radiello passive sampler (CHO and VOCs), Passam Ag passive sampler ($NO_2$), Q-Trak (Temperature, humidity, $CO_2$) | No |
| [59] | PM2.5, PM10 | During rush hours (8:00 a.m.–12:00 p.m.) for one week per each season from June 2015–June 2016 | Yes | Dust-Trak | No |

## References


1. Ana, G.R.; Alli, A.S.; Uhiara, D.C.; Shendell, D.G. Indoor air quality and reported health symptoms among hair dressers in salons in Ibadan, Nigeria. *J. Chem. Health Saf.* **2019**, *26*, 23–30. [CrossRef]
2. Tham, K.W. Indoor air quality and its effects on humans—A review of challenges and developments in the last 30 years. *Energy Build.* **2016**, *130*, 637–650. [CrossRef]
3. Kiurski, J.S.; Aksentijević, S.M.; Mandarić, S.D. Statistical approach for characterization of photocopying indoor pollution. *Air Qual. Atmos. Health* **2018**, *11*, 867–881. [CrossRef]
4. EPA. Why Indoor Air Quality is Important to Schools. Available online: https://www.epa.gov/iaq-schools/why-indoor-air-quality-important-schools (accessed on 24 September 2019).
5. Fisk, W.J.; Rosenfeld, A.H. Estimates of Improved Productivity and Health from Better Indoor Environments. *Indoor Air* **1997**, *7*, 158–172. [CrossRef]
6. Hadei, M.; Hopke, P.K.; Rafiee, M.; Rastkari, N.; Yarahmadi, M.; Kermani, M.; Shahsavani, A. Indoor and outdoor concentrations of BTEX and formaldehyde in Tehran, Iran: Effects of building characteristics and health risk assessment. *Environ. Sci. Pollut. Res.* **2018**, *25*, 27423–27437. [CrossRef] [PubMed]

7. WHO. Air Pollution and Health. Available online: https://www.who.int/airpollution/en/ (accessed on 24 September 2019).
8. Can, E.; Üzmez, Ö.Ö.; Döğeroğlu, T.; Gaga, E.O. Indoor air quality assessment in painting and printmaking department of a fine arts faculty building. *Atmos. Pollut. Res.* **2015**, *6*, 1035–1045. [CrossRef]
9. Ramos, C.A.; Wolterbeek, H.T.; Almeida, S.M. Exposure to indoor air pollutants during physical activity in fitness centers. *Build. Environ.* **2014**, *82*, 349–360. [CrossRef]
10. Liu, J.; Dai, X.; Li, X.; Jia, S.; Pei, J.; Sun, Y.; Lai, D.; Shen, X.; Sun, H.; Yin, H.; et al. Indoor air quality and occupants' ventilation habits in China: Seasonal measurement and long-term monitoring. *Build. Environ.* **2018**, *142*, 119–129. [CrossRef]
11. Yurdakul, S.; Civan, M.; Özden, Ö.; Gaga, E.; Döğeroğlu, T.; Tuncel, G. Spatial variation of VOCs and inorganic pollutants in a university building. *Atmos. Pollut. Res.* **2017**, *8*, 1–12. [CrossRef]
12. Kalimeri, K.K.; Saraga, D.E.; Lazaridis, V.D.; Legkas, N.A.; Missia, D.A.; Tolis, E.I.; Bartzis, J.G. Indoor air quality investigation of the school environment and estimated health risks: Two-season measurements in primary schools in Kozani, Greece. *Atmos. Pollut. Res.* **2016**, *7*, 1128–1142. [CrossRef]
13. EPA. *Compendium of Methods for the Determination of Air Pollutants in Indoor Air*; Project Summary; EPA: Washington, DC, USA, 1990.
14. Ishizaka, T.D.; Kawashima, A.; Hishida, N.; Hamada, N. Measurement of total volatile organic compound (TVOC) in indoor air using passive solvent extraction method. *Air Qual. Atmos. Health* **2019**, *12*, 173–187. [CrossRef]
15. SKC. IP-10A Method Update. Available online: https://www.skcinc.com/catalog/pdf/instructions/1660.pdf (accessed on 24 September 2019).
16. Mardonova, M.; Choi, Y. Toward Open-Source Hardware and Software for the Mining Industry: A Case Study of Low-Cost Environmental Monitoring System for Non-Metallic Underground Mines. *Min. Metall. Explor.* **2019**, *36*, 657–674. [CrossRef]
17. Zanni, S.; Lalli, F.; Foschi, E.; Bonoli, A.; Mantecchini, L. Indoor Air Quality Real-Time Monitoring in Airport Terminal Areas: An Opportunity for Sustainable Management of Micro-Climatic Parameters. *Sensors* **2018**, *18*, 3798. [CrossRef] [PubMed]
18. Zakaria, N.A.; Abidin, Z.Z.; Harum, N.; Hau, L.C.; Ali, N.S.; Jafar, F.A. Wireless Internet of Things-Based Air Quality Device for Smart Pollution Monitoring. *Int. J. Adv. Comput. Sci. Appl.* **2018**, *9*. [CrossRef]
19. Benammar, M.; Abdaoui, A.; Ahmad, S.H.; Touati, F.; Kadri, A. A Modular IoT Platform for Real-Time Indoor Air Quality Monitoring. *Sensors* **2018**, *18*, 581. [CrossRef] [PubMed]
20. Castell, N.; Dauge, F.R.; Schneider, P.; Vogt, M.; Lerner, U.; Fishbain, B.; Broday, D.; Bartonova, A. Can commercial low-cost sensor platforms contribute to air quality monitoring and exposure estimates? *Environ. Int.* **2017**, *99*, 293–302. [CrossRef] [PubMed]
21. Zhu, Q.; Wang, R.; Chen, Q.; Liu, Y.; Qin, W. Iot gateway: Bridgingwireless sensor networks into internet of things. In Proceedings of the 8th International Conference on Embedded and Ubiquitous Computing (EUC), Hong Kong, China, 11–13 December 2010; pp. 347–352.
22. Chen, H.; Jia, X.; Li, H. A brief introduction to IoT gateway. In Proceedings of the ET International Conference on Communication Technology and Application (ICCTA 2011), Beijing, China, 14–16 October 2011; pp. 610–613.
23. Nakamoto, S. Bitcoin: A Peer-to-Peer Electronic Cash System. Available online: https://bitcoin.org/bitcoin.pdf (accessed on 24 September 2019).
24. Brogan, J.; Baskaran, I.; Ramachandran, N. Authenticating health activity data using distributed ledger technologies. *Comput. Struct. Biotechnol. J.* **2018**, *16*, 257–266. [CrossRef] [PubMed]
25. Ethereum Foundation. Ethereum Blockchain App Platform. Available online: https://www.ethereum.org/ (accessed on 24 September 2019).
26. IOTA. What Is IOTA? Available online: https://www.iota.org/get-started/what-is-iota (accessed on 24 September 2019).
27. Popov, S.; Saa, O.; Finardi, P. Equilibria in the Tangle. *Comput. Ind. Eng.* **2019**, *136*, 160–172.
28. Handy, P. *Introducing Masked Authenticated Messaging*; IOTA: Berlin, Germany, 2017.
29. NIOSH. *NIOSH Pocket Guide to Chemical Hazards*; U.S. Department of Health Human Services: Atlanta, GA, USA, 2016.

30. EPA. EPA Air Quality Standards. Available online: https://www.epa.gov/criteria-air-pollutants/naaqs-table (accessed on 24 September 2019).
31. EEA. European Union Air Quality Standards. 2019. Available online: https://ec.europa.eu/environment/air/quality/standards.htm (accessed on 24 September 2019).
32. Moreno-Rangel, A.; Sharpe, T.; Musau, F.; McGill, G. Field evaluation of a low-cost indoor air quality monitor to quantify exposure to pollutants in residential environments. *J. Sens. Sens. Syst.* **2018**, *7*, 373–388. [CrossRef]
33. AirVisual. How Often Does the AirVisual Pro's Sensor Take Measurements? What Is the Difference between "Continuous" and "Default" Mode? Available online: https://support.airvisual.com/en/articles/3029368-how-often-does-the-airvisual-pro-s-sensor-take-measurements-what-is-the-difference-between-continuous-and-default-mode (accessed on 24 September 2019).
34. Sun, S. Indoor Air Quality. Available online: https://gitlab.com/sunshengjing/iaq (accessed on 24 September 2019).
35. Circulate. EnvCon App. Available online: https://apps.apple.com/ca/app/envcon/id1045648840 (accessed on 24 September 2019).
36. Gubb, C.; Blanusa, T.; Griffiths, A.; Pfrang, C. Can houseplants improve indoor air quality by removing $CO_2$ and increasing relative humidity? *Air Qual. Atmos. Health* **2018**, *11*, 1191–1201. [CrossRef]
37. Meattle, K. Green Buildings: A Step Towards Sustainable Development. Available online: https://www.nbmcw.com/tech-articles/tall-construction/30066-green-buildings-a-step-towards-sustainable-development.html (accessed on 24 September 2019).
38. Sulewska, M.J.; Gładyszewska-Fiedoruk, K.; Sztulc, P. Analysis of the results of empirical research and surveys of perceived indoor temperature depending on gender and seasons. *Environ. Sci. Pollut. Res.* **2018**, *25*, 31205–31218. [CrossRef] [PubMed]
39. CBRE. Spain Occupier Report. Available online: https://www.cbre.es/en/services/business-lines/global-workplace-solutions/workplace-strategy/cbre-lab (accessed on 24 September 2019).
40. Yu, F.R.; Liu, J.; He, Y.; Si, P.; Zhang, Y. Virtualization for Distributed Ledger Technology (vDLT). *IEEE Access* **2018**, *6*, 25019–25028. [CrossRef]
41. Román, V.; Ordieres-Meré, J. [WiP] IoT Blockchain Technologies for Smart Sensors Based on Raspberry Pi. In Proceedings of the 11th Conference on Service-Oriented Computing and Applications (SOCA), Paris, France, 20–22 November 2018; pp. 216–220. [CrossRef]
42. Kitchenham, B.A.; Charters, S. *Guidelines for performing Systematic Literature Reviews in Software Engineering*; Technical Report EBSE-2007-01; Keele University: Keele, UK, 2007.
43. Fathallah, H.; Lecuire, V.; Rondeau, E.; Le Calvé, S. Development of an IoT-based system for real time occupational exposure monitoring. In Proceedings of the Tenth International Conference on Systems and Networks Communications, Barcelona, Spain, 15–20 November 2015.
44. Maragkidou, A.; Arar, S.; Al-Hunaiti, A.; Ma, Y.; Harrad, S.; Jaghbeir, O.; Faouri, D.; Hämeri, K.; Hussein, T. Occupational health risk assessment and exposure to floor dust PAHs inside an educational building. *Sci. Total Environ.* **2017**, *579*, 1050–1056. [CrossRef]
45. Kiurski, J.S.; Marić, B.B.; Aksentijević, S.M.; Oros, I.B.; Kecić, V.S.; Kovačević, I.M. Indoor air quality investigation from screen printing industry. *Renew. Sustain. Energy Rev.* **2013**, *28*, 224–231. [CrossRef]
46. Chiang, C.M.; Su, H.J.; Lai, C.M.; Chou, P.C.; Li, Y.Y.; Tu, Y.F. Indoor Air Quality Assessment in an Office Building in an Industrial Park in Taiwan. In Proceedings of the Asia-Pacific Conference on the Built Environment, Taipei, Taiwan, 1999. Available online: http://citeseerx.ist.psu.edu/viewdoc/download?doi=10.1.1.614.2821&rep=rep1&type=pdf (accessed on 24 September 2019).
47. Loupa, G. Case study. Health hazards of automotive repair mechanics: Thermal and lighting comfort, particulate matter and noise. *J. Occup. Environ. Hyg.* **2013**, *10*, 35–46. [CrossRef] [PubMed]
48. Abdel Hameed, A.A.; Khoder, M.I.; Farag, S.A. Organic dust and gaseous contaminants at wood working shops. *J. Environ. Monit.* **2000**, *2*, 73–76. [CrossRef] [PubMed]
49. Keskin, S.S.; Sinan Keskin, S.; Dilmac, E. Indoor air particulate matter exposure of commuter bus passengers in Istanbul, Turkey. *Indoor Built Environ.* **2016**, *26*, 337–346. [CrossRef]
50. Goel, A.; Wathore, R.; Chakraborty, T.; Agrawal, M. Characteristics of Exposure to Particles due to Incense Burning inside Temples in Kanpur, India. *Aerosol Air Qual. Res.* **2017**, *17*, 608–615. [CrossRef]

51. Dai, H.; Jing, S.; Wang, H.; Ma, Y.; Li, L.; Song, W.; Kan, H. VOC characteristics and inhalation health risks in newly renovated residences in Shanghai, China. *Sci. Total Environ.* **2017**, *577*, 73–83. [CrossRef]
52. Singh, D.; Kumar, A.; Kumar, K.; Singh, B.; Mina, U.; Singh, B.B.; Jain, V.K. Statistical modeling of $O_3$ , $NO_x$, CO, PM2.5 , VOCs and noise levels in commercial complex and associated health risk assessment in an academic institution. *Sci. Total Environ.* **2016**, *572*, 586–594.
53. Mainka, A.; Kozielska, B. Assessment of the BTEX concentrations and health risk in urban nursery schools in Gliwice, Poland. *AIMS Environ. Sci.* **2016**, *3*, 858–870. [CrossRef]
54. Kwon, S.B.; Jeong, W.; Park, D.; Kim, K.T.; Cho, K.H. A multivariate study for characterizing particulate matter (PM(10), PM(2.5), and PM(1)) in Seoul metropolitan subway stations, Korea. *J. Hazard. Mater.* **2015**, *297*, 295–303. [CrossRef] [PubMed]
55. Huang, L.; Mo, J.; Sundell, J.; Fan, Z.; Zhang, Y. Health risk assessment of inhalation exposure to formaldehyde and benzene in newly remodeled buildings, Beijing. *PLoS ONE* **2013**, *8*, e79553. [CrossRef] [PubMed]
56. de M. Ochs, S.; de O. Grotz, L.; Factorine, L.S.; Rodrigues, M.R.; Pereira Netto, A.D. Occupational exposure to formaldehyde in an institute of morphology in Brazil: A comparison of area and personal sampling. *Environ. Sci. Pollut. Res.* **2012**, *19*, 2813–2819.
57. Guo, H.; Lee, S.C.; Chan, L.Y.; Li, W.M. Risk assessment of exposure to volatile organic compounds in different indoor environments. *Environ. Res.* **2004**, *94*, 57–66. [CrossRef]
58. Roda, C.; Barral, S.; Ravelomanantsoa, H.; Dusséaux, M.; Tribout, M.; Le Moullec, Y.; Momas, I. Assessment of indoor environment in Paris child day care centers. *Environ. Res.* **2011**, *111*, 1010–1017. [CrossRef] [PubMed]
59. Bolourchi, A.; Atabi, F.; Moattar, F.; Ehyaei, M.A. Experimental and numerical analyses of particulate matter concentrations in underground subway station. *Int. J. Environ. Sci. Technol.* **2017**, *15*, 2569–2580. [CrossRef]

*sensors*

MDPI

*Article*

# ADAPTS: An Intelligent Sustainable Conceptual Framework for Engineering Projects

**Amalia Luque *, Ana De Las Heras, María Jesús Ávila-Gutiérrez and Francisco Zamora-Polo**

Dpto. Ingeniería del Diseño. Escuela Politécnica Superior. Universidad de Sevilla. Virgen de África, 7. 41011 Sevilla, Spain; adelasheras@us.es (A.D.L.H.); mavila@us.es (M.J.Á.-G.); fzpolo@us.es (F.Z.-P.)

* Correspondence: amalialuque@us.es

Received: 28 January 2020; Accepted: 7 March 2020; Published: 11 March 2020

**Abstract:** This paper presents a conceptual framework for the optimization of environmental sustainability in engineering projects, both for products and industrial facilities or processes. The main objective of this work is to propose a conceptual framework to help researchers to approach optimization under the criteria of sustainability of engineering projects, making use of current Machine Learning techniques. For the development of this conceptual framework, a bibliographic search has been carried out on the Web of Science. From the selected documents and through a hermeneutic procedure the texts have been analyzed and the conceptual framework has been carried out. A graphic representation pyramid shape is shown to clearly define the variables of the proposed conceptual framework and their relationships. The conceptual framework consists of 5 dimensions; its acronym is ADAPTS. In the base are: (1) the Application to which it is intended, (2) the available DAta, (3) the APproach under which it is operated, and (4) the machine learning Tool used. At the top of the pyramid, (5) the necessary Sensing. A study case is proposed to show its applicability. This work is part of a broader line of research, in terms of optimization under sustainability criteria.

**Keywords:** conceptual framework; sensors; approaches; tools; data; application; project engineering; LCA; SDG 9; SDG 11

---

## 1. Introduction

In recent years concern for sustainability has grown, becoming one of the main problems worldwide [1,2]. The 2030 Agenda for Sustainable Development sets out 17 Sustainable Development Goals with 169 goals of an integrated and indivisible nature that cover the economic, social and environmental spheres. An example of the importance that environmental sustainability has at the moment is that several of the Sustainable Development Goals are directly related to the concepts of sustainability [3,4].

Many of the interpretations of what sustainable development should be agree that, in order to achieve this, the policies and actions to achieve economic growth must respect the environment and also be socially equitable to achieve economic growth: it is the model of Triple E [5,6].

The main objective of this work is to propose a conceptual framework to help researchers to approach optimization under the criteria of sustainability of engineering projects, making use of current Machine Learning techniques.

Likewise, the growing development in collaborative methodologies such as BIM (a methodology that integrates a growing number of disciplines and processes involved in the life cycle of a project), is something to consider. The sixth dimension of BIM is not only about energy saving and sustainable design (although they are the most recognized aspects), but also about the concept of value engineering, which consists in the optimization of construction systems, structures and facilities, so that with a few key modifications in strategic items or in certain systems or equipment it could be possible to obtain a significant reduction in costs, in the construction phase and / or in the exploitation phase, without losing the essence of the project. In a project that incorporates the sixth dimension of the BIM, analytical models are generated to perform analysis, calculations and simulations in order to improve the quality of the project [7,8].

For the optimization of sustainability throughout the entire life cycle of a particular product, process or industrial installation, it is necessary to use some methodology for quantification and evaluation of sustainability.

There are techniques aimed primarily at controlling effects (for example, life cycle analysis-LCA) [9,10] and techniques more focused on eliminating the causes (among which is Cradle to Cradle-C2C) [11,12].We can also find the circular economy approach, which proposes a new model of society that uses and optimizes stocks and flows of materials, energy and waste, with the aim of maximizing the efficiency of resource use [13,14] (Figure 1).

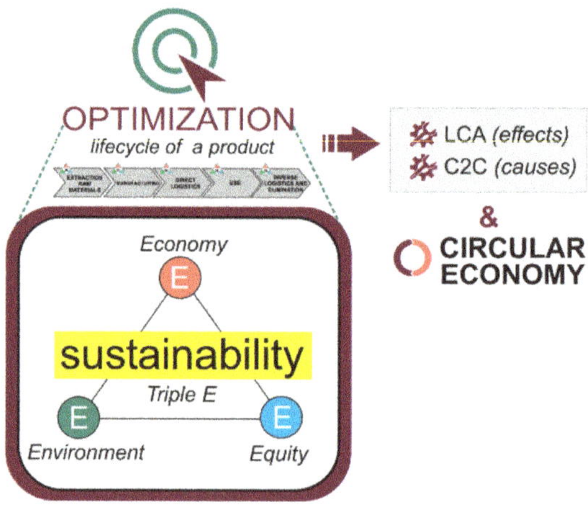


**Figure 1.** Sustainability, Triple Bottom Line and Optimization. LCA/C2C/Circular Economy.

However, these techniques, more oriented to modify the causes of sustainability inefficiencies, do not provide rigorous quantitative techniques for their evaluation (although they can be very useful in the decision-making process) [15,16]. That is why it seems appropriate to deepen the study of the LCA as a tool for evaluating potential impacts.

Life Cycle Analysis (LCA) is an objective process that allows evaluating the environmental loads associated with a product, process or activity, identifying and quantifying both the use of matter and energy and the emissions to the environment, to determine the impact of that use of resources and those emissions [17,18].

On the other hand, industry is currently immersed in an evolution, consisting of its digital transformation [19,20]. To understand the keys to this transformation it is necessary to know the available tools and other emerging ones of new application. The term Industry 4.0. is a recent term, which consists in the use of new technologies and the integration with some other evolved ones, to achieve the total or partial digitalization of the current productive models, or to create new models that allow a substantial reduction of the terms in all the phases of the affected project or services and efficiency improvements of all kinds [21,22].

Among the solutions related to Industry 4.0 with more future are artificial intelligence and machine learning. Artificial intelligence techniques have evolved vertiginously recently [23], becoming a very useful tool to address complex problems in many different fields. These types of techniques have been applied to problems in the fields of sound classification [24], image processing [25,26], risk prevention [27,28], air conditioning [29,30], in estimation of project parameters [31,32], and in many other fields of research. We understand very important to deepen the study of possible fields of application of these tools.

One of the challenges is that machine learning algorithms need to have a large volume of data in order to be trained, validated and generalized. There are multiple technologies that are framed within Industry 4.0. However, we can circumscribe the processes of digitization of industrial environments around three elements (Figure 2):

- Collection of data from machines, warehouses and articles, achieved through the Internet of Things (IoT).
- Analysis and exploitation of this huge amount of data through big data and business intelligence (BI) techniques.
- Predictive analytics based on data through machine learning.

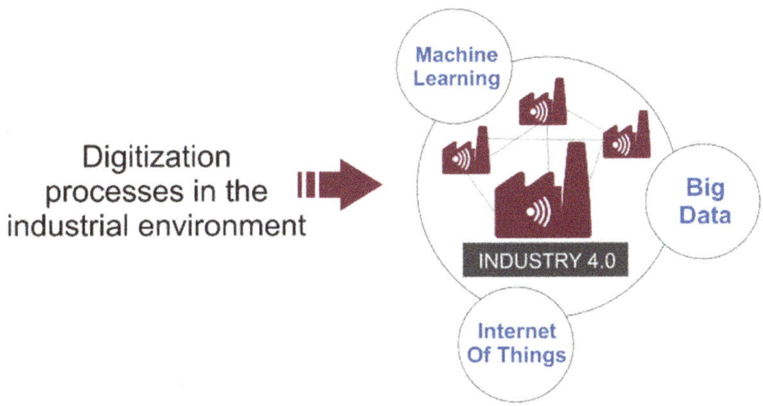


**Figure 2.** Three digitalization process.

Information is of crucial importance on these three stages. Obtaining, storing and managing relevant data intelligently plays a decisive role in the so-called Industry 4.0. [33,34]. In this way, Big Data becomes the axis on which the rest of actions must pivot in terms of digitalization. However, the avalanche of data faced by organizations may pose a threat to the viability of the project.

In the first phase of industrial digitalization, companies need to capture in real time the maximum possible information, structured and accessible, about what is happening in their business. The development of intelligent sensors, capable of being located in multiple locations of the industrial processes, allows to capture a large number of parameters based on various indicators.

These systems are complemented with cloud technology (Figure 3). The emergence of cloud solutions allows companies to store and manage in real time the multiple measurements obtained from sensors. This process is what we call the Internet of things (IoT). There are a number of advantages inherent to IoT that could be taken advantage of immediately by the industry, such as the detection of possible failures, the forecast of wear of parts or the reconfiguration of parameters and calibrations. However, many professionals are still cautious about their actual application in the industry. In this sense, there is a widespread perception that the real industrial world is not so prepared for hyper connectivity [35,36].

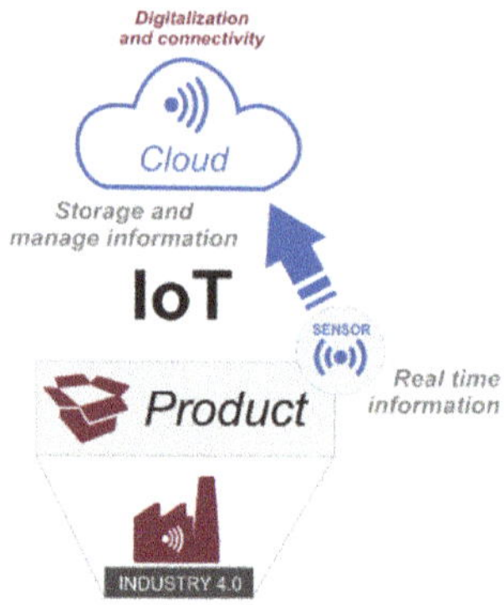


**Figure 3.** Sensors/Cloud/(connectivity)/ Storage (connectivity).

It is necessary to rely on agents that cover this gap from analog systems to intelligent ones where the technology allows to connect the real world to communicate it to the cloud through the so-called cyber-physical systems. In any case, it is an unstoppable trend since several studies estimate that by 2020 there will be 212 billion devices connected with sensors in the world [37].

The second phase consists in analyzing what is happening through tools that identify patterns and inefficiencies. Big data solutions allow the collection and systematized treatment of relevant data, obtained through sensorization, to make decisions that affect both the immediate future of organizations (to solve a breakdown or replace a part) and its development in the long term (change supplier, modify packaging or renew machinery) (Figure 4).

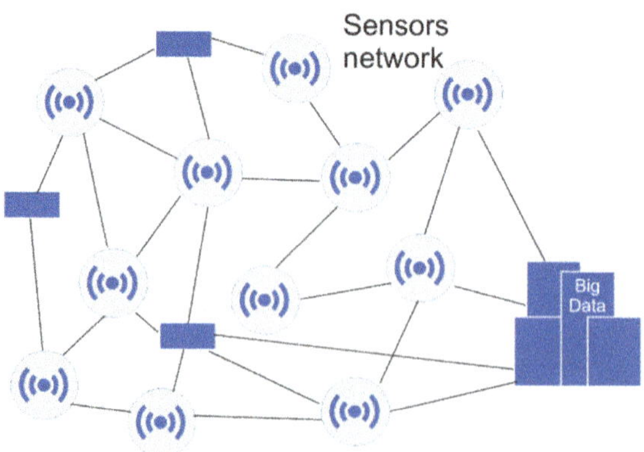


**Figure 4.** Sensors network.

It is a very complex process due to two factors: the huge volume of data and the heterogeneity of the sources from where come the data.

In addition to this, we do not only want to know what it is that has happened or is happening in those moments, but what is going to happen in the near future. This is achieved by providing the manufacturing equipment of intelligent applications that make measurements along all processes by combining the historical data and predictive models. Machine learning can be then understood as the last phase of the evolution of Industry 4.0 [38,39].

The predictive analysis, based on artificial intelligence, requires the design and implementation of algorithms that learn to represent data and to detect trends. The objective of the system is to develop models of future behaviors from the data. In this sense, the quality and quantity of information it is essential to take the next steps towards the Fourth Industrial Revolution. As we see, this brings us back to Big Data.

At this point we will return to the objective approach to the optimization under the criteria of sustainability of engineering projects, making use of the current techniques of Machine Learning. We will focus on the evaluation of the sustainability using the technique of LCA, because it uses a few indicators that allow to quantify the environmental impacts [9,40].

Given that the techniques of artificial intelligence are a very useful tool for dealing with complex problems in diverse fields, it seems interesting to raise the possibility of using them as an aid in this goal. Therefore, it is essential to take account of the need to collect and make a systematic treatment of the relevant data, obtained through smart sensing.

As far as we know, the sensorization of industrial plants and the treatment of data through machine learning algorithms is not yet sufficiently extended in the field of sustainability optimization. We detect a gap of opportunity (Figure 5) in the investigation of the state of the art, with the objective of proposing a conceptual framework that can help in the approach to this type of problems.

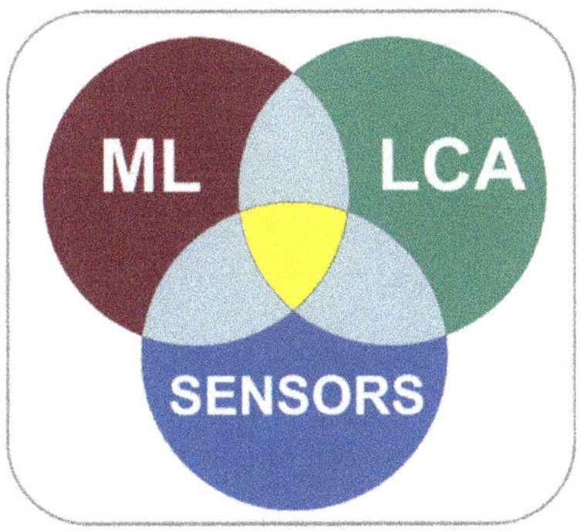


**Figure 5.** ML-LCA-SENSORS.

Conceptual frameworks are a very useful tool widely used for various applications. Figure 6 shows the evolution in the number of articles contained "conceptual framework" in the title indexed in the SCOPUS database over the last 10 years. As can be seen, there is a growing interest in the development of this type of work by the scientific community.

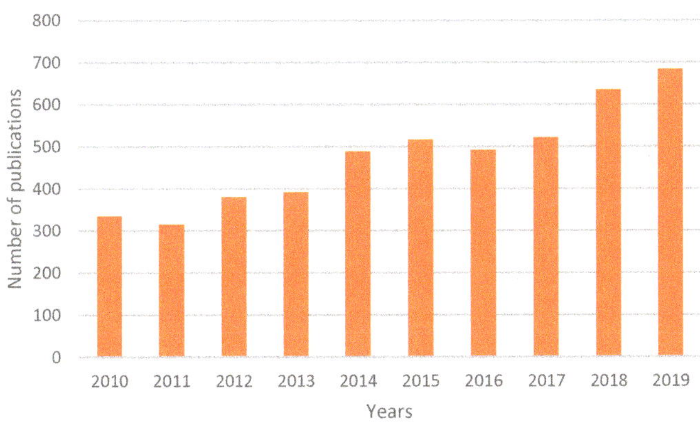


**Figure 6.** Number of published articles containing "conceptual framework" in the title indexed in Scopus. Source: Scopus (2020).

In [41] the use of portable sensors to provide an adaptation based on affection in Environmental Intelligence systems is considered, and a proposal for a conceptual design framework for games is presented. Zupančič et al. [42] defines a conceptual framework that considers human participation in mobile crowd detection systems and takes into account that users provide their opinions and other subjective data in addition to unprocessed detection data generated by your smart devices. Mordecai et al. [43] proposes a conceptual approach based on models to capture, explain and mitigate CPG, which improves the systems engineer's ability to cope with CPGs, mitigate them by design and avoid decisions and wrong actions. González et al. [44] presents a new architecture based on OPC to implement automation systems dedicated to R&D and educational activities. The proposal is a new conceptual framework, structured in four functional layers where the various components are classified with the objective of promoting the systematic design and implementation of automation systems that involve OPC communication. Yoo et al. [45] describe a conceptual framework for exchanging closed cycle life cycle information for the service of products on the Internet of Things (IoT). The framework is based on the product-service ontology model and a standard IoT message type, Open Messaging Interface (O-MI) and Open Data Format (O-DF), which guarantees data communication. Varela et al. [46] states that human interaction environments (HIE) should be understood as any place where people carry out their daily lives, including their work, family life, leisure and social life, interacting with technology to improve or facilitate the experience. The integration of technology in these environments has been achieved in a disorderly and incompatible way, with devices that operate on isolated islands with artificial borders delimited by manufacturers. A framework is presented that constitutes an integral solution for the development of systems that require the integration and interoperation of devices and technologies in HIE. In this work a conceptual framework for the integration of artificial intelligence and life cycle assessment (LCA) will be proposed.

## 2. Methodology

The objective of this work is the development of a conceptual framework for the integration of artificial intelligence and LCA. A conceptual framework is a tool that allows the analysis and organization of information related to a field of knowledge. Thus, it is easier to carry out future research [47,48].

An important part of academic texts has to do with integrating concepts, ideas, arguments or theories of our discipline that allow us to fulfill the objectives of a writing work. Sometimes, these concepts and ideas work to briefly explain the object or theme of our text, but in other cases a more extensive conceptual framework must be developed to meet the requirements of the task.

A conceptual framework is a section of a text written in the academic field that details the theoretical models, concepts, arguments and ideas that have been developed in relation to a topic. The conceptual framework is generally oriented to define this object, describe its characteristics and explain possible processes associated with it. In some more extensive texts, the conceptual framework also works to recognize and describe "the state of the art", that is, to point out the main theoretical lines in relation to this topic, in order to propose a new theoretical view that is considered relevant in relationship with the object.

All research needs to use concepts to be able to organize your data and perceive the relationships between them. Borsotti [49] suggests that scientific knowledge is entirely conceptual, since; ultimately, it is constituted by interrelated systems of concepts in different ways. Hence, to access the ideas of science, it is necessary to manage the concepts and languages of science. These concepts cannot cease to be subjective; they are necessarily conditioned by ideological positions and by evaluative positions that are logical assumptions of all knowledge. Borsotti adds, that "when you think about it, it is irremediable to resort to notions drawn from common language, generated in historical and social life, and that are loaded with ideological connotations and full of ambiguity and vagueness. Science cannot be managed with these concepts. It does not seek to be exact, but to be precise, in order to achieve the elaboration, the construction of unique concepts, that is, concepts whose intention and extension are as precise as possible." A concept is an abstraction obtained from reality and, therefore, its purpose is to simplify by summarizing a series of observations that can be classified under the same name.

The information that is integrated into the conceptual framework must be systematically organized so that it can be better understood. An important principle is to start from the most general to the most particular. A starting point can be the definition of the object or topic and then describe its characteristics, functions and indicate the parts that compose it or the associated concepts that are relevant.

The diagram representing the research topic or problem is sometimes called the conceptual framework, this diagram could be useful to analysis and interpret the results [47,48,50]. It is a visual scheme that represents the concept or idea. It is the way in which the work will be carried out and integrates the elements. It also influences the research problem as it is associated with the literature used. A part of this framework will offer a synopsis of the main points of the study. In addition, the diagram will show the central factors that influence the relationship of the primary variables, elements or constructions, as well as the hypothesis. After reading the literature of the corresponding area, it has to be shown what the theories state about it and support the relationship.

The first phases followed in the methodology for developing the conceptual framework include investigating the main variables or elements that correspond to those contextual factors that are related to the research work. The technique used in this initial stage for constructing the conceptual framework is the hermeneutics. In hermeneutics, the texts are read and analyzed in order to delve into them obtaining a better understanding of reality [51]. Although the origin of hermeneutics is associated with the study and interpretation of religious texts, its use has been extended to other disciplines such as pedagogy or philosophy [52]. With the expression hermeneutic circle, the relationship between the text and the context from which the research is revealed [50,52]. In our case, it has been successfully applied to the construction of a conceptual framework for the teaching of Sustainable Development Goals in Higher Education [50].

For the search and selection of the texts a systematic search of the literature has been carried out following the sequence proposed by Pawson [53]. The first step is to clarify the purpose of the review. In the second step, it aims to search for documents. This stage was divided into three sub-stages: the search for bibliographic references proper, the filtering of the documentation and the synthesis of the documents.

The review was carried out on the main collection of the Web of Science, in documents written in English and published in the last 5 years (2015-19) [48,54,55]. Keywords used in the search are shown in Table 1.

**Table 1.** Keywords used during systematic literature review.

| Keywords | Search Criteria |
|---|---|
| "Machine Learning" and "LCA" | I |
| "Machine Learning" and "Life Cycle Assessment" | II |
| "Artificial Intelligence" and "Life Cycle Assessment" | III |
| "Artificial Intelligence" and "LCA" | IV |

Once this step was finished, the actual hermeneutic work began with the evaluation of the results, the synthesis of the documentation and the creation of the conceptual framework.

The methodology used to build the proposed conceptual framework consists of the following main phases [56], as shown in Figure 7.

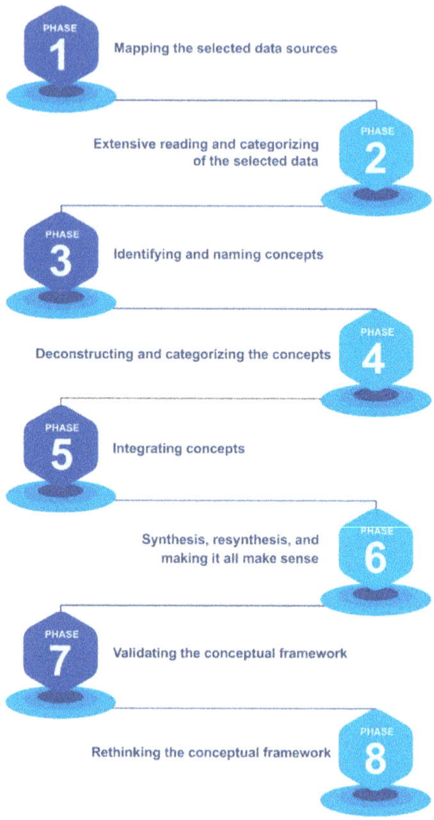


**Figure 7.** Methodology used to build the proposed conceptual framework [56].

Phase 1: Identification of the selected data sources. The first task is to review the spectrum of multidisciplinary literature regarding the phenomenon in question. This process includes the identification of text types and other data sources.

Phase 2: Detailed reading and categorization of the selected data. The objective in this phase is to categorize the data by discipline and by a scale of importance.

Phase 3: Identification and denomination of concepts. The objective in this phase is to reread the selected data and identify the concepts that group them [57,58].

Phase 4: Build and categorize concepts. The objective of this phase is to find each concept, identify its main attributes, characteristics, assumptions and role. Subsequently it organizes and categorizes the concepts according to their characteristics and ontological, epistemological and methodological role.

Phase 5: Integration of concepts. The objective in this phase is to group conceptions that have similarities in a new concept. This phase dramatically reduces the number of definitions and allows a reasonable number of them to be manipulated.

Phase 6: Synthesis The objective in this phase is to synthesize concepts in a theoretical framework. The researcher must be open, tolerant and flexible with the theorizing process and the emerging new theory. This process is iterative and includes repetitive synthesis until the researcher recognizes a general theoretical framework that makes sense.

Phase 7: Validation of the conceptual framework. The objective in this phase is to test the conceptual framework. The question is whether the proposed framework and its concepts make sense not only for the researcher but also for other academics and professionals.

Phase 8: Rethink the conceptual framework. A theory or theoretical framework that represents a multidisciplinary phenomenon will always be dynamic. It should be reviewed according to new knowledge, comments, literature.

## 3. Results

In this study, it has been detected that the sensorization of industrial plants and the treatment of data through Machine Learning algorithms has not yet been extended enough in the field of sustainability optimization. As a result of this research on the state of the art, five fundamental dimensions are obtained in the approach to these types of problems: applications, data, approaches, tools and sensors. These five aspects will be integrated into a proposed conceptual framework, which aims to be a contribution when facing sustainability engineering projects.

We propose a conceptual framework that may help to understand and situate the research in life cycle analysis using techniques of machine learning, as well as apply the proposed framework to a case study.

The search result according to the criteria shown in the previous section was 39 documents. Of these documents, 15 were discarded because they were false positives: from the abstract and the title it could be deduced that there was no relation with the topic analyzed in the work. The remaining 24 documents were read in depth. Figure 8 shows the distribution of the documents according to the year of publication and the type of publication (journal or conference proceedings or book chapters).

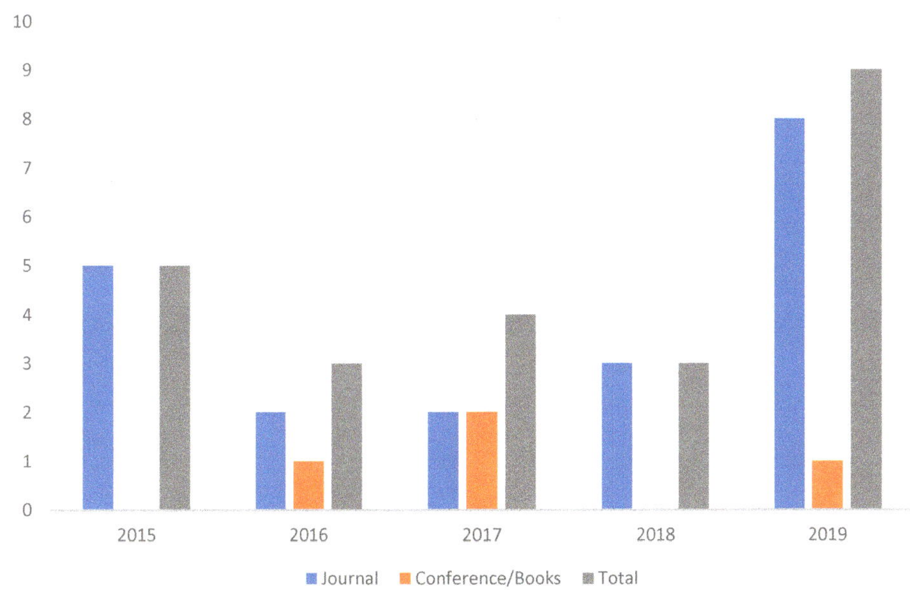


**Figure 8.** Evolution of the articles published in the last 5 years.

As can be seen in the figure, most of the 24 documents that have been reviewed correspond to articles published in journals. An increase in the number of publications that address this topic could be inferred from the data, this aspect shows the interest of the work.

From the reading of the previous documents, a total of 11 articles were eliminated because they were outside the scope. For example, for dealing with steam turbine operating conditions [59] or improving the energy use of a farm [60]. Thus, the articles that were finally used for the construction of the framework are shown in Table 2.

**Table 2.** Documents used to construct the conceptual framework.

| ID [ref] | Tittle | Year | Search Criteria | | | |
|---|---|---|---|---|---|---|
| | | | I | II | III | IV |
| A [61] | Machine learning for toxicity characterization of organic chemical emissions using USEtox database: Learning the structure of the input space | 2015 | 1 | | 1 | |
| B [62] | Extending life cycle assessment normalization factors and use of machine learning - A Slovenian case study | 2015 | 1 | | 1 | |
| C [63] | Limitations of toxicity characterization in life cycle assessment: Can adverse outcome pathways provide a new foundation? | 2016 | 1 | | 1 | |
| D [64] | Quantifying the impact of sustainable product design decisions in the early design phase trough machine learning | 2016 | 1 | | 1 | |
| E [65] | A Data-Driven Approach for Improving Sustainability Assessment in Advanced Manufacturing | 2017 | 1 | | 1 | 1 |
| F [66] | Computational design optimization of concrete mixtures: A review | 2018 | | 1 | | |
| G [67] | Integration of artificial intelligence methods and life cycle assessment to predict energy output and environmental impacts of paddy production | 2018 | | | 1 | 1 |
| H [68] | Developing surrogate ANN for selecting near-optimal building energy renovation methods considering energy consumption, LCC and LCA | 2019 | 1 | 1 | | |
| I [69] | Machine Learning for Sustainable Structures: A Call for Data | 2019 | 1 | 1 | 1 | 1 |
| J [70] | Model uncertainty analysis using data analytics for life-cycle assessment (LCA) applications | 2019 | 1 | | 1 | |
| K [71] | Assessing environmental performance in early building design stage: An integrated parametric design and machine learning method | 2019 | | 1 | | |
| L [72] | A machine learning approach for the estimation of fuel consumption related to road pavement rolling resistance for large fleets of trucks | 2019 | | 1 | | |
| M [73] | Combined life cycle assessment and artificial intelligence for prediction of output energy and environmental impacts of sugarcane production | 2019 | | | 1 | 1 |

As can be inferred from Table 2, only one document 17 meets the four search criteria, one document 13 covers three search criteria. Most of the documents [61–64,68,70,73] cover two search criteria, the most common being the conjunction of criteria I and II. Only two documents [71,73] meet a single search criterion.

### 3.1. ADAPTS: A Proposal of Conceptual Framework for Engineering Projects

Results have been extracted from the bibliographic study (shown in Table 1). The most relevant characteristics detected in the works analyzed are: (1) the application to which the work refers, (2) the data used, (3) the approach that has been given to the problem addressed, (4) the machine learning tool used and 5) the sensors used or proposed for implementation. These five aspects detected are what form the basis of our conceptual framework. Therefore, the proposed conceptual framework starts from the bibliographic study carried out, which has allowed us to identify the key aspects when addressing the optimization of engineering projects from the perspective of sustainability, using LCA.As previously described in the methodology section, after a detailed reading of the above-mentioned bibliographical references (phase 2 of Figure 7), authors of this article constructed and categorized the concepts (phase 4), integrated the concepts (phase 5) and proposed a pyramid-shaped structure that integrates all the results (phase 6).

The conceptual framework will be validated through a practical application exercise, a case study demonstrating its usefulness (phase 7), shown in the following section. This paper describes a new conceptual framework to be applied in addressing project problems in engineering, from a point of view of sustainability optimization. The conceptual framework provides tools to approach engineering projects in an intelligent and sustainable way. The proposed tools are based on the analysis of the state of the art in the areas of sustainability, life cycle analysis, sensing and machine learning. Five main dimensions have been detected: Applications, Data, APproaches, Tools and Sensors. The results of the "state of the art" study carried out are shown on Table 3.

**Table 3.** Results for State of the art.

| ID | Application | Data | Approach | Tools | Sensors |
|---|---|---|---|---|---|
| A [61] | Predict energy consumption of buildings | TRNSYS simulation data. Data collected on existing buildings. | Energy. Performance prediction | ANN + SBMO (genetic algorithms) | Literature review |
| B [62] | Reduce the impact of Structures | Geometry, material, building type and other key parameters | A more sustainable built environment | Machine Learning + Artificial Neural Networks | Resource efficient built environment lab |
| C [63] | Predict the sources of uncertainty in the LCA: Chicago Pavement LCA | Traffic data report | Objective uncertainty quantification (UQ) | Various data analytics methods were used to conduct a thorough model uncertainty analysis | Traffic, Speed IRI Collected from 2015 Traffic data report |
| D [64] | Sustainability in manufacture | Manufacture data using simulation models | Data-driven modeling | Data-model-decision network | Cheaper monitoring tools and pervasive wireless technology enables environmental data to be collected. Manufacturing process data is most often proprietary |
| E [65] | To asses biological effects using a tool quantitative outcome pathway (qAOP) | Toxicity data. The emission levels. Data of inventory analysis | Toxicological LCIA models and assumptions | Mechanistic; Probabilistic supervised machine learning models; and Weight of evidence | Experimental toxicity data |
| F [66] | Estimate LCA results from product properties. 37 case study | LCA data. Data generated during conceptual design. | Guidelines, Heuristics, Standards Methods Preferences | Multi-layer perception neural network with back propagation training | Product attributes |
| G [67] | Toxicity characterization of chemical emissions in Life Cycle Assessment (LCA) | Properties of the chemical compounds being assessed (databases) buildings. | Usetox model | Dimensionality reduction techniques. | Environmental properties |
| H [68] | LCA normalization factors | A pesticides properties database PPDB, ReciPe .08 and FURS. | LCA normalization | Linear regression using Java program Package | Environmental indicators |
| I [69] | Estimate LC environmental impacts and output energy of sugarcane production (planted or ratoon farms) | Ecoinvent 2.2 databases | Cradle to grave approach | Artificial neural networks (ANNs) and adaptive neuro fuzzy inference system (ANFIS) model | Used resources emissions, Used electricity |
| J [70] | Estimate LC and energy of paddy production | Agricultural input parameters from 240 paddy producers. | CExD cumulative. Energy Demand | Artificial neural networks (ANNs) and adaptive neuro fuzzy inference system (ANFIS) | Paddy production process |
| K [71] | Evaluate environmental impact in early building design stage | Generated samples | Parametric design | Fuzzy C-means clustering and extreme learning machine | Properties of the building |
| L [72] | Energy consumption of the trucks to evaluate the operation phase of the pavements. | Database of Micrilise Ltd. Road geometry and condition of the road surface for each vehicle in the databases | Enveloping methods (Boruta) | Boruta algorithm and Neural Networks | Standard sensors (SAE International 2016) that keep track of various parameters (including consumption) |
| M [73] | Design and optimization of concrete structures | Literature review | Optimization Decision Making | ANNs, instance-based learning, decision-trees and SVMs. | Concrete mixture parameters |

A conceptual framework is proposed that integrates these five dimensions as shown in Figure 9. At the base of this pyramid will be the applications, data, approaches and tools. At the top of the pyramid is the sensorization. As a complement to the proposed conceptual framework, this proposal will be developed for a specific case (a case of a food industry), a development that can be found in the discussion section.

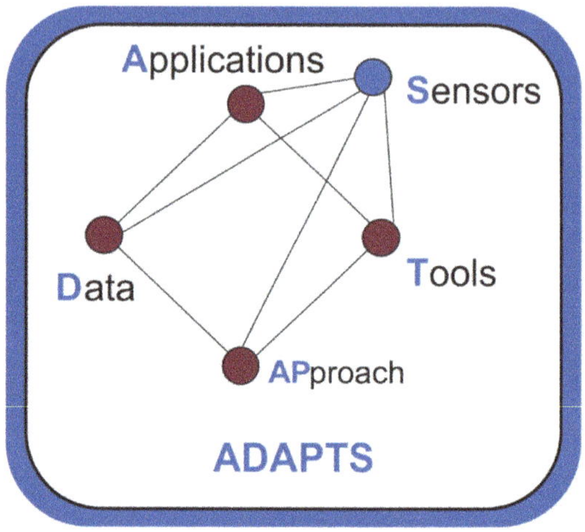


**Figure 9.** Proposed conceptual framework.

### 3.1.1. Applications

The first dimension of the proposed conceptual framework is the application of artificial intelligence and machine learning technologies. A first classification of the applications can be referred to the sectors in which they are applied.

Among the 13 articles analyzed; six of them are focused on the construction sector and civil engineering. Traditionally, the construction sector has been quite conservative and resistant to change. However, the emergence of technologies such as Building Information Modelling are causing a change in it. LCA criteria could be used for design structures. This was explored in a review article on the design of concrete structures [66] or in a call for data for the evaluation of structures [69]. Environmental criteria can be used for the design of buildings in the early design stage [71] or for the estimation of total energy consumption from environmental life cycle analysis (LCA) and in cost life cycle analysis (LCC) [68]. In the field of civil engineering, environmental assessment of roads (in its operational phase) was explored by analyzing truck traffic [72] or vehicle speed and road roughness data in Chicago [70].

The design and production of products has been analyzed. For this purpose, LCA was obtained from the data generated in the conceptual design [64] or by analyzing sustainability in manufacturing [65].

Environmental assessment of agricultural activities using artificial intelligence techniques has been analyzed jointly with the energy consumption for the cultivation of sugar cane (planted or ratoon farm) [73] or rice [67].

Finally, some applications consist of using artificial intelligence techniques to address specific aspects of the LCA such as sensitivity to certain factors [70], to asses biological effects using a tool quantitative outcome pathway (qAOP) [63], toxicity characterization of chemical emissions [61] or assess normalization factors in LCA methodology [62].

#### 3.1.2. Data

The data is crucial for the implementation of Machine Learning and Artificial Intelligence methodologies. Data are required for training and making predictions with both supervised and unsupervised techniques.

Obtaining data is not always simple in fact, some authors warn of the need to work in scenarios with little data (austere data environments). This justifies the need for call for data. For example, D'Amico made a request for data geometry, material, type of building and other aspects in the field of structures [69].

In road environmental impact assessment studies, the data came from a company database (Microlise) [72] or from mobility studies in cities such as Chicago [70].

In the field of agriculture, data such as the amount of pesticides, fertilizers, or seeds are needed to determine the environmental impact. This can be done by randomly obtaining data, as was done in [67] to analyze the environmental impact of rice or in [73] for sugarcane farms.

In some investigations, data come from simulations. For example, in Sharif and Hammad [68] extensive data is collected on existing buildings related to several factors including TEC, outside temperature, building envelope components, HVAC and lighting systems; in other occasions the data are obtained using a data generator these data are later validated with experimental data [65].

The conceptual design of products [64] or the early design stage of building [71] are a source of data that can be used in the environmental assessment of products [64] or buildings [65].

Finally, to perform the toxicological characterization of chemical emissions [61], the authors used databases such as USEtox [74], for the normalization of factors [62] the authors used databases such as PPDB, ReciPe.08 or FURs.

#### 3.1.3. Approaches

In the study of the state of the art carried out as part of the process of construction of the proposed conceptual framework, various work approaches have been shown. For example, several of these works [63,66,68,69,71] use the LCA life cycle analysis technique to improve the design. There are also works that focus on the exploitation phase [67,70,72,73], while others focus on the study of the methodology followed in the LCA [61,62,65].

#### 3.1.4. Tools

The use of artificial neural networks is currently a trend in the scientific literature [75,76]. In this area, neural networks have been used to predict energy consumption [68], as a surrogate model to replace simulation software. [69], to obtain LCA results from product characteristics [64], to obtain toxicity with fewer parameters [61], to evaluate energy consumption and environmental impact of agricultural activities [67,73] and to evaluate the energy consumption in order to evaluate environmental impacts of roads [72].

Artificial Neural Networks are often used in combination with other tools such as Simulation-Based Multi-Objective Optimization [68], Bayesian analysis and orthogonal basis polynomial basis system [70], dimensionality reduction techniques and linear regression [61]; adaptive Neuro fuzzy inference system (ANFIS) model and Boruta algorithm [72].

Another similar tool is the Extreme Machine Learning (feedforward neural networks), that together with fuzzy C-means clustering was used to valuate environmental impact in early building design stage. Bayesian Network Models were used too in several applications [63,65]. Linear regression was used to estimate normalization LCA factors [62].

#### 3.1.5. Sensors

Throughout this study the enormous relevance of using sensing when addressing an objective of intelligent sustainability in engineering projects has emerged.

This sensorization is essential to be able to train models, validate and generalize them. It is also useful to have intelligent sensors that allow us to have control of the data in the exploitation process.

Several of the works analyzed use simulation data, data taken from databases or public data. For example, [63] works with toxicity data, in [71] it deals with properties of the buildings or in [70] traffic data is used. The enormous utility of having data from sensorization is evident.

### 3.2. Case Study

A new conceptual framework has been described that could be applied to address the problems of engineering projects, from the point of view of sustainability optimization. The proposed conceptual framework integrates five dimensions: applications, data, approaches, tools and sensing. This conceptual framework is developed below for a specific case (olive oil sector), showing its applicability and usefulness.

The case study intends to answer the five questions that constitute the validation phase of the conceptual framework [77].

(1) Is this framework useful? [78,79].
(2) Does it provide a common language from which to describe the situation under scrutiny and to report the findings about it [79].
(3) Does it develop a set of guiding principles against which judgments and predictions might be made?
(4) Does it act as a series of reference points from which to locate the research questions within contemporary theorizing? Does it provided a structure within which to organize the content of the research and to frame conclusions within the context? [78].
(5) Below is an application of the proposed conceptual framework to a specific case study, the olive oil sector. Each of the dimensions of the ADAPTS pyramid will be discussed in this example (Figure 10).

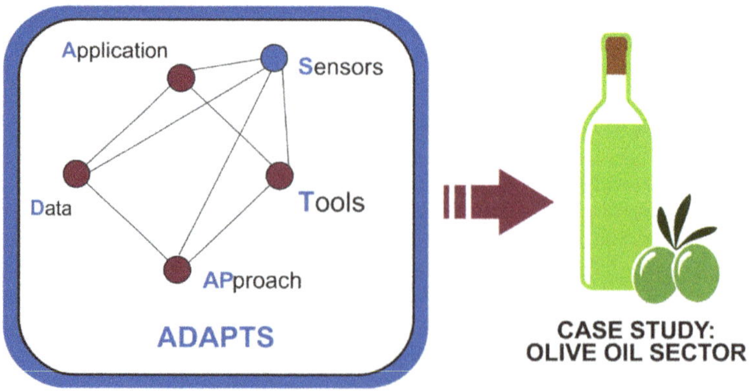


**Figure 10.** Conceptual framework. Study case.

Olive oil production is a very important activity in the Mediterranean area. Oil processing influences the environment by causing resource depletion, land degradation, air emissions and waste generation [80]. Figure 11 illustrates the total volume of olive oil exports within the European Union, by country.

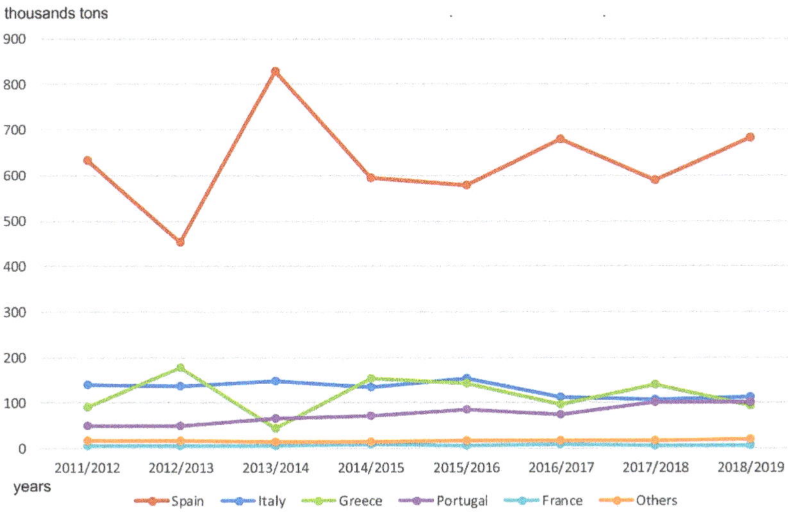


**Figure 11.** Total exports volume. Compiled by the authors based on [81].

Different phases must be considered to carry out the LCA of oil production. Firstly, in the agricultural phase, the cultivation of the olive trees is considered, as well as the pruning and harvesting. In the phase of production, oil extraction must be analyzed. Some studies also consider aspects such as packaging, distribution, consumption and transport. Finally, the management of the residues must be considered. There is a consensus in the scientific literature that the phase that has the greatest impact is agriculture. This is due to the use of fertilizers, phytosanitary products and irrigation [82].

Thus, it is necessary to consider that the processes are compatible with both environmental protection and efficiency, throughout the entire product life cycle. This extends to the handling, packaging and labeling of products. It is necessary to take into account the reduction of inputs such as fertilizers, phytosanitary products or fossil fuels. The development of technologies is sought to optimize the use of valuable water resources in an environment with water scarcity. It is advisable to use climate monitoring stations through olive groves, making extensive use of soil moisture sensors, salinity sensors and reporting systems to ensure that water is used for maximum efficiency. Carbon emissions play an important role in atmospheric conditions and climate change, so it is necessary to reduce emissions. It is also necessary to reduce the energy use of the electricity grid, seeking to reduce the carbon footprint.

### 3.2.1. Application

The olive trees produce the olive that is transported to the oil mills, where after a few mechanical processes the virgin olive oil is extracted. This oil is packaged directly in packaging machines belonging to oil mills or in independent packaging machines, in the case of extra virgin olive oil. If not, it is sold to refineries where refined olive oil is obtained. From the mixture of extra virgin olive oil and the refined olive oil is obtained which will be packaged in the refineries. Oil distribution can be done through distribution platforms, hypermarkets, supermarkets and traditional stores [83], being able to start in olive crops with different forms of exploitation.

There are three cultivation modalities: traditional or extensive, intensive and superintensive cultivation. The first cultivation modality is the usual one in the areas of olive tradition; they can be irrigated or dry. Its planting density is around 80–120 trees/ha, with one or several feet. This makes the collection is mostly done manually through the help of machinery. In the intensive cultivation system, always in better soils and irrigated land, we work with a planting density of 200–400 trees/ha.

The collection systems are very similar to those of the traditional olive grove. In the superintensive (or "in hedge") the planting density is more than 800 trees/ha. These systems constitute what has come to be called "new olive growing" [83]. The olive harvest in this type of plantation is fully mechanized thanks to the existence of machines designed for this type of olive grove. The impact of this first stage is the highest according to most studies [82].

Once the olive has been collected using the methods required for each type of crop (traditional, intensive and extensive), the industrialization process begins. To do this, the olive is cleaned well on the farm itself where it is collected or, it is taken to the mills and there it will undergo the cleaning process. In the oil mills, the olives caught in flight are separated, that is, from the tree, or from the ground since, the quality of the oil varies depending on the origin and possible damage that it may have suffered. Once separated, the oil extraction process begins by grinding, shaking, horizontal and vertical centrifugation and decanting. Once these phases are finished, the oil is stored until the packaging process begins, which can be done in the mills themselves, if they have the capacity to do so, or in independent packaging machines. A third option is packing machines linked to refineries where the lampante oil is taken to undergo a neutralization process. This oil is the result of a last centrifugation which makes it very acidic and not suitable for human consumption. It is called that because it was formerly used for the combustion of oil lamps.

Olive oil packaging must go through the filling and capping, labeling and packaging phases. The distribution of olive oil can be carried out on different supports depending on what will be your final recipient. The bulk distribution involves selling the unpacked oil, so that the buyer is responsible for its bottling and subsequent distribution. Packaged oil, in the mills themselves or in independent packaging machines, is usually sold directly to the final consumer or packed to small businesses. Finally, pallet oil is sold wholesale to new forms of commercial distribution such as supermarkets and hypermarkets.

In the last ten years, the olive oil value chain has benefited from innovations introduced with the idea of making oil more efficient and profitable. The most significant innovations have been exposed in the work, helping us to do so with the specific value chain mentioned above [84].

### 3.2.2. Data

One of the main difficulties in carrying out an adequate LCA of oil production is the need to have public databases with information about all stages of the process [82].

In this way, information about soil salinity and climatic characteristics can be crucial to develop an optimization of the impact of this activity. This information could be collected by sensors.

The main technological variables that influence the elaboration process are:

(1) *Degree of grinding*. The degree of grinding indicates the average size in which the hardest parts of the paste remain. Grinding too thick means a weak breakage of the tissues that leads to a decrease in exhaustion. On the other hand, too fine grinding causes a greater increase in the temperature of the paste that has a negative impact on the quality of the oil, and can generate more emulsions in the pasta that deplete exhaustion. Additionally, too fine grinding causes problems of bindings in the mill and increases energy consumption [85].

(2) *Temperature and beat time*. These parameters are, perhaps, the most decisive in the quality of the oil to be obtained. The increase in the temperature of the pasta in the blender reduces its viscosity, which favors the aggregation of the drops of oil and therefore improves extraction performance. On the other hand, the increase in shaking time also favors the change in the structure of the paste that allows increasing the depletion of the pomace. However, both parameters have a negative impact on the quality of the oil obtained, since the increase in temperature accelerates the speed of the reactions that take place in the blender and favors the loss of volatile components.

(3) *Composition and structure of the pasta at the exit of the blender*. In the shaking of the so-called difficult pastes, which are those pastes that present difficulties in extracting the oil, it is necessary to use

adjuvants (natural microtalco and, where appropriate, water) to improve their behavior. A repair of the deficient pulp entails substantial increases in the oil contained in the pomace, while the addition of adjuvants has no influence on the quality of the oils obtained [86].

(4) *Degree of moisture of the paste in decanter.* This parameter has great relevance in depletion, since it will determine the thickness of the rings inside the decanter and, therefore, the operating conditions of the machine.

(5) *Residence time in decanter.* The residence time in the decanter is determined by the established production rate, which is generally imposed by the olive oil entering the mill and the capacity of the installation. Operating the decanter at higher rates than recommended implies a significant loss of fat in the pomace.

(6) *Parameters of the operation within the decanter.* The differential screw-bowl speed and the discharge height of the oil phase determine the width of the different rings within the decanter [87]. A correct choice of these parameters makes it possible to improve depletion without influencing the quality of the oil obtained.

(7) *Parameters specific to the operation of the vertical centrifuge.* The temperature of the addition water must be adjusted to the temperature of the oil so as not to affect its organoleptic properties and avoid the formation of emulsions that induce the loss of oil with the wash waters. Likewise, the water flow must be adjusted to that of oil for the proper functioning of the machine in terms of losses. Finally, the discharge frequency of the cumulative strips is an important parameter since it influences the quality of the oil obtained and the oil losses in the operation.

(8) *Parameters of the decantation in stainless steel tanks.* The main parameter is the residence time of the oil in the tanks and the frequency of the purges of the erasures. A short residence time means that the oil remains with a high level of moisture and impurities, while a residence time that is too high and a poor purge frequency can be supposed to damage its organoleptic characteristics [88].

These variables are related to the quality of the olive oil, but also to other aspects such as the energy consumption or the waste generated in the process. In this way, with a suitable sensing, the impact that the activity has on the environment can be optimized.

#### 3.2.3. Approach

As a result of the growth of the food and beverage industries, a particularly demanding sector with production management is found. Economic behavior (rigid supply, inelastic demand), administrative intervention in primary productions, food safety requirements, diversity of products, variability of productions, etc. to which we must add those that also affect the rest of the economy: financial fluctuations, acceleration of applicable technologies, globalization of markets, etc. [89].

The agro-food industry is a very important strategic sector for our economy. It generates more than half a million direct jobs, above the total manufacturing industry and the Spanish economy as a whole [90]. For this reason, the case study has been focused on this sector, due to the great potential. These companies show and the possibilities they provide. Thanks to the new Industry 4.0 approach, making use of information technology, it is now easier to convert data into useful information for decision making.

Tools such as data mining and predictive techniques organizations have information that helps them raise more precise, effective and applicable business strategies in shorter periods of time. Before they can interpret the process data, companies must treat them to reduce the problem to be treated and optimize the available resources. Data mining provides the means for the treatment of productive data.

On the other hand, there are different predictive techniques, each with its benefits and deficiencies, which provide a new way for companies to make decisions. The Spanish agri-food industry is likely to benefit from the Industry 4.0 approach. In a globalized market, any small advantage over the competition can make a big difference. As the food and beverage market is very demanding regarding production management, the tools discussed above offer organizations a competitive advantage to value [91].

### 3.2.4. Tools

As shown in the section dedicated to tools, the use of artificial neural networks is currently a growing trend in recent academic literature [75,76]. In the field of sustainability applied to engineering projects, neural networks have been used to predict energy consumption [68], as a surrogate model to replace simulation software. [69], to obtain LCA results from product characteristics [64], to obtain toxicity with fewer parameters [61], to evaluate energy consumption and environmental impact of agricultural activities [67,73] and to evaluate the energy consumption in order to evaluate environmental impacts of roads [72], among many other applications.

Artificial Neural Networks are often used in combination with other tools such as Simulation-Based Multi-Objective Optimization [68], Bayesian analysis and orthogonal basis polynomial basis system [70], dimensionality reduction techniques and linear regression [61]; adaptive Neuro fuzzy inference system (ANFIS) model and Boruta algorithm [72].

In this case of application it has been decided to use ANN as a tool due to the reasons already stated: because the use of artificial neural networks is currently a growing trend, because in the field of sustainability applied to engineering projects ANN have been used in numerous applications and because ANNs are often used in combination with other tools.

Artificial neural networks (ANN) are a machine learning tool that can be useful for predicting one or more variables in complex systems. ANNs consist of an input layer, a variable number of hidden layer(s), an output layer, weights and connection biases, an activation function and an addition node. Each neuron constitutes a computational unit, integrated in a layer. Each layer takes as input values those calculated in the previous layer and generates an output value for the next layer. The input layer provides the input values of the network, which are fed to the hidden layer. Each hidden layer consists of several neurons that calculate an output using all the inputs of the input layer and a predefined set of weights and biases. During the learning process, each neuron calculates a single output value based on its input data from the previous layer. This result can be fed to the next hidden layer or to the output layer. The output layer takes as inputs all outputs of the last hidden layer and produces the final output of the ANN [92].

### 3.2.5. Sensors

As we have mentioned before, in order to perform an adequate LCA of the oil manufacturing process it is essential to have a reliable database about the variables that influence the process. In this sense, a correct sensor network arranged throughout the process can contribute to improve the LCA and with it, the process optimization can be carried out crucial aspect for the optimization of the LCA of olive oil is the cultivation phase. In this respect, Previous studies have shown that sensing can help optimize olives drip irrigation by controlling soil moisture and knowing the weather using a weather station [93,94]. LED Scanner Sensor have been used for measuring olive oil canopies [95].

One of the problems that arise in the automatic control of oil mills is the difficulty of having the necessary information about the process. In fact, in order to adapt the operating conditions of the plant from a global point of view, it would be necessary to know the characteristics of the input fruit, the characteristics of the pasta in the blender, the composition and flow of the flows of entry and exit of the decanter, etc. To control the mill with the objective of maximizing quality, it would be necessary to be able to measure this variable, which in general would be a combination of the values of different chemical and organoleptic parameters.

Many of these variables are qualitative and difficult to measure online, so the use of indirect measures or the use of sensory fusion techniques are intuited as necessary alternatives to be able to estimate the values of the parameters. An important sensor technology for the automatic control of oil mills are Near Infrared Spectrocopy (NIR) sensors, since this technique allows the construction of sensors to estimate the moisture and fat content of the pulp and pomace. In addition, it allows characterizing the oil obtained from the process in terms of quality by estimating a series of chemical parameters, such as acidity, peroxide index, K270 and total polyphenol content [96].

The use of this type of sensors together with neural networks it allows to improve data obtained from this type of sensors [97,98]., which together with the possibility of using these sensors for measurements online makes them fundamental tools for automatic control of the oil mill. Another technology of relevance sensors is the arrays of voltmetric sensors, which allow evaluating the polyphenol content of oil [99]. The construction of sensors in line with this technology can provide very valuable information for the control of oil mills in order to maximize the quality of the oils obtained, since they allow information on parameters sensitive to the elaboration process and very related to the oil quality In this regard, they have been applied this same type of sensors to monitor online the accumulation of volatile components in the mixer [100], which opens the doors to its use for automatic control.

The first reference of using neural networks to building a virtual sensor is located in [101], where a neural network is designed and implemented to infer depletion and moisture from the alpeorujo. The use of neural networks to infer characteristics of the oil produced from characteristics of the input fruit and the process parameters can be consulted in [102], as well as the use of artificial vision to capture information from the input olives, in this case the index of maturity. In the same line of behavior prediction of the installation from neural networks, build a neural network to predict the depletion of the pomace from variables characteristic of the fruit (fat and moisture content) and technological variables such as the beat temperature, the addition of micro-total, paste inlet flow into the decanter, paste moisture and oil outlet height from the decanter [103]. These works present the bases for the construction of virtual sensors that allow variables to be included in control loops that otherwise would not be possible to measure online [88].

The Figure 12 shows the result of applying the proposed conceptual framework to the case study.

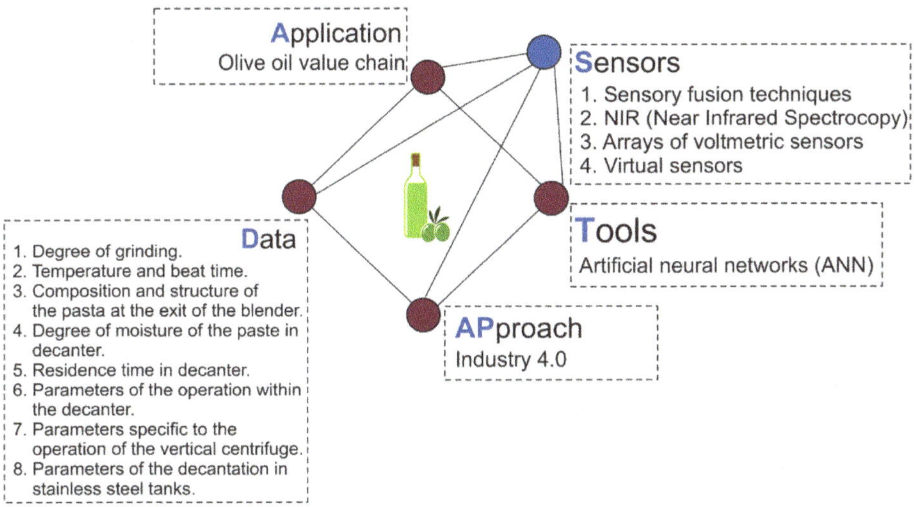


**Figure 12.** Conceptual framework. Study case.

The case study is a validation of the conceptual framework proposed in Section 3.1. The conceptual framework is a useful tool to analyze the production of olive oil from an environmental perspective. It allows to create a common language for the analysis of the LCA using machine learning tools.

The framework can be a reference point that will allow to guide future research and to organize the content of future investigations. In this way, it can be stated that the conceptual framework answers the questions proposed by Smith [77] (see Figure 13).

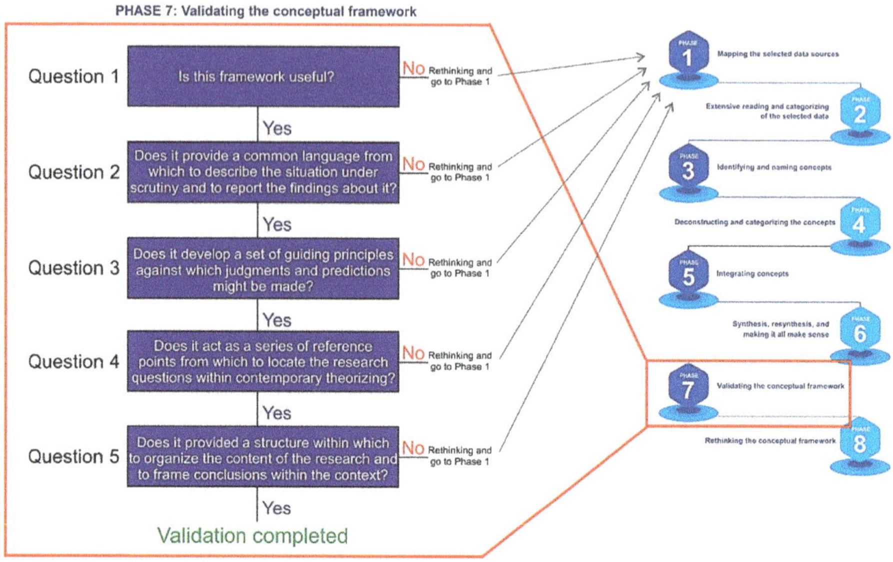


**Figure 13.** Validation of the Conceptual Framework.

Rykiel [104] argues that models can be validated pragmatically, while theoretical validity is always provisional. In this regard, he, like Matalas et al. [105], distinguishes between theoretical and conceptual frameworks. According to Rykiel [104], validation is not a procedure to test the conceptual framework, but rather a proof of its suitability for its intended use. The domain of applicability (of the conceptual model) will be the conditions for which the conceptual model has been tested, that is, compared to reality as far as possible and considered suitable for use [106].While a theoretical framework is used to test theories, to predict and control the situations within the context of a research inquiry, a conceptual framework is aimed at development of a theory that would be useful to practitioners in the field [107]. In this sense, this case study remarks that the proposed conceptual framework develops a set of guiding principles against which judgments and predictions might be made. Specifically, the conceptual framework proposes to focus the study on five axes: the application, the data, the approach, the machine learning tools to be used and the necessary sensing.

In the case studied, using these guiding principles proposed, it is concluded that for the application in the case of olive oil it is useful to have data related to the quality of the olive oil, but also to other aspects such as the energy consumption or the waste generated in the process. It is also claimed that the agri-food industry is likely to benefit from the Industry 4.0 approach, and it is proposed that use of ANN In this case of application it has been decided to use ANN as a tool, and address the need for adequate sensing, because to perform an adequate LCA of the oil manufacturing process it is essential to have a reliable database about the variables that influence the process. In this sense, a correct sensor network arranged throughout the process can contribute to improve the LCA and with it, the process optimization can be carried out crucial aspect for the optimization of the LCA of olive oil is the cultivation phase.

The results obtained from the bibliographic study (shown in Table 3) provide the most relevant characteristics detected in the analyzed works: 1) the application to which the work refers, 2) the data used, 3) the approach that has been given to the problem addressed, 4) the machine learning tool used and 5) the sensors used or proposed for implementation. These five aspects detected are those that form our conceptual framework. Therefore, the proposed conceptual framework starts from the bibliographic study carried out, which has allowed us to identify the key aspects when addressing the optimization of engineering projects from the perspective of sustainability, using LCA. As far as we know, industrial plant sensing and data processing through Machine Learning algorithms has not yet been extended sufficiently in the field of sustainability optimization for engineering projects. The way to bridge this opportunity gap detected in the investigation of the state of the art (Figure 5) constitutes our research question, for which the proposed conceptual framework aims to constitute a reference point that helps to locate the research question within the contemporary theorizing.

## 4. Discussion

The main objective of this work is the development of a conceptual framework for the integration of artificial intelligence and life cycle assessment (LCA). In the literature review that has been carried out, it has been detected that the sensorization of industrial plants and the treatment of data through Machine Learning algorithms has not yet been extended enough in the field of sustainability optimization.

This work has focused on the evaluation of sustainability using the LCA technique, because it uses some indicators that allow quantifying environmental impacts.

As far as we know, industrial plant sensorization and data processing through machine learning algorithms have not yet been extended enough in the field of sustainability optimization. An opportunity gap has been detected in the investigation of the state of the art.

As shown in Figure 5, our work is part of the triple coincidence between the sectors of sustainability (especially through life cycle analysis), sensorization and the application of machine learning techniques. In the bibliographic study conducted, the confluence between machine learning tools and the life cycle analysis technique has been enhanced, and the results obtained are shown in the corresponding section. It has not deepened the binomials machine learning-sensors and sensors-LCA, because the searches of these binomials in Web Of science give a huge number of results, some of them not very relevant, because they are very closely related terms.

In Pérez et al. [108], sustainability is taken into account from the stage of conceptualization and design of an engineering project. This paper presents a review of the state of knowledge and project design methodology to obtain a first comprehensive approach and an initial structure of a generic nature, as the first step to provide a practical way to facilitate analysis and application of sustainability criteria in the design of an engineering project.

In García et al. [109] a model is shown, in consecutive stages, for sustainability analysis: definition, interpretation, conception of goals and specifications, measurement and evaluation. Specifically, these are principles that integrate a philosophy of sustainable design around innovation and creativity in engineering in general, and in chemical engineering in specific.

Vanegas et al. [110] proposes a model to incorporate sustainability criteria and principles in the design, construction and management of infrastructures, which he proposes applicable to any sustainability discussion in engineering, architecture and construction. Its model encompasses three visions of sustainability (a global vision; a sector vision and a project vision); three maps for the implementation of sustainability (strategic, tactical and operational) and the indication of sustainability principles from specific sources, manifesting a freedom in their adoption as long as these principles can be made effective by expressing them in terms of specific goals; quantifiable objectives associated with the goal; and an application plan, for specific projects.

The sustainability evaluation model of engineering projects using specific sustainability criteria proposed by Segalas et al. [111], associates measurement and evaluation variables in the different stages of the life cycle of a project; and a learning assessment model that engineering students acquire in different subjects through the specific use of concept maps.

Vezzoli et al. [112] propose the use of guides and checklists for the design of a certain type of product with an eco-efficient approach, pointing out the importance of developing specific guides and checklist for each type of product, as tools to realize the design sustainable of an object.

In Labus et al. [113], the application of sustainability indicators in the design process of an engineering project is proposed. Based on the analysis of current computer frameworks, it establishes a framework of indicators that can guide the different stages of a project, a product or a system;

to link sustainability principles throughout the project life cycle and between the different stages that comprise it. It also brings the qualitative importance of sustainability assessment with decision analysis techniques.

Other elements of consideration from a project management point of view are provided in Fernandez et al. [114], to identify sustainability factors and indicators in engineering projects in general and civil engineering projects in particular.

The results of the study conducted in Armenia et al. [115], indicate that the academic literature on this subject is still in diapers, but that the attention of academics is growing and opens new directions of research. Based on the results of the literature review, a new conceptual framework is proposed that links five key dimensions of sustainable project management: corporate policies and practices, resource management, life cycle guidance, stakeholder participation and organizational learning.

In none of the existing conceptual frameworks, as far as the authors know, a conceptual framework is proposed that integrates the aspects of sustainability through the application of Machine Learning techniques in engineering projects.

A conceptual framework is proposed that can help in the approach to these types of problems. This paper has described a new conceptual framework that could be applied to address the problems of engineering projects, from the point of view of optimization of sustainability.

In a research work not only influences the choice of the topic and the approach of the problem, but also affects the selection made of the research procedures, the underlying theories that explain the topic of interest, and the specific way in which results are analyzed and disseminated.

When carrying out the work, the researchers incorporate and make initial formulations of the research problem, which should be based on the empirical evidence that best supports the existing theoretical perspective(s). It is convenient to develop the research project based on a conceptual framework, related to the subject in question, which makes reference to the explanations given for the research problem of interest, the most appropriate procedures to answer the research questions, as well as the strength of the evidence achieved in terms of methodological instrumentation.

The initial plan for the development of a framework that supports the research to be carried out, includes not only the assumptions from which the research starts, but also shapes the way in which the data is collected, which in turn determines or establishes the limits of the kinds of analysis that can be used.

Certain techniques are more compatible with some assumptions than with others, which means that at the time of selecting a series of research methods, a certain theoretical position is necessarily assumed.

The scientific method in general, favors the scope of objective knowledge, has a basic methodology that uses research logic and research procedures, and is invariable regardless of the kind of data studied. On the other hand, the researcher can observe, relate and make sense of the events he/she can remember, imagine, compare, differentiate, integrate, and thereby place them in his/her proper perspective. And part of other assumptions too, it has the means to create instruments that extend these capabilities or reduce their restrictions. In a broad sense, scientific theory refers to a series of logically interrelated propositions or assertions that empirically make sense, as well as the assumptions the researcher makes.

The conceptual framework is actually a bibliographic investigation that talks about the variables that will be studied in the research, or the relationship between them, described in similar or previous studies. It refers to perspectives or approaches used in related studies, its goodness or property and its relevance to the current study is analyzed.

More specifically, it leads to the establishment of hypotheses, suggests ways of analysis, or new perspectives to be considered, and at the same time, helps interpret the results of the study [116].

The conceptual framework proposed in this work provides tools to address engineering projects in an intelligent and sustainable way. The proposed tools are based on the analysis of the state of the art in the areas of sustainability, life cycle analysis, detection and machine learning.

A conceptual framework that integrates five dimensions is proposed. At the base of the proposed pyramid will be the applications, data, approaches and tools. At the top of the pyramid is the sensorization. As a complement to the proposed conceptual framework, this proposal has been developed for a specific case (olive oil sector), showing its applicability and usefulness.

## 5. Conclusions

This paper proposes a conceptual framework applicable to optimization problems under sustainability criteria in engineering projects, making use of current machine learning techniques.

A systematic literature review has been carried out. From the selected documents, the texts were analyzed, and the conceptual framework was proposed. A graphic representation is also proposed to clearly define the variables of the proposed conceptual framework and their relationships.

The proposed conceptual framework consists of five dimensions. At the base are: (1) the application to which it is intended, (2) the available data, (3) the approach and (4) the tool used. At the top of the pyramid, (5) the necessary sensing.

The first dimension of the proposed conceptual framework is the application to which the conceptual framework is applied. A first classification of applications may refer to the sectors in which they are applied.

Data is crucial for the implementation of machine learning and artificial intelligence methodologies. Data is necessary to train supervised algorithms and make predictions in unsupervised algorithms.

In the study of the state of the art carried out as part of the process of construction of the proposed conceptual framework, various work approaches have been shown.

Another very important dimension of the proposed framework is the artificial intelligence and machine learning tools used.

Throughout this study, the enormous relevance of using sensing when addressing an objective of intelligent sustainability in engineering projects has emerged. This sensorization is essential to be able to train models, validate them and generalize them. It is also useful to have intelligent sensors that allow us to have control of the data in the exploitation process.

This work is part of a broader line of research, in terms of optimization under sustainability criteria. We hope that the proposed framework will serve as a basis for future research related to this topic.

**Author Contributions:** Conceptualization, methodology, formal analysis and investigation: A.L. and F.Z.-P.; writing—original draft preparation, A.L., A.D.L.H., M.J.Á.-G. and F.Z.-P.; writing—review and editing, A.L., A.D.L.H., M.J.Á.-G. and F.Z.-P.; funding acquisition, A.L. All authors have read and agreed to the published version of the manuscript.

**Funding:** This work has been supported by the Telefónica Chair "Intelligence in Networks" of the University of Seville (Spain).

**Conflicts of Interest:** The authors declare no conflict of interest.

## References

1. Kuhlman, T.; Farrington, J. What is Sustainability? *Sustainability* **2010**, *2*, 3436–3448. [CrossRef]
2. Mebratu, D. Sustainability and sustainable development: Historical and conceptual review. *Environ. Impact Assess. Rev.* **1998**, *18*, 493–520. [CrossRef]
3. Lélé, S.M. Sustainable development: A critical review. *World Dev.* **1991**, *19*, 607–621. [CrossRef]
4. Baker, S.; Kousis, M.; Young, S.; Richardson, D. *The Politics of Sustainable Development: Theory, Policy and Practice within the European Union*; Psychology Press: London, UK, 1997.
5. Reike, D.; Vermeulen, W.J.V.; Witjes, S. The circular economy: New or Refurbished as CE 3.0?-Exploring Controversies in the Conceptualization of the Circular Economy through a Focus on History and Resource Value Retention Options. *Resour. Conserv. Recycl.* **2018**, *135*, 246–264. [CrossRef]
6. Elkington, J. Accounting for the Triple Bottom Line. *Meas. Bus. Excell.* **1998**, *2*, 18–22. [CrossRef]
7. Chong, H.Y.; Lee, C.Y.; Wang, X. A mixed review of the adoption of Building Information Modelling (BIM) for sustainability. *J. Clean. Prod.* **2017**, *142*, 4114–4126. [CrossRef]

8. Eleftheriadis, S. BIM Integrated Optimisation Framework for Environmentally Responsible and Structurally Efficient Design Systems: A Holistic Cloud Based Approach BIM Integrated Optimisation Framework for Environmentally Responsible and Structurally Efficient Design Syste. Ph.D. Thesis, University College London, London, UK, 2014.
9. Shi, J.; Liu, Z.; Zhang, H.; Jiang, Q.; Li, T. Life Cycle Assessment: State of the Art and Future Perspectives. *Recent Patents Mech. Eng.* **2015**, *8*, 211–221. [CrossRef]
10. Rebitzer, G.; Ekvall, T.; Frischknecht, R.; Hunkeler, D.; Norris, G.; Rydberg, T.; Schmidt, W.P.; Suh, S.; Weidema, B.P.; Pennington, D.W. Life cycle assessment Part 1: Framework, goal and scope definition, inventory analysis, and applications. *Environ. Int.* **2004**, *30*, 701–720. [CrossRef]
11. McDonough, W.; Braungart, M. *Cradle to Cradle: Remaking the Way We Make Things*, 1st ed.; North Point Press: New York, NY, USA, 2002; ISBN 9780865475878.
12. Aguayo González, F.; Peralta Álvarez, M.E.; Lama Ruiz, J.; Soltero Sánchez, V. *Ecodiseño: Ingeniería Sostenible de la Cuna a la Cuna (C2C)*; RC Libros: Madrid, Spain, 2011; ISBN 9788493831264.
13. Prieto-Sandoval, V.; Jaca, C.; Ormazabal, M. Towards a consensus on the circular economy. *J. Clean. Prod.* **2018**, *179*, 605–615. [CrossRef]
14. Ghisellini, P.; Cialani, C.; Ulgiati, S. A review on circular economy: The expected transition to a balanced interplay of environmental and economic systems. *J. Clean. Prod.* **2016**, *114*, 11–32. [CrossRef]
15. Bjørn, A.; Hauschild, M.Z. Cradle to Cradle and LCA–is there a Conflict. In *Glocalized Solutions for Sustainability in Manufacturing*; Springer: Berlin/Heidelberg, Germany, 2011; pp. 599–604.
16. Peralta-Álvarez, M.E.; Aguayo-Gonzálezz, F.; Lama-Ruiz, J.R.; Ávila-Gutiérrez, M.J. MGE2: Un marco de referencia para el diseño de la cuna a la cuna. *DYNA* **2015**, *82*, 137–146.
17. Chang, D.; Lee, C.K.M.; Chen, C.H. Review of life cycle assessment towards sustainable product development. *J. Clean. Prod.* **2014**, *83*, 48–60. [CrossRef]
18. Jacquemin, L.; Pontalier, P.Y.; Sablayrolles, C. Life cycle assessment (LCA) applied to the process industry: A review. *Int. J. Life Cycle Assess.* **2012**, *17*, 1028–1041. [CrossRef]
19. Del Val Román, J.L. Industria 4.0: La transformación digital de la industria. In Proceedings of the Conferencia de Directores y Decanos de Ingeniería Informática, Informes CODDII, Valencia, Spain, 18 March 2016; p. 10.
20. Schweer, D.; Sahl, J.C. The Digital Transformation of Industry—The Benefit for Germany. In *The Drivers of Digital Transformation*; Springer: Cham, Switzerland, 2017; pp. 23–31. ISBN 978-3-319-31823-3.
21. Kagermann, H. Change through digitization—Value creation in the age of industry 4.0. In *Management of Permanent Change*; Springer Science + Business Media: Norwell, MA, USA, 2015; pp. 23–45. ISBN 9783658050146.
22. Wang, S.; Wan, J.; Li, D.; Zhang, C. Implementing Smart Factory of Industrie 4.0: An Outlook. *Int. J. Distrib. Sens. Networks* **2016**, *2016*, 3159805. [CrossRef]
23. Al-Jarrah, O.Y.; Yoo, P.D.; Muhaidat, S.; Karagiannidis, G.K.; Taha, K. Efficient Machine Learning for Big Data: A Review. *Big Data Res.* **2015**, *2*, 87–93. [CrossRef]
24. Palaniappan, R.; Sundaraj, K.; Ahamed, N.U. Machine learning in lung sound analysis: A systematic review. *Biocybern. Biomed. Eng.* **2013**, *33*, 129–135. [CrossRef]
25. Madabhushi, A.; Lee, G. Image analysis and machine learning in digital pathology: Challenges and opportunities. *Med. Image Anal.* **2016**, *33*, 170–175. [CrossRef]
26. Komura, D.; Ishikawa, S. Machine Learning Methods for Histopathological Image Analysis. *Comput. Struct. Biotechnol. J.* **2018**, *16*, 34–42. [CrossRef]
27. Arano, K.A.G.; Sun, S.; Ordieres-Mere, J.; Gong, B. The use of the internet of things for estimating personal pollution exposure. *Int. J. Environ. Res. Public Health* **2019**, *16*, 3130. [CrossRef]
28. Steyerberg, E.W.; van der Ploeg, T.; Van Calster, B. Risk prediction with machine learning and regression methods. *Biom. J.* **2014**, *56*, 601–606. [CrossRef]
29. Gholami, B.; Phan, T.S.; Haddad, W.M.; Cason, A.; Mullis, J.; Price, L.; Bailey, J.M. Replicating human expertise of mechanical ventilation waveform analysis in detecting patient-ventilator cycling asynchrony using machine learning. *Comput. Biol. Med.* **2018**, *97*, 137–144. [CrossRef] [PubMed]
30. Kashnikov, A.V.; Levin, L. Applying machine learning techniques to mine ventilation control systems. In Proceedings of the 2017 20th IEEE International Conference on Soft Computing and Measurements, SCM 2017, St. Petersburg, Russia, 24–26 May 2017; Institute of Electrical and Electronics Engineers Inc.: Interlaken, Switzerland, 2017; pp. 391–393.

31. Van Peteghem, V.; Vanhoucke, M. A genetic algorithm for the preemptive and non-preemptive multi-mode resource-constrained project scheduling problem. *Eur. J. Oper. Res.* **2010**, *201*, 409–418. [CrossRef]
32. Vanhoucke, M.; Coelho, J.; Debels, D.; Maenhout, B.; Tavares, L.V. An evaluation of the adequacy of project network generators with systematically sampled networks. *Eur. J. Oper. Res.* **2008**, *187*, 511–524. [CrossRef]
33. Cai, H.; Xu, B.; Jiang, L.; Vasilakos, A.V. IoT-Based Big Data Storage Systems in Cloud Computing: Perspectives and Challenges. *IEEE Internet Things J.* **2017**, *4*, 75–87. [CrossRef]
34. Adamson, G.; Wang, L.; Holm, M.; Moore, P. Cloud manufacturing—A critical review of recent development and future trends. *Int. J. Comput. Integr. Manuf.* **2017**, *30*, 347–380. [CrossRef]
35. De Carolis, A.; Macchi, M.; Kulvatunyou, B.; Brundage, M.P.; Terzi, S. Maturity Models and tools for enabling smart manufacturing systems: Comparison and reflections for future developments. In *IFIP Advances in Information and Communication Technology*; Springer New York LLC: New York, NY, USA, 2017; Volume 517, pp. 23–35.
36. Kost, G.J. Connectivity: The millennium challenge for point-of-care testing. *Arch. Pathol. Lab. Med.* **2000**, *124*, 1108–1110. [PubMed]
37. Puyol Moreno, J. Una aproximación a Big Data. *RDUNED. Rev. Derecho UNED* **2014**, *14*, 471–506.
38. Diez-Olivan, A.; Del Ser, J.; Galar, D.; Sierra, B. Data fusion and machine learning for industrial prognosis: Trends and perspectives towards Industry 4.0. *Inf. Fusion* **2019**, *50*, 92–111. [CrossRef]
39. Sarvari, P.A.; Ustundag, A.; Cevikcan, E.; Kaya, I.; Cebi, S. Technology Roadmap for Industry 4.0. In *Industry 4.0: Managing the Digital Transformation*; Springer Series in Advanced Manufacturing; Springer: Cham, Switzerland, 2018; Volume 95, 103, ISBN 978-3-319-57869-9.
40. Guinée, J.B.; Heijungs, R.; Huppes, G.; Zamagni, A.; Masoni, P.; Buonamici, R.; Ekvall, T.; Rydberg, T. Life cycle assessment: Past, present, and future. *Environ. Sci. Technol.* **2011**, *45*, 90–96. [CrossRef]
41. Nalepa, G.J.; Kutt, K.; Zycka, B.G.; Jemioło, P.; Bobek, S. Analysis and use of the emotional context with wearable devices for games and intelligent assistants. *Sensors* **2019**, *19*, 2509. [CrossRef]
42. Zupančič, E.; Žalik, B. Data trustworthiness evaluation in mobile crowdsensing systems with users' trust dispositions' consideration. *Sensors* **2019**, *19*, 1326. [CrossRef] [PubMed]
43. Mordecai, Y.; Dori, D. Minding the cyber-physical gap: Model-based analysis and mitigation of systemic perception-induced failure. *Sensors* **2017**, *17*, 1644. [CrossRef] [PubMed]
44. González, I.; Calderón, A.J.; Barragán, A.J.; Andújar, J.M. Integration of sensors, controllers and instruments using a novel OPC architecture. *Sensors* **2017**, *17*, 1512. [CrossRef] [PubMed]
45. Yoo, M.J.; Grozel, C.; Kiritsis, D. Closed-loop lifecycle management of service and product in the internet of things: Semantic framework for knowledge integration. *Sensors* **2016**, *16*, 1053. [CrossRef]
46. Varela, G.; Paz-Lopez, A.; Becerra, J.A.; Vazquez-Rodriguez, S.; Duro, R.J. UniDA: Uniform device access framework for human interaction environments. *Sensors* **2011**, *11*, 9361–9392. [CrossRef]
47. Succar, B. Building information modelling framework: A research and delivery foundation for industry stakeholders. *Autom. Constr.* **2009**, *18*, 357–375. [CrossRef]
48. Zamora-Polo, F. Conceptual Framework for the Use of Building Information Modeling in Engineering Education. *Int. J. Eng. Educ.* **2019**, *35*, 744–755.
49. Borsotti, C.A. *Temas de Metodología de la Investigación*; Argentina: Miño y Dávila: Buenos Aires, Argentina, 2006.
50. Zamora-Polo, F.; Sánchez-Martín, J. Teaching for a better world. Sustainability and Sustainable Development Goals in the construction of a change-maker university. *Sustainability* **2019**, *11*, 4224. [CrossRef]
51. Heidegger, M. *Sein und Zeit (Ser y Tiempo)*; Trotta S.A.: Madrid, Spain, 2005; ISBN 9788498790474.
52. Lozano, R.; Merrill, M.; Sammalisto, K.; Ceulemans, K.; Lozano, F. Connecting Competences and Pedagogical Approaches for Sustainable Development in Higher Education: Review and Framework Proposal. *Sustainability* **2017**, *9*, 1889. [CrossRef]
53. Pawson, R.; Greenhalgh, T.; Harvey, G.; Walshe, K. Realist review-a new method of systematic review designed for complex policy interventions. *J. Health Serv. Res. Policy* **2005**, *10*, 21–34. [CrossRef]
54. Soust-Verdaguer, B.; Llatas, C.; García-Martínez, A. Critical review of bim-based LCA method to buildings. *Energy Build.* **2017**, *136*, 110–120. [CrossRef]
55. Anand, C.K.; Amor, B. Recent developments, future challenges and new research directions in LCA of buildings: A critical review. *BMJ Case Rep.* **2017**, *67*, 408–416. [CrossRef]
56. Jabareen, Y. Building a Conceptual Framework: Philosophy, Definitions, and Procedure. *Int. J. Qual. Methods* **2009**, *8*, 49–62. [CrossRef]

57. Strauss, A.; Corbin, J. *Basics of Qualitative Research*; Sage Publications, Inc.: Newbury Park, CA, USA, 1967; ISBN 0-8039-5939-7.
58. Strauss, A.; Corbin, J. Grounded theory research: Procedures, canons, and evaluative criteria. *Qual. Sociol.* **1990**, *13*, 3–21.
59. El Hamzaoui, Y.; Rodríguez, J.A.; Hernández, J.A.; Salazar, V. Optimization of operating conditions for steam turbine using an artificial neural network inverse. *Appl. Therm. Eng.* **2015**, *75*, 648–657. [CrossRef]
60. Khoshnevisan, B.; Rafiee, S.; Omid, M.; Mousazadeh, H.; Shamshirband, S.; Hamid, S.H.A. Developing a fuzzy clustering model for better energy use in farm management systems. *Renew. Sustain. Energy Rev.* **2015**, *48*, 27–34. [CrossRef]
61. Marvuglia, A.; Kanevski, M.; Benetto, E. Machine learning for toxicity characterization of organic chemical emissions using USEtox database: Learning the structure of the input space. *Environ. Int.* **2015**, *83*, 72–85. [CrossRef]
62. Slapnik, M.; Istenič, D.; Pintar, M.; Udovč, A. Extending life cycle assessment normalization factors and use of machine learning—A Slovenian case study. *Ecol. Indic.* **2015**, *50*, 161–172. [CrossRef]
63. Gust, K.A.; Collier, Z.A.; Mayo, M.L.; Stanley, J.K.; Gong, P.; Chappell, M.A. Limitations of toxicity characterization in life cycle assessment: Can adverse outcome pathways provide a new foundation? *Integr. Environ. Assess. Manag.* **2016**, *12*, 580–590. [CrossRef]
64. Wisthoff, A.; Huynh, T.; Ferrero, V.; Dupont, B. Quantifying the impact of sustainable product design decisions in the early design phase through machine learning. In Proceedings of the ASME 2016 International Design Engineering Technical Conferences and Computers and Information in Engineering Conference, Charlotte, NC, USA, 21–24 August 2016; Volume 4, pp. 1–10.
65. Li, Y.; Zhang, H.; Roy, U.; Lee, Y.T. A data-driven approach for improving sustainability assessment in advanced manufacturing. In Proceedings of the 2017 IEEE International Conference on Big Data (Big Data), Boston, MA, USA, 11–14 December 2017; pp. 1736–1745.
66. DeRousseau, M.A.; Kasprzyk, J.R.; Srubar, W.V. Computational design optimization of concrete mixtures: A review. *Cem. Concr. Res.* **2018**, *109*, 42–53. [CrossRef]
67. Nabavi-Pelesaraei, A.; Rafiee, S.; Mohtasebi, S.S.; Hosseinzadeh-Bandbafha, H.; Chau, K. Wing Integration of artificial intelligence methods and life cycle assessment to predict energy output and environmental impacts of paddy production. *Sci. Total Environ.* **2018**, *631–632*, 1279–1294. [CrossRef] [PubMed]
68. Sharif, S.A.; Hammad, A. Developing surrogate ANN for selecting near-optimal building energy renovation methods considering energy consumption, LCC and LCA. *J. Build. Eng.* **2019**, *25*, 100790. [CrossRef]
69. D'Amico, B.; Myers, R.J.; Sykes, J.; Voss, E.; Cousins-Jenvey, B.; Fawcett, W.; Richardson, S.; Kermani, A.; Pomponi, F. Machine Learning for Sustainable Structures: A Call for Data. *Structures* **2019**, *19*, 1–4. [CrossRef]
70. Ziyadi, M.; Al-Qadi, I.L. Model uncertainty analysis using data analytics for life-cycle assessment (LCA) applications. *Int. J. Life Cycle Assess.* **2019**, *24*, 945–959. [CrossRef]
71. Feng, K.; Lu, W.; Wang, Y. Assessing environmental performance in early building design stage: An integrated parametric design and machine learning method. *Sustain. Cities Soc.* **2019**, *50*, 101596. [CrossRef]
72. Perrotta, F.; Parry, T.; Neves, L.C.; Mesgarpour, M. A machine learning approach for the estimation of fuel consumption related to road pavement rolling resistance for large fleets of trucks. In *Life Cycle Analysis and Assessment in Civil Engineering: Towards an Integrated Vision, Proceedings of the Sixth International Symposium on Life-Cycle Civil Engineering (IALCCE 2018), Ghent, Belgium, 28–31 October 2018*; CRC Press: Boca Raton, FL, USA, 2019; pp. 2011–2015.
73. Kaab, A.; Sharifi, M.; Mobli, H.; Nabavi-Pelesaraei, A.; Chau, K. Wing Combined life cycle assessment and artificial intelligence for prediction of output energy and environmental impacts of sugarcane production. *Sci. Total Environ.* **2019**, *664*, 1005–1019. [CrossRef]
74. Huijbregts, M.; Margni, M.; Van de Meent, D.; Jolliet, O.; Rosenbaum, R.; McKone, T.E.; Hauschild, M.Z. USEtoxTM Chemical-Specific Database: Organics. Available online: https://usetox.org/ (accessed on 2 March 2020).
75. Walczak, S. Artificial neural networks. In *Advanced Methodologies and Technologies in Artificial Intelligence, Computer Simulation, and Human-Computer Interaction*; IGI Global: Hershey, PA, USA, 2019; pp. 40–53.
76. Färber, M.; Jatowt, A. Finding Temporal Trends of Scientific Concepts. In Proceedings of the BIR@ ECIR, Cologne, Germany, 14 April 2019; pp. 132–139.
77. Smyth, R. Exploring the usefulness of a conceptual framework as a research tool: A researcher's reflections. *Issues Educ. Res.* **2004**, *14*, 167–180.

78. Minichiello, V.; Sullivan, G. *Handbook for Research Methods in Health Sciences.*; Pearson Ecuation Australia: Melbourne, Australia, 2004.
79. Bishop, A.J.; Clements, K.; Keitel, C.; Kilpatrick, J.; Laborde, C. *The Role of Theory in Mathematics Education and Research*; Bishop, A.J.; Clements, K.; Keitel, C.; Kilpatrick, J.; Laborde, C. Springer: Dordrecht, The Netherlands, 1996.
80. Guarino, F.; Falcone, G.; Stillitano, T.; De Luca, A.I.; Gulisano, G.; Mistretta, M.; Strano, A. Life cycle assessment of olive oil: A case study in southern Italy. *J. Environ. Manag.* **2019**, *238*, 396–407. [CrossRef]
81. Directorate-General for Agriculture and Rural Development. Olive Oil Trade Data. Available online: http://data.europa.eu/88u/dataset/olive-oil-trade-data (accessed on 18 December 2019).
82. Espadas-Aldana, G.; Vialle, C.; Belaud, J.P.; Vaca-Garcia, C.; Sablayrolles, C. Analysis and trends for Life Cycle Assessment of olive oil production. *Sustain. Prod. Consum.* **2019**, *19*, 216–230. [CrossRef]
83. Food Price Observatory MARM. Value Chain Study and Olive Oil Price Formation. Available online: https://www.internationaloliveoil.org/wp-content/uploads/2019/12/CADENADEVALOR-ENG.pdf (accessed on 12 January 2020).
84. De Latorre, P.; del Pilar, M. *Innovación en la Cadena de Valor del Aceite de Oliva: Análisis de una Cadena de Valor Concreta*; Tesis doctoral, Universidad de Comillas: Madrid, Spain, 2019.
85. Civantos, L. *El Olivo, el Aceite, la Aceituna*, 2nd ed.; Consejo Oleícola Internacional: Madrid, Spain, 1998.
86. Cert, A.; Moreda, W.; León-Camacho, M.; Pérez-Camino, M.C. Determinación de absorción de luz UV a 232 nm, composición de ácidos grasos, trilinoleína y triglicéridos con numéro equivalente de carbonos igual a 42, en aceites de oliva y de orujo de oliva: Determinación de precisión de los métodos analíticos mediante. *Grasas Aceites* **1996**, *47*, 401–410. [CrossRef]
87. Leung, W.W.F. Torque requirement for high-solids centrifugal sludge dewatering. *Filtr. Sep.* **1998**, *35*, 883–887. [CrossRef]
88. Cano Marchal, P.; Gómez Ortega, J.; Aguilera Puerto, D.; Gámez García, J. Situación actual y perspectivas futuras del control del proceso de elaboración del aceite de oliva virgin. *RIAI Rev. Iberoam. Autom. Inform. Ind.* **2011**, *8*, 258–269. [CrossRef]
89. Ministerio de Agricultura, Pesca y Alimentación. *Marco Estratégico para la Industria de Alimentación y Bebidas*; Ministerio de Agricultura, Pesca y Alimentación, Federación Española de Industrias de la alimentación y la bebida (FIAB): Madrid, Spain, 2018.
90. Ciruela-Lorenzo, A.M.; Del Aguila-Obra, A.R.; Padilla-Meléndez, A.; Plaza-Angulo, J.J. Digitalization of Agri-cooperatives in the Smart Agriculture Context. Proposal of a Digital Diagnosis Tool. *Sustainability* **2020**, *12*, 1325. [CrossRef]
91. Guerrero, M.; Luque Sendra, A.; Lama-Ruiz, J.R. Técnicas de predicción mediante minería de datos en la industria alimentaria bajo el paradigma de Industria 4.0. In *Avances en la Investigación en Ciencia e Ingeniería*; Área de Innovación y Desarrollo, S.L., Ed.; 3Ciencias: Alcoy, Alicante, 2019; pp. 149–157. ISBN 978-84-120057-2-1.
92. Malekjafarian, A.; Golpayegani, F.; Moloney, C.; Clarke, S. A machine learning approach to bridge-damage detection using responses measured on a passing vehicle. *Sensors* **2019**, *19*, 4035. [CrossRef] [PubMed]
93. Perea, R.G.; García, A.M.; García, I.F.; Poyato, E.C.; Montesinos, P.; Díaz, J.A.R. Middleware to operate smart photovoltaic irrigation systems in real time. *Water* **2019**, *11*, 1508. [CrossRef]
94. Capraro, F.; Tosetti, S.; Rossomando, F.; Mut, V.; Serman, F.V. Web-based system for the remote monitoring and management of precision irrigation: A case study in an arid region of Argentina. *Sensors* **2018**, *18*, 3847. [CrossRef]
95. Sola-Guirado, R.R.; Bayano-Tejero, S.; Rodríguez-Lizana, A.; Gil-Ribes, J.A.; Miranda-Fuentes, A. Assessment of the accuracy of a multi-beam LED scanner sensor for measuring olive canopies. *Sensors* **2018**, *18*, 4406. [CrossRef]
96. Hermoso, M.; Uceda, M.; Frias, L.; Beltrán, G. *Maduración. el Cultivo del Olivo*; Barranco, D., Fernández-Escobar, D., Rallo, L., Eds.; Junta de Andalucía y Ediciones Mundi-Prensa: Madrid, Spain, 1997.
97. Marquez, A.J.; Díaz, A.M.; Reguera, M.I.P. Using optical NIR sensor for on-line virgin olive oils characterization. *Sens. Actuators B Chem.* **2005**, *107*, 64–68. [CrossRef]
98. Jiménez, A.; Beltrán, G.; Aguilera, M.P.; Uceda, M. A sensor-software based on artificial neural network for the optimization of olive oil elaboration process. *Sens. Actuators B Chem.* **2008**, *129*, 985–990. [CrossRef]

99. Rodríguez-Méndez, M.L.; Apetrei, C.; de Saja, J.A. Evaluation of the polyphenolic content of extra virgin olive oils using an array of voltammetric sensors. *Electrochim. Acta* **2008**, *53*, 5867–5872. [CrossRef]
100. Sonia, E.; GianFrancesco, M.; Roberto, S.; Ibanez, R.; Agnese, T.; Stefania, U.; Maurizio, S. Monitoring of virgin olive oil volatile compounds evolution during olive malaxation by an array of metal oxide sensors. *Food Chem.* **2009**, *113*, 345–350. [CrossRef]
101. Bordons, C.; Zafra, M.L. Inferential sensor for the olive oil industry. In Proceedings of the European Control Conference, ECC 2003, Cambridge, UK, 1–4 September 2003; Institute of Electrical and Electronics Engineers Inc.: Interlaken, Switzerland, 2003; pp. 1940–1946.
102. Furferi, R.; Carfagni, M.; Daou, M. Artificial neural network software for real-time estimation of olive oil qualitative parameters during continuous extraction. *Comput. Electron. Agric.* **2007**, *55*, 115–131. [CrossRef]
103. Jiménez Marquez, A.; Aguilera Herrera, M.P.; Uceda Ojeda, M.; Beltrán Maza, G. Neural network as tool for virgin olive oil elaboration process optimization. *J. Food Eng.* **2009**, *95*, 135–141. [CrossRef]
104. Rykiel, E.J. Testing ecological models: The meaning of validation. *Ecol. Model.* **1996**, *90*, 229–244. [CrossRef]
105. Matalas, N.C.; Landwehr, J.M.; Wolman, M.G. *Prediction in Water Management, Scientific Basis of Water Management*; Scientific basis of water resource management, National Research Council, National Academy Press: Washington, DC, USA, 1982.
106. Refsgaard, J.C.; Henriksen, H.J. Modelling guidelines—Terminology and guiding principles. *Adv. Water Resour.* **2004**, *27*, 71–82. [CrossRef]
107. Adom, D.; Adu-Gyamfi, S.; Agyekum, K.; Ayarkwa, J.; Dwumah, P.; Abass, K.; Osei-Poku, P. Theoretical and conceptual framework: Mandatory ingredients of a quality research. *J. Educ. Hum. Dev.* **2016**, *5*, 158–172.
108. Pérez, S.G.; Villar, S.G.; Carrillo, Á.G.; López, L.D. Sostenibilidad, energía y gestión urbana: Enfoque integral para el diseño de proyectos de ingeniería en el contexto de formación MDP-UPC. In Proceedings of the XIV International Congress on Project Engineering, Madrid, Spain, 30 June–2 July 2010; pp. 2927–2938.
109. García-Serna, J.; Pérez-Barrigón, L.; Cocero, M.J. New trends for design towards sustainability in chemical engineering: Green engineering. *Chem. Eng. J.* **2007**, *133*, 7–30. [CrossRef]
110. Vanegas, J.A. Road Map and Principles for Built Environment Sustainability. *Environ. Sci. Technol.* **2003**, *37*, 5363–5372. [CrossRef]
111. Segalàs Coral, J. *Engineering Education for a Sustainable Future*; Universitat Politècnica de Catalunya: Barcelona, Spain, 2009.
112. Vezzoli, C.; Sciama, D. Life Cycle Design: From general methods to product type specific guidelines and checklists: A method adopted to develop a set of guidelines/checklist handbook for the eco-efficient design of NECTA vending machines. *J. Clean. Prod.* **2006**, *14*, 1319–1325. [CrossRef]
113. Labuschagne, C.; Brent, A.C.; Van Erck, R.P.G. Assessing the sustainability performances of industries. *J. Clean. Prod.* **2005**, *13*, 373–385. [CrossRef]
114. Fernández-Sánchez, G.; Rodríguez-López, F.; Hruškovič, P. Identificación de factores e indicadores de sostenibilidad genéricos en los proyectos de ingeniería civil. In Proceedings of the XIII Congreso Internacional de Ingeniería de Proyectos, Badajoz, Spain, 8–10 July 2009; pp. 12–25.
115. Armenia, S.; Dangelico, R.M.; Nonino, F.; Pompei, A. Sustainable project management: A conceptualization-oriented review and a framework proposal for future studies. *Sustainability* **2019**, *11*, 2664. [CrossRef]
116. Reidl, L.M. Marco conceptual en el proceso de investigación. *Investig. Educ. Médica* **2012**, *1*, 146–151.

*sensors*

MDPI

*Article*

# Local Wireless Sensor Networks Positioning Reliability Under Sensor Failure

**Javier Díez-González [1,*], Rubén Álvarez [2,*], Natalia Prieto-Fernández [1] and Hilde Perez [1]**

1 Department of Mechanical, IT and Aerospace Engineering, Universidad de León, 24071 León, Spain; nprief02@estudiantes.unileon.es (N.P.-F.); hilde.perez@unileon.es (H.P.)

2 Positioning Department, Drotium, Universidad de León, 24071 León, Spain

* Correspondence: jdieg@unileon.es (J.D.-G.); ruben.alvarez@drotium.com (R.Á.)

Received: 31 January 2020; Accepted: 3 March 2020; Published: 5 March 2020

**Abstract:** Local Positioning Systems are collecting high research interest over the last few years. Its accurate application in high-demanded difficult scenarios has revealed its stability and robustness for autonomous navigation. In this paper, we develop a new sensor deployment methodology to guarantee the system availability in case of a sensor failure of a five-node Time Difference of Arrival (TDOA) localization method. We solve the ambiguity of two possible solutions in the four-sensor TDOA problem in each combination of four nodes of the system by maximizing the distance between the two possible solutions in every target possible location. In addition, we perform a Genetic Algorithm Optimization in order to find an optimized node location with a trade-off between the system behavior under failure and its normal operating condition by means of the Cramer Rao Lower Bound derivation in each possible target location. Results show that the optimization considering sensor failure enhances the average values of the convergence region size and the location accuracy by 31% and 22%, respectively, in case of some malfunction sensors regarding to the non-failure optimization, only suffering a reduction in accuracy of less than 5% under normal operating conditions.

**Keywords:** cramer rao lower bound; localization; LPS; multi-objective optimization; sensor failure; wireless sensor networks

## 1. Introduction

Autonomous navigation has meant a challenge for scientific development over the last few years. The high accuracy required has entailed the interest in Local Positioning Systems (LPS) where the positioning signal paths are reduced between targets and architecture sensors. This fact significantly reduces noise and uncertainties by minimizing the global architecture errors with respect to Global Navigation Satellite Systems (GNSS).

GNSS provide global coverage but the distortion of their signals in their travel affects the stability and the accuracy of the localization over time. In addition, GNSS navigation is denied in indoor environments, where Automatic Ground Vehicles (AGVs) mostly operate, as signals deteriorate crossing large buildings. This causes Non-Line-of-Sight (NLOS) connections between satellites and targets which makes position determination impractical. The application of also GNSS has limitations in outdoor environments such as low-altitude flights in Unmanned Aerial Vehicles (UAVs) due to the higher uncertainty in the vertical coordinate of the global systems. It is a consequence of the similar altitude of the satellites in their constellations.

These reasons have promoted this new localization concept based on LPS especially for high accuracy automated navigation [1,2]. LPS require the deployment of architecture sensors in a defined and known space where the capabilities of the system are maximized. The characteristics of the LPS for a defined space rely on the measurement of the physical magnitude used for the determination of the target location: time [3], power [4], frequency [5], angle [6], phase [7] or combinations of them [8].

Among these systems, the most extended are time-based models due to their reliability, stability, robustness and easy-to-implement hardware architectures. Time-based positioning has two main systems that differ in time measurements computed: Time of Arrival (TOA) [9] and Time Difference of Arrival (TDOA) [10] systems.

TOA systems measure the total time of flight of a positioning signal from an emitter to a receiver. It requires the synchronization of the clocks of all the system elements (i.e. targets and sensors). This leads to the generation of a sphere of possible locations in the 3-D space for each received signal in a different architecture sensor. The intersection of spheres determines the target location. Mathematical standards show that the unequivocal target location is achieved in TOA systems with at least four sensors.

TDOA systems compute the relative time between the reception of the positioning signal in two different architecture sensors. The synchronization of these systems is optional considering asynchronous TDOA architectures in which the time differences are computed in a single clock of a coordinator sensor [11] and synchronous TDOA where all architecture sensors must be synchronized. Time relative measurements lead to hyperboloid surfaces of possible location of targets. A hyperboloid equation is obtained every two architecture sensors while only ($n$-$1$) independent equations can be processed from $n$ different sensors [12]. The required number of sensors to determine unequivocally the target location is five sensors for 3-D positioning in these methodologies.

However, the intersection of three different spheres -3 architecture sensors- in TOA systems and three different hyperboloids -4 architecture sensors- in TDOA systems leads to two different potential solutions. Nevertheless, these solutions are not able to be discarded from a mathematical point of view.

In one of our previous works [13], we have demonstrated that a reliable unique solution to the intersection of three hyperboloids or spheres can be obtained through the maximization of the distance between the two potential solutions in a defined environment by means of Genetic Algorithms (GA). We achieve this result by applying Taylor-based algorithms [14] from an initial iteration point which must be close enough to the final solution. Results show that the node deployment has a direct impact in this finding.

The sensor distribution also has relation with the global accuracy of the LPS. Traditionally, the Position Dilution of Precision (PDOP) has been used to determine the achievable accuracy of time-based positioning systems in GNSS [15] by considering satellite location with respect to target nodes. This methodology considers the homoscedasticity of the satellite signals as they actually travel similar distances from satellites to target nodes. This consideration is impractical for LPS since the paths traveled can significantly differ from one architecture sensor to another producing the heteroscedasticity in the time measurements [16].

This fact promotes the use of Cramer Rao Lower Bound (CRLB) [17,18] derivations to characterize the White Gaussian Noise (WGN) present in the time measurements. In practice, CRLB determines the minimum achievable error in positioning systems [19]. We have computed these derivations for asynchronous and synchronous TDOA positioning methodologies in our recent works [20,21] in order to define the beauty of a node deployment in terms of accuracy. This has allowed us to perform the node deployment optimization in TDOA systems by means of GA. The reason of the use of heuristic techniques relies on the NP-Hard problem solution of the 3D sensor deployment in LPS and it is widely considered in the literature [22–27].

However, any of the approaches presented considers a possible sensor failure during the node distribution optimization addressed. This means that in these sensor deployments a sensor fault will cause the unavailability of TOA architectures with 4 sensors and TDOA architectures with 5 sensors. However, our finding in [13] has determined that an unequivocal solution for these systems with a possible sensor failure -3 sensors in TOA and 4 sensors in TDOA- can be achieved under an optimized node localization. As a consequence, an optimized sensor distribution can guarantee the availability of the system in sensor failure conditions through the consideration of a methodology to enhance the system properties in these situations.

In this paper, we propose for the first time a GA optimization for the 3D node deployment in a TDOA system with five architecture sensors with failure consideration, maximizing the performance during regular operation and in any possible sensor malfunction (see Figure 1). For that purpose, we performed a multi-objective optimization in which we looked for a trade-off between the global accuracy of the system with five sensors and every combination of four nodes in a defined environment of an LPS. Additionally, we ensured the unequivocal position determination for every distribution of four sensors by maximizing the distance between the two possible mathematical solutions of the target location [11]. Based on [19] a 3D sensor distribution in irregular environments is provided, enabling the application of this failure-consideration approach to outdoor and indoor scenarios. This methodology will also ensure the availability of the system with acceptable accuracy in case of a sensor failure in any of the architecture nodes.

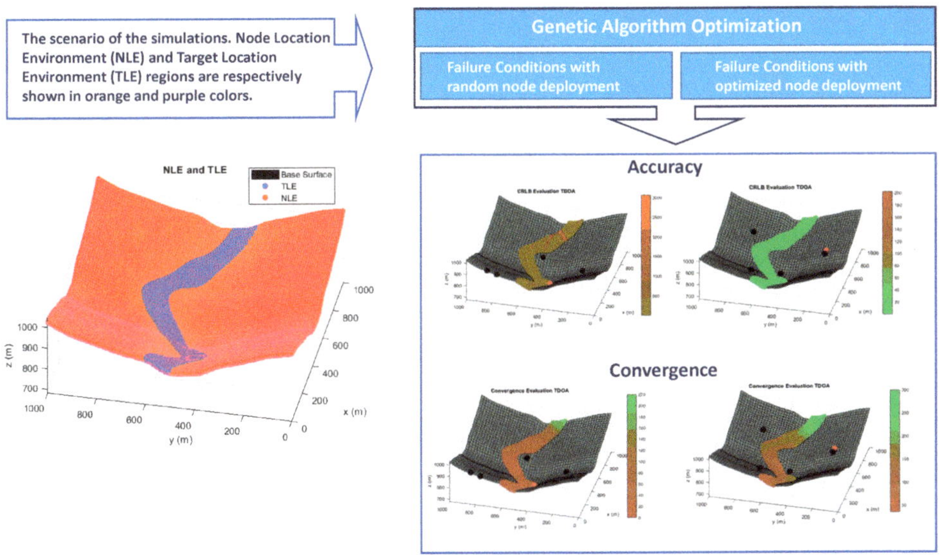


**Figure 1.** Graphical Abstract.

The remainder of the paper is organized as follows: the algorithm for the target unequivocal location determination is presented in Section 2, the CRLB modeling is introduced in Section 3, the GA and the fitness function are presented in Sections 4 and 5 and Section 6 show the results and conclusions of the presented paper.

## 2. Taylor-Based Positioning Algorithm in Time Difference of Arrival (TDOA) Systems

Relative time measurements in TDOA systems lead to hyperboloid equations of possible target locations. These equations are non-linear so numerical methods are required to solve the intersection of the hyperboloids. The algorithms used have been classified in two main categories: closed-form algorithms and iterative methods.

Closed-form algorithms [28,29] provide a direct final solution by solving a linearization of the hyperboloid equations. Iterative methods perform a gradient descent to achieve the solution through Taylor-Based linearization. These methods start from an initial position which must be closed enough to the final solution [30] to iteratively converge to the target location. The convergence of the algorithm depends on the initial position -usually the last known position of the target- which promotes a constant updating of the target location.

The position calculation with four architecture sensors in TDOA systems provides two possible ambiguous target localizations. The achievement of an unequivocal position cannot be determined according to mathematical standards. As a consequence, the position determination by means of iterative methods provides a unique solution that it might not match with the real target location. Nevertheless, we have shown in [13] that the optimal solution can be achieved by maximizing the radius of convergence of the initial iteration point which forces the iterative method to converge to the real solution in a high confidence interval. It has been demonstrated that this fact coincides with the maximization of the distance between the two possible solutions in LPS. This allows us to solve the 3-D TDOA problem with 4 nodes through Taylor-Based positioning algorithms with enough confidence under the optimization proposed.

This finding enables LPS architectures of 5 sensors -minimum number of sensors to supply unequivocal target location- to provide stable and accurate service in case of sensor failure or temporal unavailability of one of the architecture nodes.

Taylor-Based algorithms in TDOA systems are linearizations of the equation of the time difference of arrival:

$$\begin{aligned} R_{ij} = d_{ij} = d_{Ei} \; - d_{Ej} = c\, t_{ij} = c\left(t_i - t_j\right) \\ = \sqrt{(x_E - x_i)^2 + (y_E - y_i)^2 + (z_E - z_i)^2} \\ - \sqrt{\left(x_E - x_j\right)^2 + \left(y_E - y_j\right)^2 + \left(z_E - z_j\right)^2} \end{aligned} \tag{1}$$

where $R_{ij}$ and $d_{ij}$ represent the distance difference of the signal travel from the emitter to sensors $i$ and $j$, $d_{Ei}$ and $d_{Ej}$ are total distance from the emitter ($E$) to sensors $i$ and $j$, $c$ is the speed of the radioelectric waves, $t_{ij}$ is the time difference of arrival measured in the architecture sensors, $t_i$ and $t_j$ is the total time of flight of the positioning signal from emitter to receivers $i$ and $j$ respectively and $(x_E\,,\ y_E\,, z_E)$, $(x_i\,,\ y_i\,,\ z_i)$ and $\left(x_j\,,\ y_j\,,\ z_j\right)$ are the Cartesian coordinates of the target and the sensors $i$ and $j$.

Taylor approximation truncated on first order is applied in Equation (1) to linearize the equation from an initial iteration point $(x_0\,,\ y_0\,,\ z_0)$:

$$R_{ij} = ct_{ij} = R_{ij_0} + \frac{\partial R_{ij}}{\partial x}\Delta x + \frac{\partial R_{ij}}{\partial y}\Delta y + \frac{\partial R_{ij}}{\partial z}\Delta z \tag{2}$$

where $R_{ij_0}$ is the range difference of arrival in the initial iteration point, $\frac{\partial R_{ij}}{\partial x}$, $\frac{\partial R_{ij}}{\partial y}$ and $\frac{\partial R_{ij}}{\partial z}$ are the partial derivatives of the range differences measured in the $i$ and $j$ architecture sensors particularized in the initial iteration point.

The application of this process to sensors $k$ and $l$ to complete the four-sensor 3D TDOA problem solution in [13] generates the range difference matrix ($\Delta\mathbf{R}$):

$$\Delta\mathbf{R} = \begin{pmatrix} \frac{\partial R_{ij}}{\partial x} & \frac{\partial R_{ij}}{\partial y} & \frac{\partial R_{ij}}{\partial z} \\ \frac{\partial R_{il}}{\partial x} & \frac{\partial R_{il}}{\partial y} & \frac{\partial R_{il}}{\partial z} \\ \frac{\partial R_{ik}}{\partial x} & \frac{\partial R_{ik}}{\partial y} & \frac{\partial R_{ik}}{\partial z} \end{pmatrix} \begin{pmatrix} \Delta x \\ \Delta y \\ \Delta z \end{pmatrix} = \mathbf{H}\Delta\mathbf{P} \tag{3}$$

where $\mathbf{H}$ is the partial derivative matrix, usually known as the visibility matrix, and $\Delta\mathbf{P}$ represents the coordinate variances in each space direction which is the unknown of the equation. The previous equation is solved and iterated until no changes in coordinate variances are appreciated by means of the least squares method as follows:

$$\Delta\mathbf{P} = \left(\mathbf{H}^{\mathbf{t}}\mathbf{H}\right)^{-1}\mathbf{H}^{\mathbf{t}}\Delta\mathbf{R} = \begin{pmatrix} \Delta x \\ \Delta y \\ \Delta z \end{pmatrix} \tag{4}$$

### 3. Cramer Rao Lower Bound (CRLB) Modeling in TDOA Systems

CRLB is an unbiased estimator of the lowest variance of a parameter. Its usage in the localization field is widespread [31–33] since it allows us to determine the minimum achievable error by the system analyzed.

It characterizes the WGN present in the time measurements of the time-based positioning systems. The uncertainties introduced in the measurements depend on the distance traveled by the positioning signal from the emitter to the architecture sensors in a heteroscedastic noise consideration. Recent studies [18] developed a matrix form of the CRLB considering heteroscedasticity in time measurements:

$$\begin{aligned} FIM_{mn} = \left(\frac{\partial h(TS)}{\partial TS_m}\right)^T \ & \mathbf{R}^{-1}(\mathbf{TS})\left(\frac{\partial h(TS)}{\partial TS_n}\right) \\ & +\frac{1}{2}tr\left\{R^{-1}(TS)\left(\frac{\partial R(TS)}{\partial TS}\right)\mathbf{R}^{-1}(\mathbf{TS})\left(\frac{\partial R(TS)}{\partial TS_n}\right)\right\} \end{aligned} \quad (5)$$

where **FIM** indicates the Fisher Information Matrix, $m$ and $n$ are the sub-indexes of the estimated parameters in **FIM**, TS is the target sensor Cartesian coordinates, $\mathbf{h}(\mathbf{TS})$ is a vector that contains the travel of the signal in the TDOA architecture to compute a time measurement:

$$\begin{aligned} h_{TDOA_i} &= \|TS - CS_i\| - \|TS - CS_j\| \\ i &= 1, \ldots, N_{CS} \\ j &= 1, \ldots, N_{CS} \end{aligned} \quad (6)$$

being $CS_i$ and $CS_j$ the coordinates of the architecture sensors $i$ and $j$ and $N_{CS}$ the number of sensors involved in the position determination. $\mathbf{R}(\mathbf{TS})$ is the covariance matrix of the time measurements in the architecture sensors. The covariance matrix is built with a heteroscedastic noise consideration in the sensors modeled by a Log-normal path loss propagation model [21] obtaining the following variances:

$$\begin{aligned} \sigma_{TDOAij}{}^2 = & \frac{c^2}{B^2\left(\frac{P_T}{P_n}\right)}PL(d_0) \\ & \left[\left(\frac{d_{Ei}}{d_0}\right)^n + \left(\frac{d_{Ej}}{d_0}\right)^n\right] \\ i = 1, \ldots, N_{CS} \quad & j = 1, \ldots, N_{CS} \quad where\ i \neq j \end{aligned} \quad (7)$$

where $B$ is the signal bandwidth, $P_T$ is the transmission power, $P_n$ is the mean noise level determined through the Johnson-Nyquist equation, $n$ is the path loss exponent, $d_0$ is the reference distance from which the path loss propagation model is applied and $PL(d_0)$ is the path-loss in the reference distance.

The inverse of the Fisher Information Matrix (**J**) provides in its diagonal the uncertainties associated with each variable to estimate, i.e. the three Cartesian coordinates of the target for a 3D positioning. The location accuracy is directly evaluated through the Root Mean Squared Error (RMSE), which is computed based on the trace of the **J** matrix.

$$RMSE = \sqrt{J_{11} + J_{22} + J_{33}} = \sqrt{\sigma_x{}^2 + \sigma_y{}^2 + \sigma_z{}^2} \quad (8)$$

This model will be applied in the GA optimization with five sensors and each distribution of four sensors in any possible target location in the defined scenario in order to compare the beauty of different node deployments.

### 4. Genetic Algorithm (GA) Optimization

The strong influence of the sensor placement in the LPS performance enables the maximization of their capabilities through the optimization of their sensor distribution. This approach is especially suitable in complex 3D environments, where the most important source of positioning error is promoted by the sensor distribution.

In this work, we developed an optimization methodology to locate the positioning sensors of a five-sensor TDOA system with the consideration of an eventual failure in some of the system nodes. This procedure must guarantee the convergence of the iterative algorithm with all the possible combinations of four nodes in every target location under coverage. Furthermore, the achievement of an optimized node distribution for the normal operating conditions with five system nodes must be accomplished. This leads to a multi-objective optimization which considers both normal and failure operating conditions.

In our previous works [21], a GA for optimizing sensor distributions in 3D irregular environments is presented. The proposed methodology allows a free definition of the optimization region and the reference surface for locating the sensors of the positioning architecture. In addition, the procedure is modular, allowing the election of different selection techniques, percentage of elitism, crossover methodologies, mutation types, and convergence criteria.

After the choice of the optimization method, the next step is the definition of the fitness function. In this case, a multi-objective optimization is carried out for maximizing the accuracy of the TDOA architecture when the minimum number of sensors for positioning is available, i.e. when some of the architecture sensors fail. Accordingly, the methodology proposed in [13] guarantees the attainment of a unique location in TDOA architectures with 4 sensors by the Taylor-based positioning algorithm described in Section 2, based on an initial iteration point closed to the target estimation. The region where this procedure converges to the final solution depends on the geometric properties of the target and the architecture sensors, i.e. the sensor placement in the environment. Based on this relation, the regions of convergence can be maximized through the optimization of the sensor distribution [13].

Consequently, the goal of the multi-objective optimization is the combined maximization of the TDOA system accuracy in 3D environments when the whole architecture is available and when only four sensors are accessible, limited by the size of the convergence regions that allow the correct execution of the Taylor-based positioning algorithm. The fulfillment of these objectives guarantees the robustness of the TDOA architectures in adverse conditions of operation. The fitness function is detailed hereafter:

$$ff = \sum_{1}^{Comb}\left\{\frac{C_1}{NT}\sum\left\{1-\frac{\left[\left(\frac{1}{RMSE_{ref}}\right)-\left(\frac{1}{\boldsymbol{RMSE_{4sensors}}}\right)\right]^2}{\left(\frac{1}{RMSE_{ref}}\right)^2}\right\}\right. \\ \left.+\frac{C_2}{NT}\sum\left\{\frac{\left[\left(\frac{1}{D_{ref}}\right)-\left(\frac{1}{\boldsymbol{D}}\right)\right]^2}{\left(\frac{1}{D_{ref}}\right)^2}\right\}\right\} \\ +C_3\sum\frac{\left\{1-\frac{\left[\left(\frac{1}{RMSE_{ref}}\right)-\left(\frac{1}{\boldsymbol{RMSE_{Ncs}}}\right)\right]^2}{\left(\frac{1}{RMSE_{ref}}\right)^2}\right\}}{NT}-C_4\frac{\sum_{i=1}^{N_{CS}}BL_i}{N_{CS}} \tag{9}$$

where *Comb* is the number of groups of four sensors which are obtainable based on the total number of architecture sensors, *NT* is the number of analyzed points, $RMSE_{ref}$ is the reference accuracy, $\boldsymbol{RMSE_{4sensors}}$ is the vector that contains the CRLB evaluation for each point at analysis with each combination of 4 sensors, $D_{ref}$ indicates the reference distance for the convergence criteria, **D** represents the vector that specifies the convergence evaluation in terms of the distance between the two possible solutions (combinations of 4 sensors) for each point at study, $\boldsymbol{RMSE_{Ncs}}$ is the vector that contains the CRLB analysis for each point at study when all architecture sensors are available, $C_1$, $C_2$, $C_3$ and $C_4$, are coefficients for calibration of the individual summands of the fitness function, and $BL_i$ is the penalization factor associated with the existence of sensors in banned regions (if they exist).

The implemented fitness function presents two important characteristics: the individual summands of the function are confined in the interval (0,1], enabling different ponderations for the optimization;

and the $RMSE_{ref}$ and $D_{ref}$ magnitudes are adaptive to the problem characteristics, facilitating the diversification and intensification phases of the GA in complex environments.

## 5. Results

In this section, the results of the optimization for sensor failure in TDOA architectures are presented. Initially, a 3D complex scenario was designed for carrying out the optimization, proving the adaptability of the proposed methodology in any environment. For this purpose, an irregular scenario of simulation was designed by considering any possible target location and extensive available zones for positioning the architecture sensors in the environment of simulations. This fact ensures the versatility of the procedure for its application to indoor and outdoor environments.

In Figure 2, the term TLE represents the Target Location Environment which defines the region where targets are possible to be located. For this simulation, the TLE region extends from 0.5 to 15 m of elevation from the base surface, emulating the operating conditions for a positioning system in the proximity of the ground. TLE region is spatially discretized based on a division of 20 m in x and y coordinates, and 2 m in z coordinate. This ensures the correct evaluation and continuity of the accuracy and convergence analysis, and the restriction in the total number of the studied points.

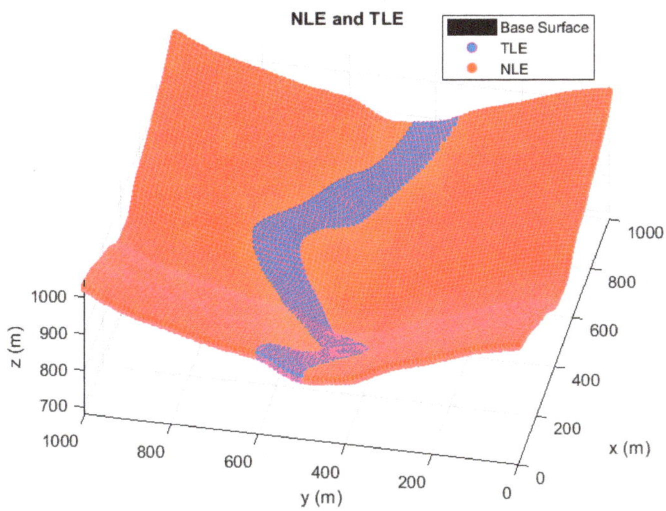


**Figure 2.** The scenario of simulations. The reference surface is depicted is grey tones. Node Location Environment (NLE) and Target Location Environment (TLE) regions are respectively shown in orange and purple colors. The discretized points of the TLE zone are the points employed for the optimization of the Time Difference of Arrival (TDOA) architecture performance. In the case of the NLE area, the points shown are only a representation of the area where every sensor can be located.

The NLE area expresses the Node Location Environment, which indicates all possible sensor locations. In the case of the NLE region, the height of the sensors is limited in the range of 3 to 10 m from the base surface, depicting for a typical outdoor LPS implementation. The discretization of the NLE region depends on the codification of the individuals of the GA, precisely on the longitude of the chromosomes implemented. In this way, the resolution of the NLE area varies in the three Cartesian coordinates from 0.5 to 1 m, alluring a fine setting in the optimization of each sensor.

Tables 1 and 2 show the principal parameters of configuration for the positioning system and the GA characteristics applied for the optimization.

**Table 1.** Parameters of configuration for the positioning system operation. Their selection is based on [19,34].

| Parameter | Value |
|---|---|
| Transmission power | 100 W |
| Mean noise power | –94 dBm |
| Frequency of emission | 1090 MHz |
| Bandwidth | 100 MHz |
| Path loss exponent | 2.05 |
| Antennae gains | Unity |
| Time-Frequency product | 1 |

**Table 2.** Configuration of the principal elements of the Genetic Algorithm (GA).

| GA | Selection |
|---|---|
| Population size | 90 |
| Selection technique | Tournament 2 |
| % Elitism | 5 |
| Crossover technique | Single-point |
| % Mutation | 3 |
| Convergence criteria | 80% individuals equals |

Values presented in Table 1 were chosen in an attempt to stand for a generic positioning technology, expressed by the typical parameters of transmission power, frequency of emission and bandwidth. The configuration of the GA shown in Table 2 has been the subject of deep analysis, looking for the trade-off between the fitness function maximization and convergence speed.

In the following paragraphs and figures, the results after the optimization process are shown for distributions of 5 sensors. Firstly, in order to highlight the importance of the sensor distribution, a random sensor placement is evaluated in terms of accuracy and convergence under a sensor failure in Figures 3 and 4.

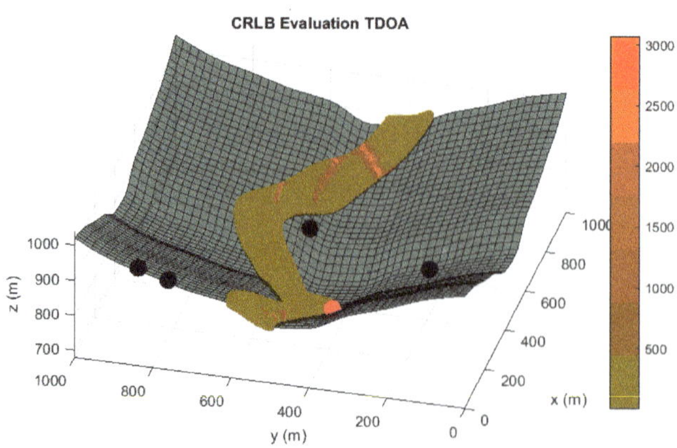


**Figure 3.** Accuracy analysis in terms of Cramer Rao Lower Bound (CRLB) in meters for a random sensor distribution of five sensors, under the assumption of one randomly malfunction sensor. Black spheres indicate the location of active sensors and red spheres highlights the sensor which is not available. Red tones in the color bar indicate bad accuracy evaluations, while green tones imply acceptable accuracy values.

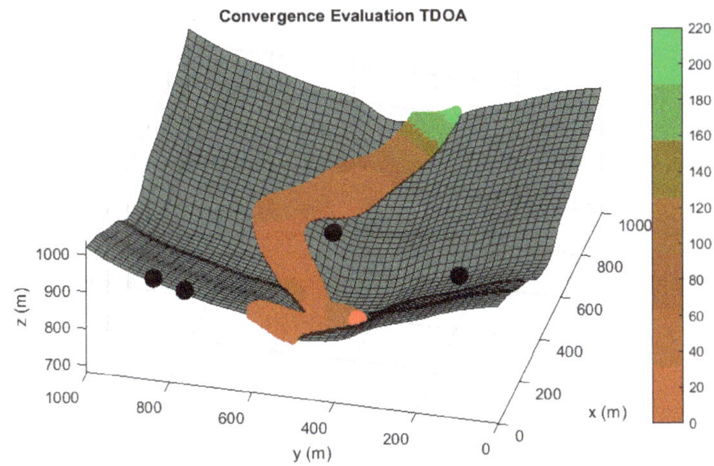


**Figure 4.** Convergence radius analysis in meters for a random sensor distribution of 5 sensors, under the assumption of one randomly malfunction sensor. The convergence radius represents the maximum radius of the sphere of convergence in which every inside point used as initial iterating point of the positioning algorithm guarantees the unequivocal position determination by using the four available sensors. It represents the same operating condition than Figure 2. Red tones in the color bar indicate bad convergence radius values, while green tones imply acceptable convergence magnitudes.

As it is shown, the performance of this sensor distribution is not acceptable for any positioning service. The results for the optimized sensor placement with failure consideration, 5 sensors nominal operating conditions and convergence maximization (Case I) are provided in Figures 5 and 6 when one of the sensors is not available.

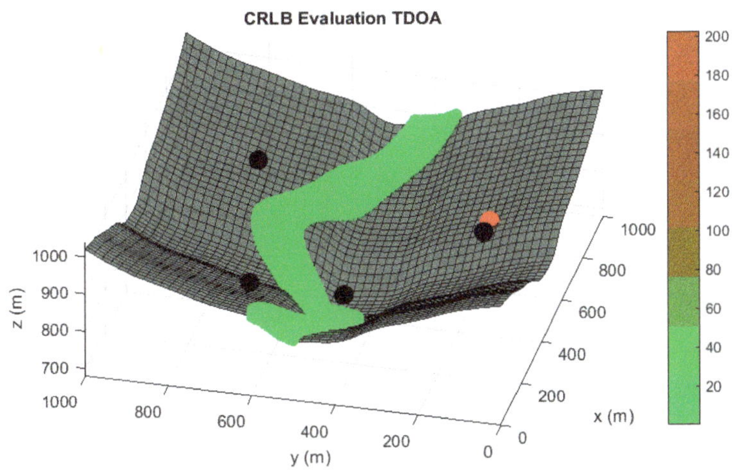


**Figure 5.** Accuracy analysis in terms of CRLB in meters for the optimized distribution of 5 sensors under possible failure. The condition represented corresponds with the Case I - Sensor Fail 1 of Table 3. Red tones in the color bar indicate badly accuracy evaluations, while green tones imply acceptable accuracy values.

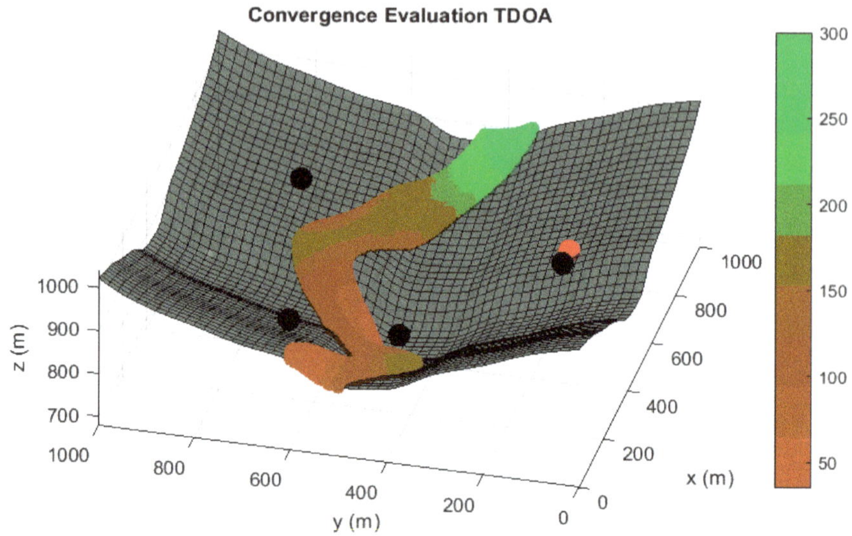


**Figure 6.** Convergence radius analysis in meters for the optimized distribution of 5 sensors under possible failure. The condition represented corresponds with the Case I - Sensor Fail 5 of Table 3. Red tones in the color bar indicate badly convergence radius values, while green tones imply acceptable convergence magnitudes.

The benefits of the consideration of the sensor failure in the architecture design have been shown through the differences in accuracy and convergence from the Figures 2–5. However, a comparison of the performance of the methodology proposed in this paper with a conventional optimized node distribution in which the failure conditions are not considered is needed to conclude the beauty of the technique. In Table 3, we set the parameters considered in each optimization considering nominal operation, failure conditions and convergence (Case I) and only nominal operating conditions (Case II). Case II match up with the GA optimization that we previously proposed in [21].

**Table 3.** Definition of the parameters considered for optimization in Case I and Case II.

| Parameter Considered | Case I | Case II |
|---|---|---|
| Nominal Operating Conditions (5 sensors distribution) | ✔ | ✔ |
| Failure Conditions (4 sensors distributions) | ✔ | X |
| Convergence Maximization | ✔ | X |

In Table 4, a comparison between the optimized sensor distribution for sensor failure (Case I) and the optimized sensor placement of 5 sensors without malfunction consideration and convergence maximization (Case II) is supplied. It should be stressed that this last optimization is carried out through a fitness function with the direct evaluation of the CRLB for 5 sensors and the last term of the Equation (8).

**Table 4.** Comparative between the optimizations of Case I and II.

| Sensor Distributions | Sensor Fail | CRLB Evaluation TDOA (meters) | | | Convergence Evaluation (meters) | | |
|---|---|---|---|---|---|---|---|
| | | Max | Mean | Min | Max | Mean | Min |
| Case I | Sensor 1 | 62.408 | 0.651 | 0.233 | 300 | 138.684 | 35 |
| | Sensor 2 | 133.556 | 0.875 | 0.216 | 240 | 125.786 | 40 |
| | Sensor 3 | 117.304 | 0.627 | 0.223 | 280 | 154.237 | 40 |
| | Sensor 4 | 191.480 | 2.005 | 0.196 | 300 | 138.851 | 35 |
| | Sensor 5 | 188.676 | 7.425 | 0.237 | 220 | 129.149 | 4 |
| | None | 0.795 | 0.326 | 0.154 | 300 | 140.229 | 40 |
| Case II | Sensor 1 | 206.049 | 1.340 | 0.225 | 240 | 103.711 | 2 |
| | Sensor 2 | 159.772 | 1.512 | 0.149 | 280 | 84.650 | 2 |
| | Sensor 3 | 65.487 | 1.688 | 0.169 | 220 | 102.037 | 4 |
| | Sensor 4 | 199.168 | 0.629 | 0.182 | 260 | 113.604 | 2 |
| | Sensor 5 | 2340.42 | 9.674 | 0.181 | 240 | 70.850 | 2 |
| | None | 0.872 | 0.312 | 0.143 | 300 | 128.306 | 10 |

Tables 4 and 5 show the importance of the optimization of the sensor distribution under possible sensor failure. This feature is especially remarkable in the analysis of the convergence radius when some of the sensors are not available for positioning.

**Table 5.** Comparative between the optimizations of Case I and II. Values presented show the comparison in relative terms of the failure consideration distribution regarding the optimization for normal operation of the system.

| Performance Analysis | | Case I | Case II | Sensor Distribution: Case I vs Case II |
|---|---|---|---|---|
| Mean CRLB Evaluation TDOA (meters) | Failure conditions | 2.316 | 2.969 | −22.0 % |
| | Non-Failure conditions | 0.326 | 0.312 | +4.3 % |
| Mean Convergence Evaluation (meters) | Failure conditions | 137.341 | 94.970 | +30.9 % |
| | Non-Failure conditions | 140.229 | 128.306 | +8.5 % |

The results of these tables reveal that the optimization carried out in Case I not only minimizes the CRLB (i.e. maximum achievable accuracy based on the conditions of operation) when only 4 sensors are accessible, it also maximizes the region where the Taylor-based positioning algorithm is able to operate (together with alliterative methods).

Optimizations with failure-consideration (Case I) increase the radius of convergence by 30.9 % in failure conditions while they also experience a boost of 8.5% in this confidence interval in the normal operating condition of five sensors availability. This is due to the convergence radius maximization in the failure-consideration optimization which is not considered in conventional sensor deployment methodologies. This shows that an increase in this confidence interval in the distributions of four sensors has also a direct effect in the convergence radius of the five-sensor normal operating distribution of the failure-consideration optimization.

The beauty of this combined multi-objective optimization is that the accuracy of the four-sensor combinations in failure conditions has been increased by 22% while the accuracy of the normal operating five sensor distribution (Case I) has been reduced by less than 5% with regards to conventional node deployments (Case II) that only consider the five-sensor optimization.

Furthermore, the achievement of higher values of the convergence radius in the failure-consideration optimization enhances availability and security in failure conditions by solving the ambiguity of two valid mathematical solutions and by increasing the confidence interval of applying Taylor-Based positioning algorithms in normal operating conditions with regards to conventional node deployment methodologies.

This new optimization procedure considering sensor failures does guarantee the robustness of the positioning system in complex conditions of operations, and the design of architectures considering these situations.

## 6. Discussion

The location of sensors in LPS has been an active topic of research over the last few years [3,13,21–24]. This is a consequence of its direct relation with the accuracy, stability and robustness of wireless local sensor networks. Conventional approaches to the optimal node distributions have considered the best location of the sensors for nominal operating conditions.

Nevertheless, in actual implementations of the LPS, some sensors are possibly denied for positioning due to the presence of obstacles that disturb signals introducing adverse effects such as multipath or signal deterioration. Furthermore, a possible sensor malfunctioning introducing noise in the measurements must be considered.

These facts have not been studied in previous sensor distribution optimizations. In this work, we propose for the first time in the authors' best knowledge a node deployment methodology that enhances position determination in case of a sensor failure. Additionally, we apply this process to the more restrictive TDOA system to unequivocally determine target location, i.e. five-sensor TDOA deployments. This leads to a sensor-failure configuration in which we first need to solve the position ambiguity determination in systems with only four nodes according to the finding that we proposed in [11].

For this purpose, we performed a multi-objective optimization in a defined 3D irregular scenario in order to extrapolate the results to normal LPS applications. This optimization reduces the CRLB while it is also maximizing the radius of convergence of the Taylor-Based algorithm that we use for the target location determination.

Results show the beauty and importance of this new technique as it is able to enhance the system behavior in failure conditions with regards to only nominal optimizations. This is particularly remarkable since conventional optimization approaches are only focused in nominal operating conditions of LPS and they can suffer from temporal unavailability that can motivate important drawbacks in autonomous navigation.

## 7. Conclusions

Local Positioning Systems have emerged over the last few years for high-demanded accurate applications. Among them, time-based positioning architectures become predominant for its robustness, stability and trade-off between accuracy and complexity.

In this paper, we propose a method to guarantee system availability under sensor failure. This is a key factor for the real operation of LPS as a consequence of the possible ineffective link between target and sensors in complex environments and possible sensor malfunctioning.

In order to simulate an actual operation environment, we have defined a 3D irregular scenario consisting of a five-sensor deployment of a TDOA architecture. This configuration validates the methodology proposed for terrestrial and aerial applications in indoor and outdoor environments. In TDOA architectures, an unequivocal target location can be determined with a minimum of five sensors according to mathematical standards. However, we have proved that the ambiguity in the position determination with four sensors can be solved by the used of Taylor-Based positioning algorithms in a convergence region around the true target location which, in practice, corresponds with the maximization of the two possible solutions distance.

The achievement of this disambiguation can be obtained through an optimized sensor distribution. The node deployment must also minimize the time measurement uncertainties which are characterized by means of the CRLB. For this reason, we implement a multi-objective optimization for the combined maximization of the accuracy and convergence under each possible sensor failure condition. In addition, the optimization needs to guarantee the reduction of the uncertainties for the nominal performance with five sensors.

Results show that the proposed method can attain both accuracy and convergence requirements under every possible sensor failure condition. The global optimization with five sensors without sensor failure consideration overcomes the five-sensor deployment optimization with failure consideration in terms of medium accuracy during nominal operation by less than 5%. In contrast, in circumstances where some of the sensors are not available and only 4 sensors can be applied in the target position calculation, the optimization considering sensor failure increases the average values of convergence region size and accuracy by 30.9% and 22% respectively, regarding the non-failure optimization. These results show the importance of considering the anomaly cases of sensor failure during the LPS node distribution optimization in order to guarantee availability and operation quality in high-demanding accuracy applications.

**Author Contributions:** Conceptualization, J.D.-G. and R.Á.; Formal analysis, H.P.; Investigation, J.D.-G. and R.Á.; Methodology, J.D.-G.; Project administration, H.P.; Resources, R.Á. and N.P.-F.; Software, R.Á. and J.D.-G.; Supervision, H.P.; Validation, H.P. and N.P.-F.; Visualization, R.Á.; Writing—original draft, J.D.-G. and R.Á.; Writing—review & editing, H.P. and N.P.-F. All authors have read and agreed to the published version of the manuscript.

**Funding:** This research was funded by the University of León under the program of stimulating open access publishing. Part of this work has been developed in the project of the Spanish Ministry of Economy, Industry and Competitiveness grant number DPI2016-79960-C3-2-P.

**Conflicts of Interest:** The authors declare no conflict of interest.

## Abbreviations

The following abbreviations are used in this manuscript:

| | |
|---|---|
| AGVs | Automatic Ground Vehicles |
| CRLB | Cramer Rao Lower Bound |
| FIM | Fisher Information Matrix |
| GA | Genetic Algorithm |
| GNSS | Global Navigation Satellite Systems |
| LPS | Local Positioning Systems |
| NLOS | Non-Line-of-Sight |
| PDOP | Position Dilution of Precision |
| RMSE | Root Mean Square Error |
| TDOA | Time Difference of Arrival |
| TOA | Time of Arrival |
| TS | Target Sensor |
| UAVs | Unmanned Aerial Vehicles |
| WGN | White Gaussian Noise |

## References

1. Lin, S.; Cheng, K.; Wang, K.; Yang, K. Visual Localizer: Outdoor Localization Based on ConvNet Descriptor and Global Optimization for Visually Impaired Pedestrians. *Sensors* **2018**, *18*, 2476. [CrossRef]
2. Cheng, R.; Wang, K.; Lin, S.; Hu, W.; Yang, K.; Huang, X.; Li, H.; Sun, D.; Bai, J. Panoramic Annular Localizer: Tackling the Variation Challenges of Outdoor Localization Using Panoramic Annular Images and Active Deep Descriptors. In Proceedings of the IEEE Intelligent Transportation Systems Conference (ITSC), Auckland, New Zealand, 27–30 October 2019.
3. Shen, H.; Ding, S.; Dasgupta, S.; Zhao, C. Multiple Source Localization in Wireless Sensor Networks Based on Time of Arrival Measurement. *IEEE Trans. Signal Process.* **2014**, *62*, 1938–1949. [CrossRef]
4. Yiu, S.; Dashti, M.; Claussen, H.; Perez-Cruz, F. Wireless RSSI Fingerprinting Localization. *Signal Process.* **2017**, *131*, 235–244. [CrossRef]

5. Lindgren, D.; Hendeby, G.; Gustafsson, F. Distributed Localization Using Acoustic Doppler. *Signal Process.* **2015**, *107*, 43–53. [CrossRef]
6. Rong, P.; Sichitiu, M.L. Angle of Arrival Localization for Wireless Sensor Networks. In Proceedings of the 2006 3rd Annual IEEE Communications Society on Sensor and Ad Hoc Communications and Networks, Reston, VA, USA, 28–28 September 2006; pp. 374–382.
7. Sackenreuter, B.; Hadaschik, N.; Faßbinder, M.; Mutschler, C. Low-complexity PDoA-based localization. In Proceedings of the 2016 International Conference on Indoor Positioning and Indoor Navigation (IPIN), Alcalá de Henares, Spain, 4–7 October 2016; pp. 1–6.
8. Yin, J.; Wan, Q.; Yang, S.; Ho, K.C. A Simple and Accurate TDOA-AOA Localization Method Using Two Stations. *IEEE Signal Process Lett.* **2016**, *23*, 144–148. [CrossRef]
9. Shen, J.; Molisch, A.F.; Salmi, J. Accurate Passive Location Estimation Using TOA Measurements. *IEEE Trans. Wireless Commun.* **2012**, *11*, 2182–2192. [CrossRef]
10. Lanxin, L.; So, H.C.; Frankie, K.W.; Chan, K.W.; Chan, Y.T.; Ho, K.C. A New Constrained Weighted Least Squares Algorithm for TDOA-based Localization. *Signal Process.* **2013**, *11*, 2872–2878.
11. He, S.; Dong, X. High-Accuracy Localization Platform Using Asynchronous Time Difference of Arrival Technology. *IEEE Trans. Instrum. Meas.* **2017**, *66*, 1728–1742. [CrossRef]
12. Priyantha, N.B.; Balakrishnan, H.; Demaine, E.D.; Teller, S. Mobile-assisted Localization in Wireless Sensor Networks. In Proceedings of the IEEE 24th Annual Joint Conference of the IEEE Computer and Communications Societies, Miami, FL, USA, 13–17 March 2005; pp. 172–183.
13. Díez-González, J.; Álvarez, R.; Sánchez-González, L.; Fernández-Robles, L.; Pérez, H.; Castejón-Limas, M. 3D Tdoa Problem Solution with Four Receiving Nodes. *Sensors* **2019**, *19*, 2892. [CrossRef]
14. Yang, K.; Xu, Z. A Quadratic Constraint Total Least-squares Algorithm for Hyperbolic Location. *I.J. Commun. Netw. Syst. Sci.* **2008**, *2*, 130–135. [CrossRef]
15. Yunlong, T.; Jinling, W.; Qi, H. Mathematical minimum of Geometric Dilution of Precision (GDOP) for dual-GNSS constellations. *Adv. Space Res.* **2016**, *57*, 183–188.
16. Huang, B.; Xie, L.; Yang, Z. TDOA-Based Source Localization With Distance-Dependent Noises. *IEEE Trans. Wireless Commun.* **2015**, *14*, 468–480. [CrossRef]
17. Lanzisera, S.; Zats, D.; Pister, K.S.J. Radio Frequency Time-of-Flight Distance Measurement for Low-Cost Wireless Sensor Localization. *IEEE Sens. J.* **2011**, *11*, 837–845. [CrossRef]
18. Kaune, R.; Hörst, J.; Koch, W. Accuracy Analysis for TDOA Localization in Sensor Networks. In Proceedings of the 14th International Conference on Information Fusion, Chicago, IL, USA, 5–8 July 2011.
19. Rappaport, T.S. *Wireless Communications-Principles and Practice*; Prentice Hall: Upper Saddle River, NJ, USA, 2002.
20. Álvarez, R.; Díez-González, J.; Alonso, E.; Fernández-Robles, L.; Castejón-Limas, M.; Perez, H. Accuracy Analysis in Sensor Networks for Asynchronous Positioning Methods. *Sensors* **2019**, *13*, 3024. [CrossRef] [PubMed]
21. Díez-González, J.; Álvarez, R.; González-Bárcena, D.; Sánchez-González, L.; Castejón-Limas, M.; Perez, H. Genetic Algorithm Approach to the 3D Node Localization in TDOA Systems. *Sensors* **2019**, *19*, 3880. [CrossRef]
22. Peng, B.; Li, L. An Improved Localization Algorithm Based on Genetic Agorithm in Wireless Sensor Networks. *Cogitive Neurodynamics* **2015**, *9*, 249–256. [CrossRef]
23. Domingo-Perez, F.; Lazaro-Galilea, J.L.; Wieser, A.; Martin-Gorostiza, E.; Salido-Monzu, D.; de la Llana, A. Sensor Placement Determination for Range-difference Positioning Using Evolutionary Multi-objective Optimization. *Expert Syst. Appl.* **2016**, *47*, 95–105. [CrossRef]
24. Zhang, Q.; Wang, J.; Jin, C.; Ye, J.; Ma, C.; Zhang, W. Genetic Algorithm Based Wireless Sensor Network Localization. In Proceedings of the Fourth International Conference on Natural Computation, Jinan, China, 18–20 October 2008.
25. Mnasri, S.; Thaljaoui, A.; Nasri, N.; Val, T. A Genetic Glgorithm-based Approach to Optimize the Coverage and the Localizationin the Wireless Audio-sensors Networks. In Proceedings of the IEEE International Symposium on Networks, Hammamet, Tunisia, 13–15 May 2015.
26. Laguna, M.; Jiménez, A.; Seco, F. Diversified Local Search for the Optimal Layout of Beacons in an Indoor Positioning System. *IIE Trans.* **2007**, *41*, 247–259. [CrossRef]

27. Rajagopal, N.; Chayapathy, S.; Sinopoli, B.; Rowe, A. Beacon Placement for Range-based Indoor Localization. In Proceedings of the 2016 International Conference on Indoor Positioning and Indoor Navigation (IPIN), Alcalá de Henares, Spain, 4–7 October 2016.
28. Stoica, P.; Li, J. Source Localization from Range-Difference Measurements. *IEEE Signal Process Mag.* **2006**, *23*, 63–69. [CrossRef]
29. Bakhoum, E.G. Closed-Form Solution of Hyperbolic Geolocation Equations. *IEEE Trans. Aerosp. Electron. Syst.* **2006**, *42*, 1396–1404. [CrossRef]
30. Bonan, J.; Xiaosu, X.; Zhang, T. Robust Time-Difference-of-Arrival (TDOA) Localization Using Weighted Least Squares with Cone Tangent Plane Constraint. *Sensors* **2018**, *18*, 778. [CrossRef] [PubMed]
31. Ruz, M.L.; Garrido, J.; Jiménez, J.; Virrankoski, R.; Vázquez, F. Simulation Tool for the Analysis of Cooperative Localization Algorithms for Wireless Sensor Networks. *Sensors* **2019**, *19*, 2866. [CrossRef] [PubMed]
32. Kowalski, M.; Willett, P.; Fair, T.; Bar-Shalom, Y. CRLB for Estimating Time-Varying Rotational Biases in Passive Sensors. *IEEE Trans. Aerosp. Electron. Syst.* **2019**, *56*, 343–355. [CrossRef]
33. Hu, D.; Chen, S.; Bai, H.; Zhao, C.; Luo, L. CRLB for Joint Estimation of TDOA, Phase, FDOA, and Doppler Rate. *The J. Eng.* **2019**, *21*, 7628–7631. [CrossRef]
34. Yaro, A.S.; Sha'ameri, A.Z. Effect of Path Loss Propagation Model on the Position Estimation Accuracy of a 3-Dimensional Minimum Configuration Multilateration System. *Int. J. Integr. Eng.* **2018**, *10*, 35–42.

sensors

MDPI

*Article*

# Accuracy Analysis in Sensor Networks for Asynchronous Positioning Methods

**Rubén Álvarez [1], Javier Díez-González [2], Efrén Alonso [1], Laura Fernández-Robles [2], Manuel Castejón-Limas [2,*] and Hilde Perez [2]**

[1] Positioning Department, Drotium, Universidad de León, 24071 León, Spain
[2] Department of Mechanical, Computer and Aerospace Engineering, Universidad de León, 24071 León, Spain
* Correspondence: manuel.castejon@unileon.es

Received: 6 June 2019; Accepted: 8 July 2019; Published: 9 July 2019

**Abstract:** The accuracy requirements for sensor network positioning have grown over the last few years due to the high precision demanded in activities related with vehicles and robots. Such systems involve a wide range of specifications which must be met through positioning devices based on time measurement. These systems have been traditionally designed with the synchronization of their sensors in order to compute the position estimation. However, this synchronization introduces an error in the time determination which can be avoided through the centralization of the measurements in a single clock in a coordinate sensor. This can be found in typical architectures such as Asynchronous Time Difference of Arrival (A-TDOA) and Difference-Time Difference of Arrival (D-TDOA) systems. In this paper, a study of the suitability of these new systems based on a Cramér-Rao Lower Bound (CRLB) evaluation was performed for the first time under different 3D real environments for multiple sensor locations. The analysis was carried out through a new heteroscedastic noise variance modelling with a distance-dependent Log-normal path loss propagation model. Results showed that A-TDOA provided less uncertainty in the root mean square error (RMSE) in the positioning, while D-TDOA reduced the standard deviation and increased stability all over the domain.

**Keywords:** sensor networks; TDOA; asynchronous; Cramér–Rao lower bound; heteroscedasticity

## 1. Introduction

Over the past few years, positioning systems have experienced a growing importance due to the wide range of applications they present in numerous civil and military fields. Positioning methods based on satellite systems, e.g., global navigation satellite systems (GNSS), offer accurate precision with global coverage but still present accuracy issues for specific crucial tasks such as high-precision trajectories or indoor navigation. These issues have recently attracted much attention with the advent of unmanned transportation.

Positioning systems have traditionally been classified into four main groups: Time of Arrival systems (TOA) [1,2], Time Difference of Arrival systems (TDOA) [3,4], Angle of Arrival systems (AOA) [5,6], Received Signal Strength Indication systems (RSSI) [7,8], or a combination of them [9,10]. Methods based on time measurement (i.e., TOA and TDOA) have been the main exponents of recent developments, on account of their robustness, universality, and reliability, in addition to their great accuracy and relative simplicity.

Time measurements have usually been obtained in two different ways. The most common one measures time intervals by synchronizing emitter and receiver clocks, which is mandatory in the case of TOA systems. The other option comes from the synchronization of receivers, and is optional in TDOA systems. This fact significantly affects the accuracy of the positioning determination process due to the appearance of clock instabilities and the introduction of small time-offsets during the process of synchronization among elements.

Owing to the challenging accuracy requirements to be met in sensor networks, the minimization of key factors that increase the uncertainty associated with the calculation of the position is an imperative task. Location systems based on TOA processes present disadvantages in this matter. Their accuracy may be in the order of 10 cm [11–13], but time errors which can occur during the synchronization process significantly increase the uncertainties associated with the position calculation [14–16].

Conventional TDOA methods have been traditionally dependent on global synchronization amongst the receivers, reaching higher accuracy levels requiring less energy than TOA systems. Nevertheless, synchronization instabilities are still present and the system complexity is higher than TOA architectures.

Notwithstanding these previous tendencies, a new pattern has been developed over the last few years, which advocates for the implementation of asynchronous architectures wherein a single clock is used to measure the time differences of arrival characteristic of TDOA systems. These new systems could overcome synchronization disadvantages in TDOA systems with less architecture complexity and higher sensor ubication flexibility, and they are key to this work. The main advantages of these new methods would include the elimination of the synchronization among receivers and the resulting error introduced in the measurement process [17,18].

In recent years, two different asynchronous systems have been proposed. Asynchronous TDOA [17] and difference-time TDOA [18]. These systems display an architecture based on a coordinator sensor and a collection of worker sensors. The coordinator sensor is in charge of processing the time measurements. The worker sensors collaborate in the determination of time differences. These new architectures avoid the necessity of a clock built into every sensor of the system. This fact reduces the overall costs and the complexity of the system and boosts accuracy by eliminating the interaction among sensor clocks. All these factors enhance indoor and low-level flight sensor positioning accuracy, a key factor that is driving the increasing popularity of these methods.

The aim of this article was to develop for the first time, to the extent of our knowledge, a methodology to select the suitability of these two asynchronous TDOA systems under different sensor placements in a 3D, real environment. This methodology must consider that vehicle navigation in local positioning systems (LPS) is highly affected by noisy environments, thus system evaluations must be performed at a high accuracy level even where time measurements are corrupted by noise.

Cramér–Rao Lower Bound (CRLB) is a commonly used estimator to determine the lowest possible uncertainty associated with a positioning process in line-of-sight (LOS) [19,20] and non-line-of-sight (NLOS) [21] conditions. This method models measurement uncertainties through the variance associated to every sensor range estimation.

Conventional models consider the presence of a constant variance associated to each time measurement [22]. However, to attain a higher level of accuracy in the results, it is imperative to introduce the distance between emitter and receiver in the model allowing for heteroscedasticity in time measurements [23,24]. This phenomenon is especially important in cases with medium and high signal-to-noise ratios (SNRs) in the receivers. If the SNR is reduced, the positioning pulse detection becomes significantly hampered, leading to drastic time measurement errors which reduce the accuracy of the positioning system [25].

Therefore, the hypothesis of heteroscedastic variances needs to be implemented on the basis of a propagation loss model over the signal path between the emitter and the receivers [26,27], depending on the positioning methodology and the characteristics of communication amongst every single sensor of the system.

The remainder of this paper is organized as follows. In Section 2, a comparison of the main characteristics of asynchronous TDOA architectures studied is developed. Section 3 covers the main path-loss models used to calculate the SNR. Section 4 includes a study of the Cramér–Rao Lower Bound, based on a matrix model implemented for each system architecture. Section 5 gathers the conclusions obtained from all the studies, along with the election of the best system. Lastly, Section 6 presents the conclusions and completes the article.

## 2. Asynchronous TDOA Methods

In this section, the asynchronous TDOA methods will be introduced. Neither of these methods need to synchronize any element of the system, using only one clock to measure the differences in times of the TDOA system. The notation used throughout the study is the one described hereafter: TS defines the location of the Target Sensor, Coordinate Sensor (CS) represents the position of the receiver in charge of the time measurements, Worker Sensors (WS) are the rest of emitters/receivers, $N$ is the total number of WS, and additionally, a CS must be considered, $t_{START}$ and $t_{END}$ represent the start and the end of the time measurement process in the CS.

### *2.1. A-TDOA*

In Figure 1, an A-TDOA architecture is presented [17]. It proposes a passive positioning system based on one single clock in the CS node, using the positioned sensor as signal repeater.

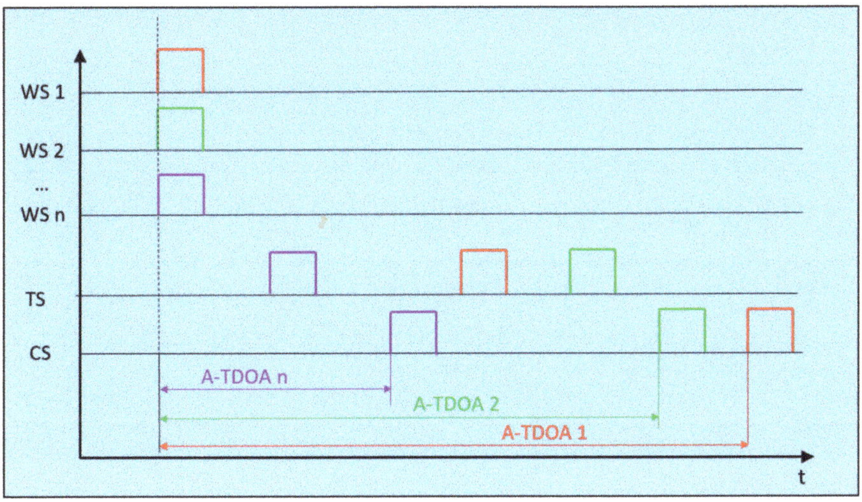


**Figure 1.** Asynchronous Time Difference of Arrival (A-TDOA) system timing diagram. Example of architecture operation with $n$ Worker sensors (WS) nodes ($n$ must be at least equal to 4). Rectangular positioning pulses are emitted from the WS nodes, and when the arrival of the signal to the Target Sensor (TS) node is produced, signals are instantaneously retransmitted to the Coordinate Sensor (CS) node. When the process is completed, A-TDOA time measurements are accomplished.

Positioning pulses are emitted by WS nodes, reaching the CS node with successive time differences which lead to the beginning of the time measurement associated with each WS–CS ($t_{START_i}$). Conversely, the signal emitted by each WS node is received by the TS node in charge of sending again these signals to the Cs node ($t_{END_i}$). When the signal is received, the time measurement process comes to an end, completing the time measurement process of each WS–CS pair. The TDOA measurement in terms of distance is represented by the following relation.

$$A - TDOA_i = c\left(t_{END_i} - t_{START_i}\right) - \|WS_i - CS\| \quad i \in [1, N] \tag{1}$$

### 2.2. D-TDOA

The D-TDOA method is based on the combination of a traditional TDOA system and a round trip time (RTT) method, accomplishing the goal of obtaining the time difference measurements with only one clock [18], as shown in Figure 2.

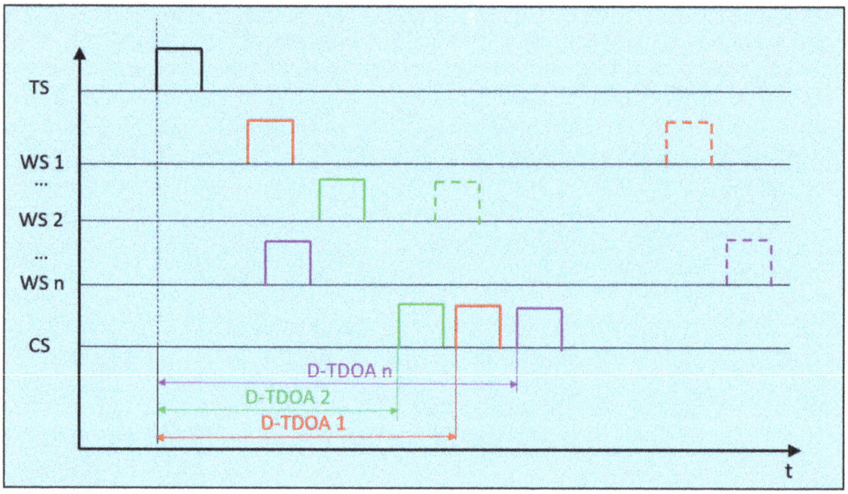


**Figure 2.** Difference-Time Difference of Arrival (D-TDOA) timing diagram. Example of architecture operation with $n$ WS nodes (with a minimum number of 4). The positioning target pulse is received at every WS node of the system that retransmits it towards the CS node. D-TDOA time measurements are completed by a round-trip transmission (RTT) process between each pair of WS–CS nodes.

Positioning pulses are broadcast by the TS node, reaching the CS node at $t_{START}$. This temporal reference is common to all the time measurements realized by the method. Meanwhile, the TS node emission is received at the WS nodes, which resend it to the CS node ($t_{END_i}$), completing the time difference measurement of each WS–CS pair of nodes. Lastly, the pulse is emitted from the CS node to WS nodes with the aim of calculating the processing time on each WS node. The TDOA measurement in terms of distance is represented by the following relation:

$$D - TDOA_i = c\left(t_{END_i} - t_{START}\right) - \|WS_i - CS\|, i \in [1, N] \tag{2}$$

While $A - TDOA_i$ and $D - TDOA_i$ hold similar equations, the time measurement recordings and positioning pulse travels differ significantly from one method to the other. These characteristics are analyzed in the following sections.

## 3. Heteroscedastic Noise Model

In this section, a noise variance distance-dependent model is implemented associated to the process of location in asynchronous TDOAs system, allowing for a better reproducibility of real conditions.

The process starts with the TOA variance range estimate due to the noisy environments. Next, the TDOA variance range estimate is defined based on time measurement correlation assumptions. The heteroscedastic noise variance model is completed with the path-loss propagation model implementation that best fit with the multiple sensor network's characteristics.

Amongst the main sources of ranging errors of positioning systems based on time measurements, the most important for TDOA asynchronous techniques is the uncertainty induced by white Gaussian noise (WGN) in the propagation channel. This problem has been deeply studied for TOA architectures, quantifying it with the CRLB [25]:

$$\sigma_i^2 \geq \frac{c^2}{(2\pi B)^2 \cdot t_s B \cdot SNR_i}, \ i = 1, \ldots, M \tag{3}$$

where $\boldsymbol{M}$ is the total number of sensors, $\sigma_i^2$ is the receptor range estimate variance, $c$ is the pulse propagation velocity, B is the bandwidth, $t_S$ is the length of time during which the bandwidth is occupied, and $SNR_i$ is the signal-to-noise ratio for each receiver.

The majority of range estimation architectures consider the product $t_s B$ approximately unitary. This, together with the hypothesis of high levels of SNR at the receivers and efficient estimator, enables the derivation of the following relation for a TOA variance estimation [23,24].

$$\sigma_i^2 = \frac{c^2}{B^2 \cdot SNR_i}, \ i = 1, \ldots, M \tag{4}$$

Based on the TOA variance estimation, the implementation for TDOA systems is made under some assumptions. He and Dong [17] proposed that the time measurements in asynchronous TDOA architectures are considered independent. Consequently, the off-diagonal elements of the covariance matrix associated with the Gaussian noise modelling are null. According to Kaune et al. [19], the variance associated with a difference distance between two nodes is the sum of the variances for each node, under the assumption of uncorrelated time measurements.

Hence:

$$\begin{gathered} \sigma_{ij}^2 = \sigma_i^2 + \sigma_j^2 \\ i = 1, \ldots, M \\ j = 1, \ldots, M \end{gathered} \tag{5}$$

Consequently,

$$\begin{gathered} \sigma_{ij}^2 = \frac{c^2}{B^2}\left(\frac{1}{SNR_i} + \frac{1}{SNR_j}\right) \\ i = 1, \ldots, M \\ j = 1, \ldots, M \end{gathered} \tag{6}$$

In Equation (6), the $SNR$ associated with each receiver mainly depends on the power emission, the transmission frequency, and environment. This last aspect is characterized by means of path-loss propagation models for indoor and outdoor environments. Large-scale models predict the mean signal strength in LOS environments based on the distance between emitter/receiver and the characteristics of the signal. Small-scale or fading models characterize the rapid fluctuations of the signal when the distance of the emitter/receiver is short, in both conditions (LOS and NLOS) [27].

Multiple sensor networks with high location accuracy are used in many applications. However, in the majority of systems, path loss during operation presents a higher level of dependency on large distances of the emitter/receiver and LOS propagation.

Consequently, large-scale models seem more appropriate for this analysis. Assuming invariant power transmission and homogeneity in the operation of receivers, the following relations are established:

$$SNR_i = \frac{P_{R_i}}{P_n} = \frac{\frac{P_T}{PL_i}}{P_n} = \frac{P_T}{P_n} \cdot \frac{1}{PL_i} \ i = 1, \ldots, N \tag{7}$$

where $P_T$ is transmission power, $P_{R_i}$ is the received power in each receiver, $PL$ is the path loss, and $P_n$ is the mean noise power, obtained from the Johnson–Nyquist equation:

$$P_n = k_B T_0 B \tag{8}$$

where $k_B$ is the Boltzmann's constant, $T_0$ is the absolute temperature of the receiver input, and B is the receiver bandwidth.

Large-scale path loss models have been deeply studied in the last decades for modelling mobile communications. The vast majority of these methods were built under some of these restrictions: emitter and receiver heights, transmission frequency, and emitter–receiver distance, among others. Under these limitations, the modelling of asynchronous TDOA architecture is not possible due to the emitter/receiver's characteristics in multiple sensor networks.

Based on the preceding assumptions, the path loss propagation model selected for the simulation is the Log-normal, which eliminates the restrictions on emitter–receiver geometry.

$$Log - normal: \ PL_i = PL(d_0)\left(\frac{d_i}{d_0}\right)^n \tag{9}$$

The noise model final implementation in the CRLB variance definition is presented below:

$$\begin{gathered} \sigma_{ij}{}^2 = \frac{c^2}{B^2\left(\frac{P_T}{P_n}\right)} PL(d_0)\left[\left[\frac{d_i}{d_0}\right]^n + \left[\frac{d_j}{d_0}\right]^n\right] \\ i = 1, \ldots, M \\ j = 1, \ldots, M \end{gathered} \tag{10}$$

where $d_0$ is the reference distance to the emitter, the basis from which the Log-normal model hypothesis is valid, $PL(d_0)$ is the path loss for this distance, and $n$ is the path loss exponent.

## 4. CRLB Derivation for A-TDOA and D-TDOA Systems

The prediction of the uncertainty associated with the position calculation process is one of the most significant accomplishments in the design and development of positioning systems.

From a statistical point of view, CRLB expresses the minimum variance value of any unbiased estimator of a deterministic parameter. In other words, the CRLB defines the minimum possible uncertainty associated with an estimation process.

$$var\left(\hat{\theta}\right) \geq \frac{1}{FIM} = \frac{1}{E\left[\left[\frac{\partial}{\partial x}\ln f[X;\theta]\right]^2\right]} \tag{11}$$

In this equation, $\hat{\theta}$ is the unbiased estimator for the parameter of study, $FIM$ is the Fisher Information Matrix, $E$ the expectation value of the denominator function, $X$ the parameter measurement vector, $\theta$ is the parameter vector to be estimated, and $f(X;\theta)$ is the probability density function of $X$ for the parameter $\theta$.

Cramér-Rao Lower Bound has proved to be especially suitable in positioning. This is due to its definition based on a prior knowledge possibility of maximum reachable exactitude in terms of the architecture geometry, the environment modelling, and the intrinsic characteristics of measurement instruments. This maximum value reached by the position estimator would be valid as long as it is unbiased and efficient.

In this section, the CRLB is adapted to A-TDOA and D-TDOA architectures. Additionally, the noise variance model introduced in Section 3 is implemented in order to estimate the RMSE in the TS location estimation.

For a TDOA system, time measurements associated with the receivers are modelled by the addition of WGN. In a real environment, the variance associated with this phenomenon depends on the distance between emitter and receiver, inducing heteroscedasticity in data management. In this context, Kaune et al. [19] includes a model of the dependent parameter's variance in the calculation of the inverse of the Fisher Information Matrix (*J*).

$$J = \frac{1}{\sigma^2(TS)}\left(\frac{\partial h(TS)}{\partial TS}\right)^T\left(\frac{\partial h(TS)}{\partial TS}\right) + \frac{1}{2}\frac{1}{\sigma^2(TS)}\left(\frac{\partial \sigma(TS)}{\partial TS}\right)^T\left(\frac{\partial \sigma(TS)}{\partial TS}\right) \tag{12}$$

That can be expressed in matrix form as:

$$J_{mn} = \left(\frac{\partial h(TS)}{\partial x_m}\right)^T R^{-1}(TS)\left(\frac{\partial h(TS)}{\partial x_n}\right) + \frac{1}{2}tr\left(R^{-1}(TS)\left(\frac{\partial R(TS)}{\partial x_m}\right)R^{-1}(TS)\left(\frac{\partial R(TS)}{\partial x_n}\right)\right) \tag{13}$$

where sub-indexes ***m*** and ***n*** refer to the respective row and column of *J*. The column matrix *h(X)* expresses the differences in the Euclidean distances among the TDOA measurements of each pair of receivers:

$$\begin{gathered} h_{A-TDOAi} = \|TS - WS_i\| + \|TS - CS\| - \|WS_i - CS\| \\ i = 1, \ldots, N \end{gathered} \tag{14}$$

$$\begin{gathered} h_{D-TDOAi} = \|TS - WS_i\| + \|WS_i - CS\| - \|TS - CS\| \\ i = 1, \ldots, N \end{gathered} \tag{15}$$

Finally, *R(x)* is the covariance matrix of the system, which is characterized by null off-diagonal elements for both systems, due to the non-correlation among time measurements. The variance modelling was implemented according to the model explained in Section 3, with the following definition for the distances between each asynchronous TDOA system.

$$\begin{gathered} d_{A-TDOA\ i} = \|TS - WS_i\| + \|TS - CS\| \\ d_{A-TDOA\ j=1} = \|WS_i - CS\| \\ i = 1, \ldots, N \end{gathered} \tag{16}$$

$$\begin{gathered} d_{D-TDOA\ i} = \|TS - WS_i\| + 2\|WS_i - CS\| \\ d_{D-TDOA\ j=1} = \|TS - CS\| \\ i = 1, \ldots, N \end{gathered} \tag{17}$$

The uncertainty is evaluated in terms of RMSE, as shown in the following equation (three-dimensional location), where the sub-indexes refer to the diagonal elements of matrix *J*:

$$RMSE = \sqrt{J_{11} + J_{22} + J_{33}} \tag{18}$$

## 5. Simulation Results

In this section, asynchronous TDOA systems A-TDOA and D-TDOA are compared for sensor network positioning. Firstly, a set of global communication parameters are defined in Table 1.

**Table 1.** Architecture parameters for Cramér-Rao Lower Bound (CRLB) study. Communication links amongst elements of Asynchronous Time Difference of Arrival (A-TDOA) and Difference-Time Difference of Arrival (D-TDOA) systems are restricted to these principal parameters. They were selected due to their utilization in similar tracking applications in the aerospace industry [26,27].

| Parameter | Magnitude |
|---|---|
| Frequency of emission | 1090 MHz |
| Bandwidth | 100 MHz |
| Transmission power | 400 W |
| Mean noise power | −94 dBm |

In addition to these parameters, the comparison among architectures was carried out based on unity gain antennas in all system transceivers and on the assumption of full-duplex communication capacity among elements. Furthermore, an assumption of the receive-and-retransmit technique in transceivers operations and a unity frequency–time product in all the architectures' communications was considered.

The results were obtained based on simulations carried out on an irregular surface of 1 km$^2$ (1000 × 1000 m) with an elevation modelled by a normal distribution $N(15,9)$ cm. The space analysis was limited to a height above ground level from 1 to 100 m. Under this assumption, the spatial discretization was 100 m for surface coordinates (Cartesian $x$ and $y$) and 10 m for coordinate $z$.

Additionally, the minimum height of sensor nodes (WS and CS) was restricted to 3 m with the objective of not inducing effects that were not considered by the Log-normal model (specially ground reflections and multipath). The maximum height was also limited to 13 m, but this restriction was related to the size of the supports (less than 10 m).

Lastly, a path loss exponent value of 2.1 was selected as highly recommended in sub-urban environments with medium frequencies [27]. Due to the theoretical approach of the problem, the Free Space Propagation Model (FSPM) was used to obtain $PL(d_0)$.

The comparison among systems (in Table 2) was carried out with five random distributions of receivers, each one with a number of five sensors. This was the minimum number of nodes for a unique three-dimensional location in TDOA architectures.

The best distributions for each system are illustrated in the following images, together with the CRLB evaluation in terms of RMSE at every point of the discretization.

**Table 2.** Node distributions in meters. Five random node distributions were defined in order to analyze the accuracy level of A-TDOA and D-TDOA architectures based on their CRLB system definition. CRLB evaluation does not require a classification of WS and CS nodes.

| Distributions | | $x$ | $y$ | $z$ |
|---|---|---|---|---|
| D.1 | Sensor 1 | 249 | 242 | 3 |
| | Sensor 2 | 254 | 759 | 4 |
| | Sensor 3 | 576 | 500 | 3 |
| | Sensor 4 | 811 | 124 | 13 |
| | Sensor 5 | 879 | 819 | 13 |
| D.2 | Sensor 1 | 72 | 156 | 3 |
| | Sensor 2 | 141 | 854 | 13 |
| | Sensor 3 | 496 | 484 | 3 |
| | Sensor 4 | 810 | 891 | 3 |
| | Sensor 5 | 876 | 133 | 13 |
| D.3 | Sensor 1 | 78 | 911 | 13 |
| | Sensor 2 | 244 | 241 | 13 |
| | Sensor 3 | 516 | 539 | 3 |
| | Sensor 4 | 624 | 655 | 13 |
| | Sensor 5 | 810 | 891 | 3 |
| D.4 | Sensor 1 | 191 | 880 | 10 |
| | Sensor 2 | 435 | 527 | 3 |
| | Sensor 3 | 482 | 198 | 9 |
| | Sensor 4 | 758 | 254 | 3 |
| | Sensor 5 | 782 | 788 | 7 |
| D.5 | Sensor 1 | 148 | 313 | 3 |
| | Sensor 2 | 469 | 621 | 13 |
| | Sensor 3 | 550 | 500 | 3 |
| | Sensor 4 | 750 | 218 | 13 |
| | Sensor 5 | 783 | 944 | 3 |

As it can be seen in Figures 3 and 4, points that are close to the surface or nodes present a higher RMSE. This phenomenon is due to the relative location between nodes and these discretization points, that causes an increase of the influence of time measurements uncertainties in total positioning accuracy.

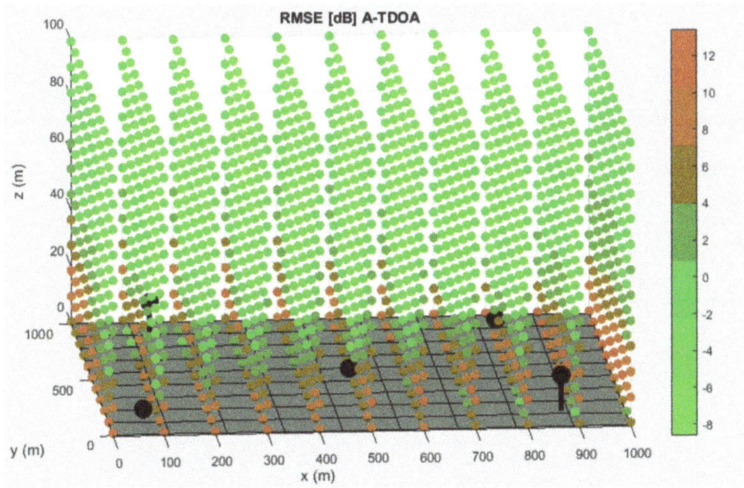


**Figure 3.** Best distribution of Worker Sensor (WS) and Coordinator Sensor (CS) nodes for the A-TDOA system. The base surface is presented as the grey hyperplane located at the bottom of the picture. The nodes are represented by black spheres with their correspondent holder that links them to the base surface. The CRLB evaluation of the discretization points is displayed according to the right-hand side legend.

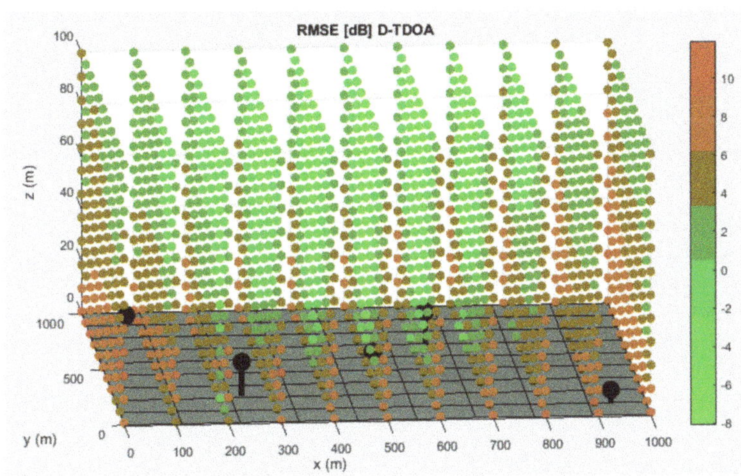


**Figure 4.** Best distribution of Worker Sensor (WS) and Coordinate Sensor (CS) nodes for the D-TDOA system. The base surface is presented as the grey hyperplane located at the bottom of the picture. The nodes are represented by black spheres with their correspondent holder that links them to the base surface. The CRLB evaluation of discretization points is displayed according to the right-hand side legend.

The final simulation results are presented in Table 3.

**Table 3.** RMSE distribution parameters for the five sensor distribution schemes in Table 2 are presented. These data were obtained based on the spatial discretization technique shown in Figures 3 and 4.

| RMSE (dB) | | A-TDOA | D-TDOA |
|---|---|---|---|
| D.1 | Mean | −0.5791 | 2.1446 |
| | Min | −9.3067 | −8.2291 |
| | Max | 21.4022 | 19.1978 |
| | SD | 5.5552 | 4.6881 |
| D.2 | Mean | −0.9528 | 2.3131 |
| | Min | −8.6153 | −7.4459 |
| | Max | 13.4399 | 19.3637 |
| | SD | 4.6718 | 4.1344 |
| D.3 | Mean | 0.0682 | 2.2769 |
| | Min | −8.9972 | −8.0968 |
| | Max | 13.2448 | 11.9421 |
| | SD | 4.9828 | 3.6965 |
| D.4 | Mean | 0.2111 | 2.6452 |
| | Min | −9.1009 | −7.4856 |
| | Max | 17.3846 | 18.3655 |
| | SD | 5.7176 | 4.5620 |
| D.5 | Mean | 0.2524 | 2.2070 |
| | Min | −9.8805 | −8.1964 |
| | Max | 13.3707 | 11.8791 |
| | SD | 5.0180 | 3.8402 |
| Mean of Means RMSE | | −0.2000 | 2.3174 |
| Mean Standard Deviations RMSE | | 5.1891 | 4.1842 |

Based on the results of the simulations, it was shown that the A-TDOA system presented a lower mean RMSE value in every distribution. The minimum RMSE values in each distribution were obtained by the A-TDOA method. In the case of maximum RMSE values, the tendency was not obvious. Finally, it can be observed that the standard deviation in every distribution was lower for the D-TDOA system, which implies a higher stability.

In terms of architecture complexity, A-TDOA systems require an initial step in the emission of the positioning pulses of the WS nodes in order to simultaneously start the process. In contrast, in D-TDOA systems, the first communication link exclusively depends on the target node emission. Energy consumption is another factor to be evaluated. Due to the lower energy requirements for amplifying the signal power at the retransmission stage in each node, A-TDOA architectures lead to better results than D-TDOA.

In summary, the A-TDOA system provides a higher accuracy than the D-TDOA method, but the latter presents a lower level of variation in the evaluation for sensor location. Although, A-TDOA architectures present more hardware complexity, they sport less energy consumption due to the reduction of the signal travel. On the basis of the information gathered, it can be concluded that the best method for multiple sensor locations is the A-TDOA system.

## 6. Discussion

The new asynchronous TDOA architectures have led to a major improvement as a consequence of the reduction of the complexity in sensor networks and the increasing accuracy of time measurements over the last few years. These methodologies have been experiencing a growing importance in LPS with particular application in robot indoor navigation and unmanned aerial vehicles (UAVs).

Amongst the asynchronous architectures, A-TDOA and D-TDOA have taken special relevance, but their novelty assumed that no previous research on the suitability of these systems had been accomplished before. This means that these architectures have not been studied in an actual common environment in order to determine a comparison among their system errors that would allow us to select the best architecture under different conditions. The error bounds must be calculated through the Cramér–Rao Lower Bound estimator all over the domain. In this context, CRLB allows to determine the minimum achievable error of a locating system with independence from the positioning algorithm used. With this parameter, the determination of the best asynchronous architecture could be done in a particular context. The extension of the usage of the LPS forces the design of an environment where CRLB must be derived in a 3D context for the first time.

This derivation includes a path-loss model propagation which depends on the distances between emitter and receiver of the positioning signal. This leads to heteroscedastic noise variances consideration that particularly fits with LPS.

The goal of this article has allowed for the development of a new methodology in order to select the best system in different contexts.

## 7. Conclusions

High accuracy requirements in modern applications lead to positioning systems where noise uncertainties must be minimized. New asynchronous positioning architectures have supposed a revolution where positioning errors have been considerably reduced. In this paper, a methodology to select the suitability of two asynchronous TDOA systems based on a CRLB evaluation under a 3D, real environment was accomplished for the first time to the best of our knowledge.

This analysis was performed based on a CRLB comparison where the uncertainties of time measurements originated by noise were distance dependent. This resulted in heteroscedasticity in the variance associated with sensor range estimation. This real model allowed us to determine the best TDOA asynchronous architecture with positioning algorithm independence.

The results showed that the A-TDOA system provided generally less uncertainty in the positioning, regardless of the node distributions. Nevertheless, the D-TDOA system achieved a better level of homogenization by reducing the RMSE standard deviation in the domain. On the basis of the information gathered, and taking into account the CRLB, it can be concluded that the best method for sensor location is the A-TDOA system.

These aspects are being treated in the current investigation, where the node distribution would be optimized for CRLB via genetic algorithms, attaining a RMSE minimization at all discretization points in future works.

**Author Contributions:** Conceptualization, R.Á., H.P., and J.D.-G.; Formal analysis, M.C.-L.; Investigation, R.Á. and J.D.-G.; Methodology, R.Á. and M.C.-L.; Resources, J.D.-G. and E.A.; Software, R.Á.; Supervision, J.D.-G. and M.C.-L.; Validation, M.C.-L.; Visualization, E.A. and L.F.-R.; Writing—original draft, R.Á. and J.D.-G.; Writing—review and editing, H.P., M.C.-L. and L.F.-R.

**Funding:** This research was funded by the Spanish Ministry of Economy, Industry and Competitiveness, grant number DPI2016-79960-C3-2-P.

**Conflicts of Interest:** The authors declare no conflict of interest.

## References

1. D'Amico, A.A.; Mengali, U.; Taponecco, L. TOA Estimation with the IEEE 802.15.4a Standard. *IEEE Trans. Wirel. Commun.* **2010**, *9*, 2238–2247. [CrossRef]
2. Shen, J.; Molisch, A.F.; Salmi, J. Accurate Passive Location Estimation Using TOA Measurements. *IEEE Trans. Wirel. Commun.* **2012**, *11*, 2182–2192. [CrossRef]
3. Ho, K.C.; Lu, X.; Kovavisaruch, L. Source Localization Using TDOA and FDOA Measurements in the Presence of Receiver Location Errors: Analysis and Solution. *IEEE Trans. Signal Process.* **2007**, *55*, 684–696. [CrossRef]
4. Xu, J.; Ma, M.; Law, C.L. Position Estimation Using UWB TDOA Measurements. In Proceedings of the 2006 IEEE International Conference on Ultra-Wideband, Waltham, MA, USA, 24–27 September 2006.

5. Xu, J.; Ma, M.; Law, C.L. AOA Cooperative Position Localization. In Proceedings of the IEEE Globecom 2008-2008 IEEE Global Telecommunications Conference, New Orleans, LA, USA, 30 November 2008.
6. Zhang, W.; Yin, Q.; Chen, H.; Gao, F. Distributed Angle Estimation for Localization in Wireless Sensor Networks. *IEEE Trans. Wirel. Commun.* **2013**, *12*, 527–537. [CrossRef]
7. Wang, G.; Yang, K. A New Approach to Sensor Node Localization Using RSS Measurements in Wireless Sensor Networks. *IEEE Trans. Wirel. Commun.* **2011**, *10*, 1389–1395. [CrossRef]
8. Weiss, A.J. On the Accuracy of a Cellular Location System Based on RSS Measurements. *IEEE Trans. Vehicular Technol.* **2003**, *52*, 1508–1518. [CrossRef]
9. Patwari, N.; Ash, J.N.; Kyperountas, S.; Hero, A.O.; Moses, R.L.; Correal, N.S. Locating the Nodes. *IEEE Signal Process. Mag.* **2005**, *22*, 54–69. [CrossRef]
10. D'Amico, A.A.; Mengali, U.; Taponecco, L. Joint TOA and AOA Estimation for UWB Localization Applications. *IEEE Trans. Wirel. Commun.* **2011**, *10*, 2207–2217.
11. Zou, Z.; Deng, T.; Zou, Q.; Sarmiento, D.; Jonsson, F.; Zheng, L.-R. Energy detection receiver with TOA estimation enabling positioning in passive UWB-RFID system. In Proceedings of the 2010 IEEE International Conference on Ultra-Wideband, Nanjing, China, 20–23 September 2010.
12. Badorrey, R.; Hernandez, A.; Choliz, J.; Valdovinos, A.; Alastruey, I. Evaluation of TOA estimation algorithms in UWB receivers. In Proceedings of the 14th European Wireless Conference, Prague, Czech Republic, 22–25 June 2008.
13. Ye, R.; Redfield, S.; Liu, H. High-precision indoor UWB localization: Technical challenges and method. In Proceedings of the 2010 IEEE International Conference on Ultra-Wideband, Nanjing, China, 20–23 September 2010.
14. Sundararaman, B.; Buy, U.; Kshemkalyani, A.D. Clock synchronization for wireless sensor networks: A survey. *Ad Hoc Netw.* **2005**, *3*, 281–323. [CrossRef]
15. Sivrikaya, F.; Yener, B. Time synchronization in sensor networks: A survey. *IEEE Netw.* **2004**, *18*, 45–50. [CrossRef]
16. Elson, J.; Estrin, D. Time Synchronization for Wireless Sensor Networks. In Proceedings of the 15th International Parallel and Distributed Processing Symposium, San Francisco, CA, USA, 1–5 May 2000.
17. He, S.; Dong, X. High-Accuracy Localization Platform Using Asynchronous Time Difference of Arrival Technology. *IEEE Trans. Instrum. Meas.* **2017**, *66*, 1728–1742. [CrossRef]
18. Zhou, J.; Shen, L.; Sun, Z. A New Method of D-TDOA Time Measurement Based on RTT. *MATEC Web Conf.* **2018**, *207*, 03018. [CrossRef]
19. Kaune, R.; Hörst, J.; Koch, W. Accuracy Analysis for TDOA Localization in Sensor Networks. In Proceedings of the 14th International Conference on Information Fusion, Chicago, IL, USA, 5 July 2011.
20. Jia, T.; Buehrer, R.M. A New Cramer-Rao Lower Bound for TOA-based Localization. In Proceedings of the MILCOM 2008-2008 IEEE Military Communications Conference, San Diego, CA, USA, 16–19 November 2008.
21. Qi, Y.; Kobayashi, H. Cramér-Rao Lower bound for geolocation in non-line-of-sight environment. In Proceedings of the 2002 IEEE International Conference on Acoustics, Speech, and Signal Processing, Orlando, FL, USA, 13–17 May 2002.
22. Chang, C.; Shai, A. Estimation Bounds for Localization. In Proceedings of the 2004 First Annual IEEE Communications Society Conference on Sensor and Ad Hoc Communications and Networks, Santa Clara, CA, USA, 4–7 October 2004.
23. Huang, B.; Xie, L.; Yang, Z. Analysis of TOA Localization with Heteroscedastic Noises. In Proceedings of the 33rd Chinese Control Conference, Nanjing, China, 28–30 July 2014.
24. Huang, B.; Xie, L.; Yang, Z. TDOA-Based Source Localization with Distance-Dependent Noises. *IEEE Trans. Wirel. Commun.* **2015**, *14*, 468–480. [CrossRef]
25. Lanzisera, S.; Zats, D.; Pister, K.S.J. Radio Frequency Time-of-Flight Distance Measurement for Low-Cost Wireless Sensor Localization. *IEEE Sens. J.* **2011**, *11*, 837–845. [CrossRef]
26. Yaro, A.S.; Sha'ameri, A.Z. Effect of Path Loss Propagation Model on the Position Estimation Accuracy of a 3-Dimensional Minimum Configuration Multilateration System. *Int. J. Integr. Eng.* **2018**, *10*, 35–42.

27. Rappaport, T.S. *Wireless Communications-Principles and Practice*; Prentice Hall: Upper Saddle River, NJ, USA, 2002.

sensors

MDPI

Article

# 3D Tdoa Problem Solution with Four Receiving Nodes

Javier Díez-González [1], Rubén Álvarez [2], Lidia Sánchez-González [1], Laura Fernández-Robles [1], Hilde Pérez [1] and Manuel Castejón-Limas [1,*]

1 Department of Mechanical, IT and Aerospace Engineering, Universidad de León, 24071 León, Spain
2 Positioning Department, Drotium, Universidad de León, 24071 León, Spain
* Correspondence: mcasl@unileon.es

Received: 8 May 2019; Accepted: 27 June 2019; Published: 29 June 2019

**Abstract:** Time difference of arrival (TDOA) positioning methods have experienced growing importance over the last few years due to their multiple applications in local positioning systems (LPSs). While five sensors are needed to determine an unequivocal three-dimensional position, systems with four nodes present two different solutions that cannot be discarded according to mathematical standards. In this paper, a new methodology to solve the 3D TDOA problems in a sensor network with four beacons is proposed. A confidence interval, which is defined in this paper as a sphere, is defined to use positioning algorithms with four different nodes. It is proven that the separation between solutions in the four-beacon TDOA problem allows the transformation of the problem into an analogous one in which more receivers are implied due to the geometric properties of the intersection of hyperboloids. The achievement of the distance between solutions needs the application of genetic algorithms in order to find an optimized sensor distribution. Results show that positioning algorithms can be used 96.7% of the time with total security in cases where vehicles travel at less than 25 m/s.

**Keywords:** TDOA; sensor networks; hyperboloids; node distribution; genetic algorithms

## 1. Introduction

Positioning is an essential factor for the correct navigation and location of vehicles. Accuracy in calculating positions has commonly determined the fields where positioning has been applied. High technological levels have been achieved when uncertainty has been sufficiently reduced. The usage of localization methods has evolved throughout the last few years from a reference object to precision applications such as farming, indoor navigation or manufacturing environments.

Positioning systems can be divided into those based on time measurements and those that measure different properties, such as angle of arrival (AOA) [1,2] or received signal strength indicators (RSSIs) [3–5]. Among them, time measurement systems are the most used, due to availability, accuracy, simplicity and robustness. In this category, TOA (time of arrival) systems [6,7] such as GPS, GLONASS or Galileo, and TDOA (time difference of arrival) systems [8,9] such as LORAN, OMEGA or WAM (wide area multilateration) [10]—which is highly widespread in aircraft environments—are considered.

TOA systems measure the total time-of-flight of a signal between a transmitter and a receptor. They require time synchronization between the transmitter and receptor and their accuracy is highly dependent on clock drift in this synchronization. These time-of-flight measurements lead to equations of three-dimensional spheres centered on the transmitter, representing possible locations of the vehicle in the space.

In contrast, TDOA systems measure the relative times between signal arrival for two different receivers. In this case, synchronization is optional, differentiating asynchronous (A-TDOA) [11] and synchronous (S-TDOA) [12] systems, which can lead to a reduction in error levels. In such a scenario, time difference measurements generate the equations of hyperboloids, whose intersection determine the position of the vehicle.

A number of $n$ equations can be obtained from $n$ different receivers in TOA systems due to global time measurements in each receptor. In contrast, relative measurements in TDOA systems must consider different combinations for the time difference of arrival measurements that originate from each pair of receivers. These combinations do not allow repetitions in pairs 1-2 or 2-1, mainly due to the duplicity of results. However, it has been proven that from a set of $n$ different receiving sensors in a TDOA problem, only a number of ($n$-1) independent equations can be obtained. In addition, the biggest limitation in the equations of spheres and hyperboloids is that they are considered to be non-linear equations. This produces a non-direct resolution of the positioning problem through these equations, a fact that causes the intersection of spheres or hyperboloids to not have a unique solution in the space. Two different solutions can therefore be obtained that cannot be distinguished through mathematical criteria.

According to rigidity theories on positioning systems [13], to completely determine the unequivocal location of an object in a three-dimensional space a minimum of four receptors are necessary in TOA systems, with a minimum of five in cases of TDOA systems. This disposition would guarantee one single solution for the positioning problem. However, global positioning systems such as GPS do not necessarily require an additional satellite for the calculation of the position, since the distances between emitter and receptor are so far-off that the sphere equations generated allow the incorrect solution to be discarded as incoherent or too separate from the previous position of the vehicle.

This problem, apparently solved in global navigation systems, poses a great importance in local positioning systems (LPSs) [14,15] such as those used in precision applications (e.g., indoor navigation or aircraft landings in nowadays airports). This is due to the proximity between the two different solutions in these cases, so that any solution can be discarded with a stable generalized criterion. In this article, a new criterion is proposed to solve this geometric problem based on the properties of certain positioning algorithms. TDOA algorithms will be considered due to their great usage in LPSs [16].

In Section 2, the TDOA positioning problem is described. In Section 3, some different algorithms are presented to solve the TDOA problem in real-time, while in Section 4 fictitious point studies based on TDOA algorithms are developed to guarantee a four-receiver TDOA solution, and the convergence sphere is defined. We show that computers have great difficulty processing convergence spheres in Section 5, and a new parameter to process the convergence radius is proposed in Section 6. Section 7 develops an optimized node localization to solve the 3D TDOA problem. The article concludes with a presentation and analysis of the results obtained and by extracting conclusions from the completed work.

## 2. The TDOA Problem

TDOA systems are based on difference time measurements between the signal arrival to different nodes or sensors in a network. These measurements can be converted to difference of distances by multiplying these times by speed emission of the radioelectric waves ($c$).

This leads in *Euclidean Geometry* to the next equation:

$$\begin{aligned} R_{ij} = d_{ij} = d_{Ii} - d_{Ij} = \sqrt{(x_I - x_i)^2 + (y_I - y_i)^2 + (z_I - z_i)^2} \\ - \sqrt{\left(x_I - x_j\right)^2 + \left(y_I - y_j\right)^2 + \left(z_I - z_j\right)^2} + h(0,\sigma) = ct_{ij} + h(0,\sigma) \end{aligned} \tag{1}$$

where $d_{Ij}$ is the distance difference between receivers $i$ and $j$—which is the result of multiplying the actual time difference of arrival ($t_{ij}$) and adding a white noise, $h(0,\sigma)$, that considers atmospheric instabilities and time error measurements. This noise is related to signal transmission and measurement of times, which cannot be controlled by TDOA algorithms and so is not considered in this paper. In addition, $(x_I,\ y_I,\ z_I)$ are space coordinates of the vehicle that are being positioned and $(x_i,\ y_i,\ z_i)$, $\left(x_j,\ y_j,\ z_j\right)$

are coordinates of the nodes $i$ and $j$, respectively, which receive the positioning signal. These equations correspond with hyperboloids that cannot be solved in an analytic direct process. Thus, numerical methods must be used to determine the problem.

## 3. Algorithms for TDOA Problem Resolution

Non-linear equations of hyperboloids must be treated in order to address the TDOA problem resolution. Generally, two main methodologies have been considered: those based on hyperboloids intersection properties with closed-form solutions, and those based on numerical methods, which offer a progressive reduction on the error gradient derivation in successive approximations leading to the final solution. Although these methods could be considered analogous, they use different properties and methodologies. However, both of them share the qualification that a univocal TDOA problem resolution must use at least five different sensors. Hence, from now on, a combined study with a method for each case is proposed to solve the TDOA problem with only four beacons.

Bucher and Misra [17] proposed a method based on the properties of the intersection of hyperboloids. They show that hyperboloid intersections can always be contained in a plane. This process increases the freedom to the problem by one degree, since a number of $n$ receivers generate a number of ($n$-1) independent hyperboloid equations and ($n$-2) independent intersection planes are obtained using this methodology. That means that to solve the 3D TDOA problem linearly, where three planes are needed, we still have to use five different receivers. Nevertheless, the fact that the intersection of two different hyperboloids is contained in a plane makes the process of obtaining this plane equation independent from the original hyperboloid equations. As a consequence, the intersection of two planes (four nodes) resulting in a line of possible vehicle localizations can be verified in any hyperboloid to finally get the two solutions that are achieved in TDOA problems with four beacons ($i, j, k, l$). This methodology leads to two different solutions that for LPS cannot be discarded by any assumable criterion.

The other method would be based on applying a Taylor approximation truncated on first order to linearize the equations and allow a real-time solution to the problem. In this way, a point with enough proximity to the final solution ($x_0$, $y_0$, $z_0$) from which a process of sequential iterations will be started is selected. These steps will finally allow the vehicle localization to be obtained through a matrix where the range differences are considered as follows:

$$R_{ij} = ct_{ij} = R_{ij_0} + \frac{\partial R_{ij}}{\partial x}\Delta x + \frac{\partial R_{ij}}{\partial y}\Delta y + \frac{\partial R_{ij}}{\partial z}\Delta z \tag{2}$$

where $R_{ij}$ is the value of the distance difference in the approximation point, and $\frac{\partial R_{ij}}{\partial x}$, $\frac{\partial R_{ij}}{\partial y}$ and $\frac{\partial R_{ij}}{\partial z}$ are partial derivatives of the range differences, particularized for the values of the approximation point. Applying this very same process to the other two nodes k and l with reference to the node $i$, $R_{ik}$ and $R_{il}$ can be estimated. This leads to the following matrix system:

$$\Delta R = \begin{pmatrix} \frac{\partial R_{ij}}{\partial x} & \frac{\partial R_{ij}}{\partial y} & \frac{\partial R_{ij}}{\partial z} \\ \frac{\partial R_{il}}{\partial x} & \frac{\partial R_{il}}{\partial y} & \frac{\partial R_{il}}{\partial z} \\ \frac{\partial R_{ik}}{\partial x} & \frac{\partial R_{ik}}{\partial y} & \frac{\partial R_{ik}}{\partial z} \end{pmatrix} \begin{pmatrix} \Delta x \\ \Delta y \\ \Delta z \end{pmatrix} \tag{3}$$

where $\Delta R$ is the range differences matrix, $H$ is the partial derivative matrix (commonly known as visibility matrix) and $P$ is the position variance matrix. Therefore, we can express the matrix system as follows:

$$H\Delta P = \Delta R \tag{4}$$

This equation is usually solved through the least squares method [18], as described below:

$$\Delta P = \left(H^t H\right)^{-1} H^t \Delta R = \begin{pmatrix} \Delta x \\ \Delta y \\ \Delta z \end{pmatrix} \tag{5}$$

The coordinates of the solution point in the first iteration would be the result of adding all the approximation coordinates to the increments obtained. After several iterations, the residual error is reduced, reaching convergence with the real solution once it has become lower than the desired precision. However, the convergence of this method depends on the initial position chosen as the start of the first iteration [19]. Regarding the resolution of the TDOA problem, four receiving sensors do not always guarantee the convergence of the method and, if produced, this can affect any of the two possible solutions (which prevents us from knowing whether the position calculation is correct). However, in contrast with the former method, the calculation of the position now guarantees a single solution instead of two possible answers.

## 4. Fictitious Point Method

Of all the methods proposed so far, it is not possible to conclude whether the TDOA System can be applied to LPS systems with four nodes with enough confidence to guarantee the correct calculation of the position. Nevertheless, it is possible to affirm that successive approximation methods do guarantee convergence—if produced—towards one of the possible of the solutions.

This means that if there were any way to ensure that the convergence occur toward the correct solution, the method would allow the problem with to be solved with four sensors. In a scenario where the process is convergent and highly dependent upon the initial point of the iterations, it is safe to say that when this initial point is close enough to the solution (i.e., the previous solution of the vehicle), the convergence should always take place toward the correct solution. To prove this statement, the behavior of any point located at a plane containing the two possible solutions is going to be proven for the TDOA problem. The solution has been calculated by applying the successive approximation method to these initial points, as presented in Figure 1.

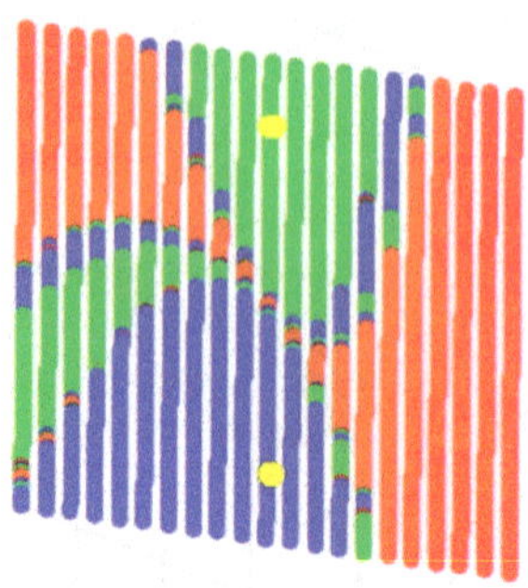

**Figure 1.** Plane of convergence containing the two solutions of a four-beacon TDOA problem.

Figure 1 represents the two potential solutions (in yellow) to the positioning problem. Their surroundings are color-coded (blue and green) in accordance with which solution these neighbors converge at. Regions in red show an absence of convergence with the successive approximation method. As it is a 3D positioning system, it is necessary to extrapolate the same reliable zone (for calculating the position with four nodes) as a 3D space to find the solution to the problem. The resulting figure would necessarily be a sphere, since the vehicle can move in any direction, with the solution as the center.

Figure 2 displays the first instabilities appearing in the surface of the convergence sphere. This guarantees that, at a maximum radius, all points on the surface of the sphere are convergent towards the inner (correct) solution.

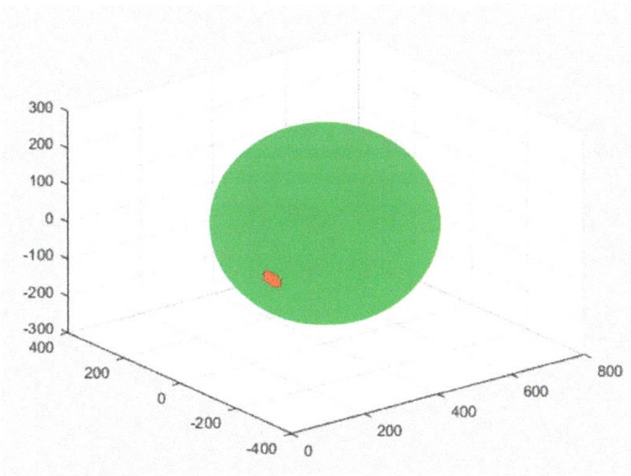


**Figure 2.** Critical convergence sphere: Surface points in green are good initial position estimates that make the successive approximation method converge at the solution in the center. Points in red fail to make the approximation method converge. This figure displays the first appearance of such instabilities when increasing the radius of the sphere from zero to a critical value marked by the appearance of these defective seeds. The axes represent the 3D environment around the solutions and their units are adimensional due to the illustrative purpose of the figure.

In this scenario, a configuration with four receiving sensors within the coverage can be defined as reliable if the distance from the initial point to the solution is inferior to the minimum radius of convergence for all points of that volume.

## 5. Convergence Parameter Modification

The convergence radius is calculated from an evaluation of the points from the sphere centered on the desired solution. In the case that all these points converge towards the inner solution, the value of the radius of convergence increases until there exists divergence at any point. This gradual process of incrementing the radius involves a higher number of calculation points for each iteration process, which cannot be assumed in a reasonable time.

Taking this into account, a different way to determine convergence is proposed in this paper. The surroundings of the solutions find a region in which convergence is not reached in the fictitious point method. This region is considered to be the border between the two intervals of convergence when sequential approximations are used to find the solution. Thus, if the two solutions could be separated enough, the discontinuity region could be ousted from the solutions, which would increase the convergence radius.

This problem leads to an association between the convergence radius and the distance between solutions. To show this, the convergence radius and distance between solutions are calculated in a representative number of points for the coverage area of a concrete node distribution. For this purpose, the spatial volume where positioning is going to be used to locate a target is divided into small steps in the three Cartesian coordinates, in order to evaluate the convergence radius and the distance between solutions at each point and show the correlation between the parameters.

The correlation between these two factors is shown in Table 1 and reaches a value of 0.999. This value allows us to conclude that any variation of these two parameters will be strongly related to the other.

**Table 1.** Correlation between radius of convergence and distance between solutions.

| Parameter | | Convergence Radius | Solutions Distance |
|---|---|---|---|
| Convergence radius | Pearson Correlation Coefficient (PCC) | 1 | 0.999 |
| | S. (bilateral) | - | 0.000 |
| | Samples | 33,306 | 33,306 |
| Solutions distance | Pearson Correlation Coefficient (PCC) | 0.999 | 1 |
| | S. (bilateral) | 0.000 | - |
| | Samples | 33,306 | 33,306 |

In this sense, the new parameter can be calculated, leading us to a new conclusion: The maximization of the distances between solutions for every coverage point of a concrete node distribution leads to an increase of the interval of confidence of the sequential approximation method to solve the four-beacon TDOA problem.

However, for a determined sensor distribution, the distances between solutions in the four-beacon TDOA problem are fixed. Hence, in order to maximize this parameter, a search for the optimum node distribution is needed. This will lead to maximizing the convergence interval of the algorithm.

## 6. Optimization of the Node Distribution for the Four-Beacon TDOA Problem

The calculation of the distance between solutions allows us to process the radius of convergence in a reasonable period of time. Due to the geometric properties of the intersection of hyperboloids, some particularities should be considered when a maximization of this parameter is performed.

A set of points with high distance between solutions values is shown in Figure 3. These points do not have a direct correlation with the radius of convergence, but they represent less than 5% of the total points. This is due to a near-tangent condition in the intersection of two different branches of the hyperboloids. The effect of this condition is the separation of the two solutions.

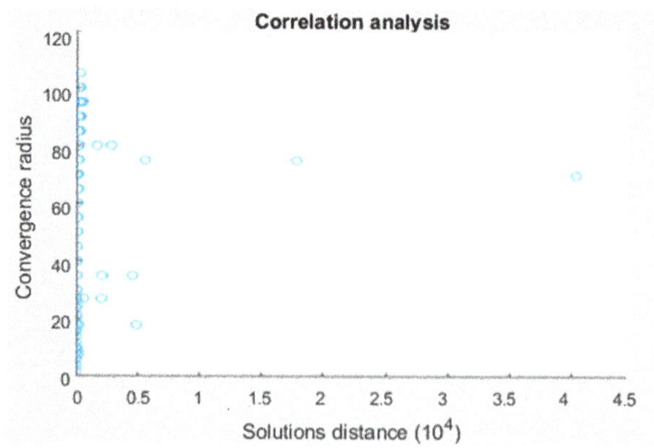


**Figure 3.** Outliers of the correlation between radius of convergence and distance between solutions.

A different circumstance occurs when it is observed at a distance between solutions of 0—which is the tangent case—and does not permit a correlation with the convergence radius in this context. The separation of the solutions or the existence of only one of them modifies the convergence problem in a four-beacon TDOA problem. The problem is converted into a different case of convergence where more receivers are concerned.

However, these points imply a great distortion for the comparison of statistical properties of the node distributions based on the distance between solutions in the four-beacon TDOA problem. In order to remove this type of point, a filter is applied before performing an optimization. The filtering process is run in two different steps:

(1) elimination of points where the distance between solutions is equal to 0;
(2) introduction of a parameter to remove the outliers where the distance between solutions is aberrant, without losing the representativeness of the sample values.

This second step is controlled with the parameter $r$, which measures the correlation between the mean of the sample values of the distance between solutions and both of their ends as a dispersion indicator.

$$r = \frac{\max(dist_{sol}) - \min(dist_{sol})}{mean(dist_{sol})} \tag{6}$$

It is concluded that node distributions with outliers show values of $r$ above 2.5, so that an elimination of points, such as the filtering process in Figure 4, must be performed until a value of $r$ smaller than 2.5 is obtained. In this case, the methodology followed is based on standard deviation. In the first steps of the filter, the standard deviation has high values as a consequence of the outliers. This circumstance allows us to define the limit of the points discarded as a sum of the media and the standard deviation.

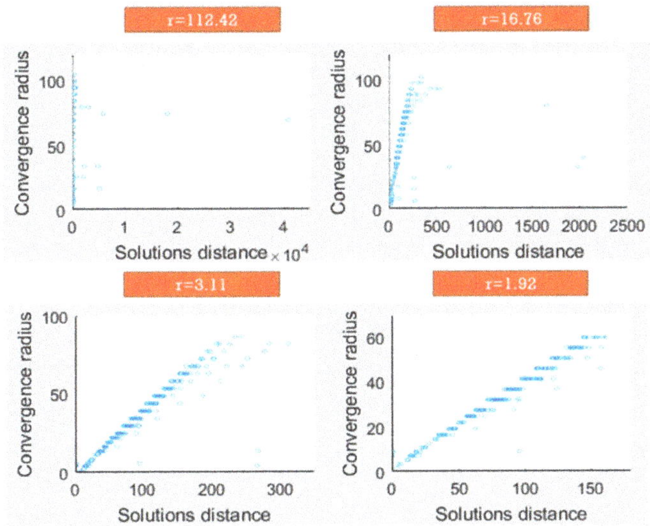


**Figure 4.** Sequential reduction of the r-correlation factor. The outliers are removed with this iteration process. The remaining distribution (r = 1.92) does not present outliers.

The process is performed iteratively until the $r$ value is reduced. In the final step of the filter, more than 85% of the sample points are preserved and the representativeness is guaranteed, as is shown in Figure 5.

Previous studies have shown a clear relationship between the radius converging towards the correct solution in a four-sensor TDOA problem and a 3D-node distribution. Assuming this hypothesis is right, a 3D space will be associated with a certain node distribution that optimizes the convergence radius.

This hypothesis was validated by means of optimization techniques, but presents two characteristics that dissuade resolution techniques based on exact algorithms—large solution space sizes (related to the required resolution level in sensor location) and an inability to apply recursive methodologies or separate the optimization into parts. Due to these circumstances, the optimization procedure is suitable to be performed by means of heuristic algorithms. Furthermore, Tekdas et al. [20] demonstrated that the node distribution problem is considered as NP-hard and must be solved with the usage of heuristic techniques.

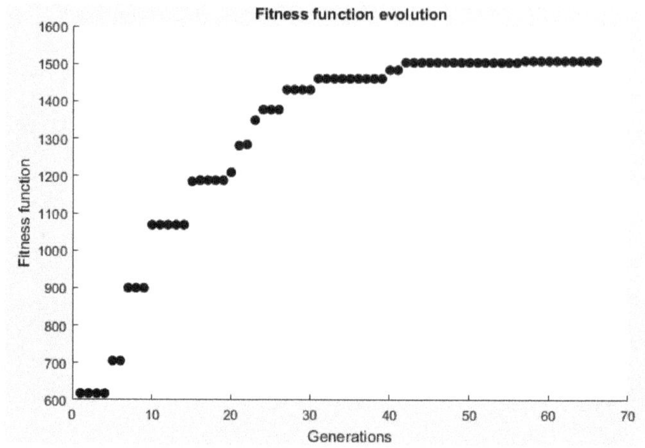


**Figure 5.** Evolution of the fitness function through several generations.

Genetic algorithms represent a robust and flexible approach that allows the possibility of using non-derivable functions and an appealing trade-off between diversification and intensification in the solution-searching process of the problem. As an alternative to genetic algorithms, techniques such as randomized search, proposed by Bergstra and Bengio [21], are also suitable for approaching this problem. The positioning problem can be seen as an optimization problem where the size of the convergence spheres plays the role of loss function while the position of the beacons can be considered as hyperparameters for the underlying positioning algorithms. This paper focuses on reporting the results obtained by using genetic algorithms.

The starting point for an analysis is the definition of the 3D experimental volume of dimensions, $1000 \times 400 \times 100$ m, described with a spatial discretization of 100 m in $x$ coordinate, 50 m in the $y$ coordinate and 10 m in the $z$ coordinate. Each of the discretization points represents a real solution to the 3D TDOA system of study. Additionally, the height of the nodes has been limited to 15 m measured from the $z = 0$ plane, similar to the conditions found in a local, terrestrial positioning system.

The genetic algorithm developed for this study is based on binary codification techniques of the population, tournament-based selection, single-point crossover, 10% elitism and a mutation probability of 4%. The fitness function has been defined as the arithmetic mean of the distance between solutions for all points at the discretization, corrected according to parameter $r$.

The stop criterion of the algorithm has been defined as the instant when the maximum of the fitness function stops improving at the same time as the solution is reached for at least half of the individuals of the population. The resolution of the genetic algorithm is shown by means of the fitness function of the problem, in relation to the number of generations.

The final result of the process can be seen in Figures 6 and 7. Figure 6 shows the evaluation of the convergence radius for the random distribution of points. The solution obtained after the maximization process is presented in Figure 7.

It is noteworthy to highlight the continuity presented by the convergence radius in all the domains and the negative influence they have on areas close to nodes. This is related to the geometry of the hyperboloids in these regions. In Table 2, a comparison between the distributions of nodes and the main statistical variables of the set of convergence radii is presented.

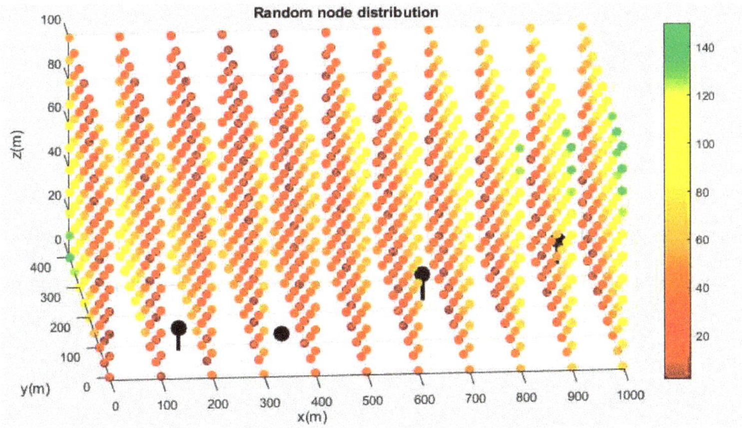


**Figure 6.** Evaluation of the convergence radius in the coverage area for a random distribution.

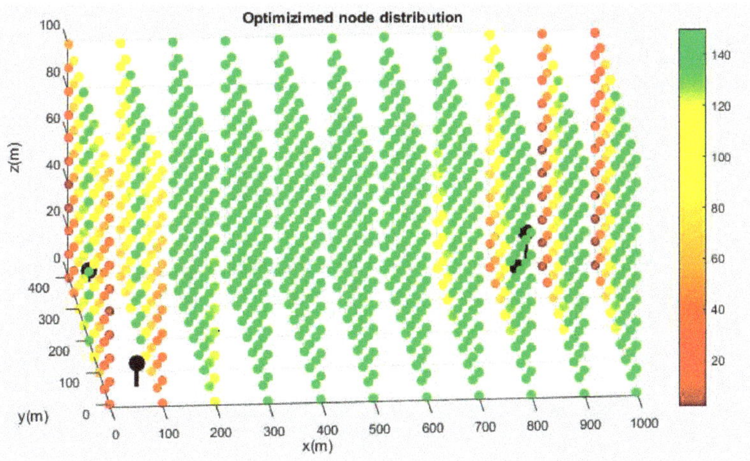


**Figure 7.** Evaluation of the convergence radius in the coverage area for the optimized distribution.

**Table 2.** Statistical parameters of the optimized and random distribution.

| Convergence Radius | Optimized Distribution | Random Distribution |
|---|---|---|
| Mean (m) | 186.03 | 45.63 |
| Min (m) | 10 | 2 |
| Max (m) | 350 | 150 |
| Std (m) | 87.06 | 30.58 |
| % Points convergence radius > 120 | 74.10% | 1.56% |

The results of the analysis lead to the conclusion that the initial hypothesis is correct, and hence a clear relationship exists between node distribution and the convergence radius of the four-node 3D-TDOA problem for the calculation of the position. Moreover, the whole procedure has been defined on the basis of genetic algorithms, making it possible to maximize the convergence radius in any environment, optimizing the product speed time refreshing rate.

## 7. Discussion

A new methodology based on convergence properties of TDOA algorithms has been proposed in order to solve the four-sensor TDOA problem. This approach considers a procedure to maximize the capabilities of the algorithms in a confidence interval without considering the existence of errors due to signal transmission, signal processing or the synchronization of the system. For this reason, in future works it is necessary to consider optimization in a context where a Non-Line-of-Sight (NLOS) scenario is presented, clock synchronization is considered and other properties related to node distribution are also contemplated.

However, this paper presents a new perspective that concludes that algorithm properties are strongly related with node distribution and that the four-node TDOA problem can be solved under certain conditions with complete security for the first time in local positioning systems. With this optimization, convergence has also been maximized, which is one of the biggest problems of gradient descent algorithms in that they are deeply dependent on the initial iteration point [19]. In practice, this point is the last estimated position. The last position can be far away from the new target localization if the vehicle is moving at high speed, which can represent a convergence uncertainty. For this reason, a confidence region around the target localization has been defined to use the gradient descent algorithm under convergence conditions. The confidence region has been maximized through the radius of convergence and the calculation of the position has been guaranteed all over the domain in the optimized distribution, which does not happen in random distribution. This has important relevance in indoor positioning and precision landings in wide area multilateration, where sensor location must be considered. The reduction of one receiver guarantees system availability in cases of sensor failure, and reduces overall costs.

## 8. Conclusions

In this paper, it has been shown that the TDOA problem can be solved with only four sensors within a confidence interval defined through the convergence radius. The great computational processing time needed to calculate this parameter has led to the search for another indicator—the distance between solutions, which permits a nearly complete explanation of the convergence radius.

This geometric factor must be filtered with the aim of allowing a statistical comparison between different node distributions. The high number of possible solutions has promoted the utilization of artificial intelligence through genetic algorithms, which have permitted the improvement of the convergence radius through optimized node distribution.

A comparison between a random and an optimized distribution shows the suitability of the methodology proposed to solve the TDOA problem with four sensors. By applying the sequential approximation algorithm between the two distributions, the confidence level is improved by over 400%. Furthermore, if a refresh rate of the positioning signal is fixed in one second, the algorithm can be used with four beacons in the optimized distribution 96.7% of the time with total security if the vehicle has a maximum speed of 25 m/s. In contrast, it can be used only in 31.2% of cases for random distribution.

The geometric statement of the problem of the intersection of hyperboloids has shown that an improvement in the space localization of the hyperboloids through node localization optimization allows the 4-sensor TDOA problem to transform into an analogous problem in which more receivers are used. This methodology ultimately provides great improvements to the positioning algorithm properties used throughout this article.

**Author Contributions:** Conceptualization, J.D.-G. and H.P.; Formal analysis, H.P. and M.C.-L.; Investigation, J.D.-G. and R.Á.; Methodology, J.D.-G. and M.C.-L.; Project administration, H.P.; Resources, R.Á.; L.S.-G. and L.F.-R.; Software, R.Á. and L.S.-G.; Supervision, H.P.; Validation, L.F.-R. and H.P.; Visualization, L.S.-G. and L.F.-R.; Writing—original draft, J.D.-G.; R.Á. and L.S.-G.; Writing—review & editing, H.P. and M.C.-L.

**Funding:** This research was funded by the Spanish Ministry of Economy, Industry and Competitiveness grant number DPI2016-79960-C3-2-P.

**Conflicts of Interest:** The authors declare no conflict of interest.

## References

1. Xu, J.; Ma, M.; Law, C.L. AOA Cooperative Position Localization. In Proceedings of the IEEE Globecom 2008 IEEE Global Telecommunications Conference, New Orleans, LO, USA, 30 November–4 December 2008. [CrossRef]
2. Zhang, W.; Yin, Q.; Chen, H.; Gao, F. Distributed Angle Estimation for Localization in Wireless Sensor Networks. *IEEE Trans. Wirel. Commun.* **2013**, *12*, 527–537. [CrossRef]
3. Weiss, A.J. On the Accuracy of a Cellular Location System Based on RSS Measurements. *IEEE Trans. Veh. Technol.* **2003**, *52*, 1508–1518. [CrossRef]
4. Wang, G.; Yang, K. A New Approach to Sensor Node Localization Using RSS Measurements in Wireless Sensor Networks. *IEEE Trans. Wirel. Commun.* **2011**, *10*, 1389–1395. [CrossRef]
5. Passafiume, M.; Maddio, S.; Cidronali, A. An Improved Approach for RSSI-Based only Calibration-Free Real-Time Indoor Localization on IEEE 802.11 and 802.15.4 Wireless Networks. *Sensors* **2017**, *17*, 717. [CrossRef] [PubMed]
6. D'Amico, A.A.; Mengali, U.; Taponecco, L. TOA Estimation with the IEEE 802.15. 4a Standard. *IEEE Trans. Wirel. Commun.* **2010**, *9*, 2238–2247. [CrossRef]
7. Shen, J.; Molisch, A.F.; Salmi, J. Accurate Passive Location Estimation Using TOA Measurements. *IEEE Trans. Wirel. Commun.* **2012**, *11*, 2182–2192. [CrossRef]
8. Xu, J.; Ma, M.; Law, C.L. Position Estimation Using UWB TDOA Measurements. In Proceedings of the 2006 IEEE International Conference on Ultra-Wideband, Waltham, MA, USA, 24–27 September 2006. [CrossRef]
9. Niitso, A.; Edelhäußer, T.; Eberlein, E.; Hadaschik, N.; Mutschler, C. A Deep Learning Approach to Position Estimation from Channel Impulse Responses. *Sensors* **2019**, *19*, 1064. [CrossRef] [PubMed]
10. Yaro, A.S. Aircraft Position Estimation Comparison of Multilateration System Lateration Algorithms with Different Reference Selection Techniques. *Elektrika* **2019**, *18*, 16–21. [CrossRef]
11. He, S. Asynchronous Time Difference of Arrival Positioning System and Implementation. Ph.D. Thesis, University of Victoria, Victoria, BC, Canada, 2016. Available online: http://hdl.handle.net/1828/7411 (accessed on 28 April 2019).
12. Ho, K.C.; Lu, X.; Kovavisaruch, L. Source Localization Using TDOA and FDOA Measurements in the Presence of Receiver Location Errors: Analysis and Solution. *IEEE Trans. Signal Process.* **2007**, *55*, 684–696. [CrossRef]
13. Priyantha, N.B.; Balakrishnan, H.; Demaine, E.D.; Teller, S. Mobile-assisted localization in wireless sensor networks. In Proceedings of the IEEE 24th Annual Joint Conference of the IEEE Computer and Communications Societies, Miami, FL, USA, 13–17 March 2005. [CrossRef]
14. Liu, H.; Darabi, H.; Banerjee, P.; Liu, J. Survey of Wireless Indoor Positioning Techniques and Systems. *IEEE Trans. Syst. Man Cybern.* **2007**, *37*, 1067–1080. [CrossRef]
15. Wang, Y.; Jia, X.; Lee, H.K. An indoors wireless positioning system based on wireless local area network infrastructure. In Proceedings of the 6th International Symposium on Satellite Navigation Technology Including Mobile Positioning & Location Services, Melbourne, Australia, 22–25 July 2003.
16. Villadangos, J.; Ureña, J.; García, J.J.; Mazo, M.; Hernández, A.; Jiménez, A.; Ruiz, D.; de Marziani, C. Measuring Time-of-Flight in an Ultrasonic LPS System Using Generalized Cross-Correlation. *Sensors* **2011**, *11*, 10326–10342. [CrossRef] [PubMed]
17. Bucher, R.; Misra, D. A Synthesizable VHDL Model of the Exact Solution for Three-dimensional Hyperbolic Positioning System. *VLSI Desgin* **2002**, *15*, 507–520. [CrossRef]
18. Yang, K.; Jianping, A.; Zhan, X.; Xiangyuan, B. A Generalized Total Least-Squares Algorithm for Hyperbolic Location. In Proceedings of the 2008 4th International Conference on Wireless Communications, Networking and Mobile Computing, Dalian, China, 12–14 October 2008.
19. Bonan, J.; Xiaosu, X.; Zhang, T. Robust Time-Difference-of-Arrival (TDOA) Localization Using Weighted Least Squares with Cone Tangent Plane Constraint. *Sensors* **2018**, *18*, 778. [CrossRef] [PubMed]

20. Tekdas, O.; Isler, V. Sensor Placement for Triangulation-Based Localization. *IEEE Trans. Autom. Sci. Eng.* **2010**, *7*, 3. [CrossRef]
21. Bergstra, J.; Bengio, Y. Random search for hyper-parameter optimization. *J. Mach. Learn. Res.* **2012**, *13*, 281–305.